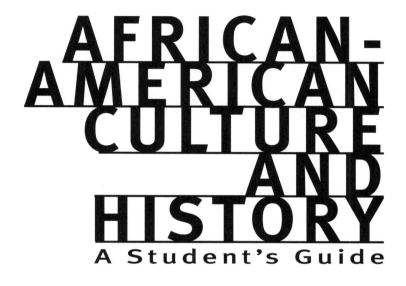

AFRICAN-AMERICAN CULTURE AND HISTORY

A Student's Guide

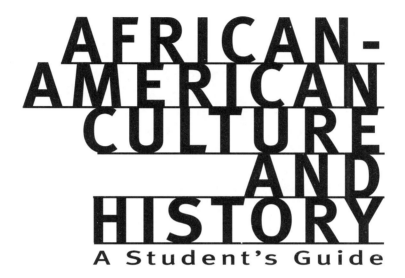

AFRICAN-AMERICAN CULTURE AND HISTORY
A Student's Guide

JACK SALZMAN
Editor-in-Chief

James S. Haskins
Consulting Editor

Evelyn Bender
Kathleen Lee
Advisors

volume 1
A - C

Macmillan Reference USA

an imprint of the Gale Group
New York • Detroit • San Francisco • London • Boston • Woodbridge, CT

Macmillan Reference USA
1633 Broadway
New York, NY 10019

Gale Group
27500 Drake Rd.
Farmington Hills, MI 48331

Editorial and Production Staff

David Galens, *Project Editor*
Kelle Sisung, *Developmental Editor*
Kathy Droste, *Illustration Editor*
Shalice Shah, *Permissions Associate*
Mark Milne, Pam Revitzer, and Larry Trudeau, *Contributing Editors*
Tim Akers, Rebecca Blanchard, Elizabeth Bodenmiller, Anne Marie Hacht, and
    Tara Atterberry, *Proofreaders*
Robert Griffin, *Copyeditor*
Tracey Rowens, *Senior Art Director*
Randy Bassett, *Imaging Supervisor*
Pam A. Reed, *Imaging Coordinator*
Dan Newell, *Imaging Specialist*
Kay Banning, *Indexer*
Geraldine Azzata, *Further Resources Compiler*

Elly Dickason, *Publisher, Macmillan Reference USA*
Jill Lectka, *Associate Publisher*

Printing number
1 2 3 4 5 6 7 8 9 10

LIBRARY OF CONGRESS CATALOGING-IN-PUBLICATION DATA

African-American culture and history: a student's guide / Jack Salzman, editor-in-chief.
    p. cm.
    Adapted from the five-volume Encyclopedia of African American culture and history published by Macmillan in 1996; revised for a sixth- to seventh-grade, middle school audience.
    Includes bibliographical references and index.
    ISBN 0-02-865531-1 (set : hardcover : alk. paper) – ISBN 0-02865532-X (vol. 1 : alk. paper) – ISBN 0-02-865533-8 (vol. 2 : alk. paper) – ISBN 0-02-865534-6 (vol. 3 : alk. paper) – ISBN 0-02-865535-4 (vol. 4 : alk. paper)
Afro-Americans—Encyclopedias, Juvenile. 2.
Afro-Americans—History—Encyclopedias, Juvenile literature. [1.
Afro-Ameridans—Encyclopedias.] I. Salzman, Jack. II. Encyclopedia of African-American culture and history.

E185 .A2527 2000
973'.0496073—dc21

Table of Contents

VOLUME 1

Table of Contents

VOLUME 2

H–I

Table of Contents

VOLUME 3

J

Table of Contents

VOLUME 4

Q–R

S

Preface

The history and culture of African Americans is to a great extent the history and culture of the United States. But as much as we may now accept this as a truism, it was not always so. It was not until the second half of the twentieth century that students and historians of the American experience began to document and carefully study the lives of people of African descent. Until then our knowledge of a people who comprise almost 15 percent of this country's population was shamefully inadequate. In 1989 Macmillan Publishing Co. decided to redress this situation by publishing a major reference work devoted to the history and culture of African Americans. I was asked to serve as editor of the new work, and in 1996 the five volume *Encyclopedia of African-American Culture and History* was published.

The encyclopedia contains close to two million words and covers all aspects of the African-American experience. In the few years since its publication it has come to be recognized as a mainstay in most high school, public, and academic libraries. *Rettig on Reference* (April 1996) found the set to be "scholarly yet accessible and immeasurably informative." *CHOICE* (1996) praised its "clear and succinct writing style" and its "breadth of coverage of general biographical and historical data." It received a Dartmouth Award Honorable Mention and appeared on every list of 1996 best reference sources. After spending six years compiling the encyclopedia it was gratifying to read, in *American Libraries* (May 1997), that the work "is of enduring value and destined to become a standard reference source."

The enthusiastic response to *Encyclopedia of African-American Culture and History* convinced us that students would benefit from a work with similar scope but one rewritten for a wider audience. *African-American Culture and History: A Student's Guide* is that work. It incorporates the same editorial criteria we used for the original encyclopedia : articles include biographies of notable African Americans, events, historical eras, legal cases, areas of cultural achievement, professions, sports, and places. Readers will find entries on all 50 states, 12 major cities, and 15 historically black colleges.

This comprehensive four-volume Student's Guide has 852 articles—arranged alphabetically—of which 597 are biographies and 255 are events, eras, genres, or colleges, states, or cities. Although for the most part articles in this set are based on entries from the original encyclopedia, our Advisory

Board recommended that we also cover several contemporary popular topics and figures. Entries were chosen to reflect the school curriculum and have been updated through Summer 2000.

African-American Culture and History: A Student's Guide has been carefully designed for younger readers, and professional writers have crafted the articles to make them accessible for the intended audience. In addition, readers will find that articles are enhanced with numerous photographs and sidebar materials. Lists, quotations, extracts from primary sources, interesting facts, and chronologies are to be found in the margins. A system of cross-references makes it easy to explore the Student's Guide. Within the text, terms and names set in boldface type indicate that there is a separate entry for this subject. Additional cross-references appear at the end of many entries. A comprehensive index for the entire set appears at the end of volume 4. A list of "Further Resources" in Volume Four includes books, articles, and web sites and will provide a starting point for students who are beginning to explore the extraordinary history and accomplishments of African Americans.

Many people have provided invaluable help with *African-American Culture and History: A Student's Guide*. In particular, I would like to single out Jill Lectka and David Galens of the Gale Group and Kelle Sisung. I would also like to thank our editorial advisors, Evelyn Bender, Librarian, Edison High School in Philadelphia; and Kathleen Lee, Librarian, John P. Turner Middle School in Philadelphia. Thanks, too, to Jim Haskins, Professor of Education, University of Florida and author of numerous books for young adults. These three professionals provided valuable guidance as I developed the article list and helped design the margin features. It was at their urging that we included curriculum-related web sites in the resources list. Finally, to Becca, Phoebe, Jonah, and Libby, who soon will be able to make use of these volumes: thank you for being as wonderful as you are and for bringing so much to me and Cec.

Jack Salzman
New York City

Contributors

The text of *African-American Culture and History: A Student's Guide* is based on the Macmillan *Encyclopedia of African-American Culture and History*, which was published in 1996. We have updated material where necessary and added new entries. Articles have been condensed and made more accessible for a student audience. Please refer to the Alphabetical List of Articles on page xi of the first volume of *Encyclopedia of African-American Culture and History* (also edited by Jack Salzman) for the names of the authors of the articles in the original set. Their academic affiliations are noted in the Directory of Contributors. This title also includes entries from the Supplement to *Encyclopedia of African-American Culture and History* published by Macmillan late in 2000. The Supplement has its own Alphabetical List of Articles and Directory of Contributors. Here we wish to acknowledge the writers who revised entries from those two publications and wrote new articles for this set:

Sheree Beaudry
Craig Collins
Stephanie Dionne
Rebecca Ferguson
David Galens
Robert Griffin
Cathy Dybiec Holm
Paul Kobel
Paula Pyzik-Scott
Ann Shurgin
Kelle Sisung
Larry Trudeau

Aaron, Henry Louis "Hank"

BASEBALL PLAYER, BASEBALL EXECUTIVE
February 5, 1934–

Perhaps best known as major league **baseball**'s career home run leader, Hank Aaron was born into poverty in Mobile, Alabama. He developed an early love for baseball, playing on vacant lots and at the racially segregated baseball diamonds in his neighborhood. Later, while playing for the Indianapolis (Indiana) Clowns of the American Negro League, Aaron quickly attracted the attention of major league scouts.

Aaron signed with the Boston Braves of the National League in 1952. In 1954 he was promoted to their major league club, which had moved to Milwaukee, Wisconsin. Aaron soon became a star for the Braves, leading them to a world championship in 1957—the same season in which he was named the National League's Most Valuable Player. From 1966 to 1974 Aaron played for the Braves in **Atlanta, Georgia,** and in 1976 he spent his final season with the Milwaukee Brewers.

In a career marked by several major league records, the most distinguished of Aaron's achievements came on April 8, 1974, when he broke Babe Ruth's home run record. The home run, his 715th in the major leagues, was not applauded by everyone. Aaron received death threats from those who did not want an African American to surpass Ruth's mark. Aaron's record, however, is still among the most celebrated in baseball and, along with his other credentials, earned him an easy induction into the Major League Baseball Hall of Fame.

After retiring as a player, Aaron returned to work in the Braves organization, eventually becoming the team's vice president. He became an outspoken critic of major league baseball's poor record of bringing minorities into leadership positions, both on and off the field. Aaron is also a vice president of Turner Broadcasting Company and maintains a number of business and charitable interests in the Atlanta area.

Hank Aaron's Career Totals

Home runs:
755 (all-time 1st)

Runs batted in:
2,297 (1st)

Extra-base hits:
1,477 (1st)

Total bases:
6,856 (1st)

Runs scored:
2,174 (2nd)

Base hits:
3,771 (3rd)

Abbott, Robert Sengstacke

NEWSPAPER EDITOR, NEWSPAPER PUBLISHER, WRITER
November 28, 1868–February 22, 1940

Robert Sengstacke Abbott, through his newspaper the *Chicago Defender*, was one of the first African Americans to provide an outlet for blacks to express their political, social, and economic concerns. First published in 1905, the paper became one of the most popular African-American newspapers. Abbott's publication was important because, at the time, racism was widespread in the United States and blacks were not always able to voice their opinions in "white" newspapers.

Robert Abbott was born on St. Simon's Island, Georgia, and became interested in African-American rights at an early age. He was a newspaper printer from 1892 to 1896. Although Abbott earned an LL.B. degree (a law degree) from Kent College of Law in Chicago, Illinois, in 1898, he decided to become a journalist instead of a lawyer.

Abbott often addressed issues that people disagreed upon. For example, the *Chicago Defender* took a position against the separation of black and white military officers. The *Defender* also reported on violence against blacks. Despite financial difficulties in January 2000, Robert Abbott's paper is still in print.

Abdul-Jabbar, Kareem

BASKETBALL PLAYER
April 16, 1947–

One of the most celebrated **basketball** players in history, Kareem Abdul-Jabbar (whose real name is Lewis Ferdinand Alcindor) was born in Harlem, New York. In 1950 his family moved to the Dyckman Street projects, city-owned middle-class housing in the Inwood section of Manhattan, where Alcindor attended Power Memorial Academy. He made All-City and All-American three times and helped Power Memorial win two New York City championships and two national crowns.

At age fourteen Alcindor was six feet eight inches tall. At maturity he stood over seven feet tall. After high school Alcindor attended the University of California at Los Angeles (UCLA), where he led the UCLA Bruins to the National Collegiate Athletic Association (NCAA) championships all three years he played. During his college years he perfected his trademark shot, the skyhook. Alcindor also popularized a rather popular shot, the dunk shot (slamming the ball into the hoop).

After college Alcindor embarked on a remarkable professional basketball career. He is not, however, merely a basketball player. He is a soft-spoken leader who is faithful to both his political and his religious beliefs. His awareness of racial injustice led him to boycott the 1968 Olympic Games. In 1968 he also converted to **Islam** in search of inner peace. His Muslim teacher named him "Kareem Abdul-Jabbar," which means "generous and powerful servant of Allah."

Kareem Abdul-Jabbar shoots over the head of Detroit Piston Rick Mahorn (AP/Wide World Photos. Reproduced by permission)

In 1969 Abdul-Jabbar began his National Basketball Association (NBA) career with a bang, winning the Rookie of the Year award with the Milwaukee Bucks. Two years later he led the Bucks to an NBA championship. He was named Most Valuable Player (MVP) three times in Milwaukee before moving to the Los Angeles Lakers in 1975. He capped off his stellar career with the Lakers with three MVP awards during his first five years with the team. Abdul-Jabbar also holds many NBA records, including the most seasons, games, and minutes played; the most field goals made; and the most points scored (44,149).

Abdul-Jabbar retired from basketball in 1989. After a long break he began pursuing a coaching career. He was hired as assistant coach for the Los Angeles Clippers basketball team in 1999 and hopes to eventually be a head coach in the NBA.

Abernathy, Ralph David

CLERGYMAN, CIVIL RIGHTS LEADER
March 11, 1926–April 17, 1990

A fellow civil rights and activist and close friend of **Martin Luther King Jr.** (1929–1968), Ralph Abernathy was born in Linden, Alabama, in 1926. His father was a successful farmer and **Baptist** deacon who inspired Abernathy to enter public service. After serving in the U.S. Army during World War II (1939–45), Abernathy was ordained a Baptist minister. He also earned a bachelor of science degree from Alabama State College (Montgomery) and a master of arts degree in sociology from Atlanta University (now Clark-Atlanta University, a member of the Atlanta University Center) in Georgia.

At Alabama State Abernathy's professors, along with his leadership of two student protests, prepared him for later work as a civil rights leader. In 1951 Abernathy became pastor of the First Baptist Church in Montgomery, Alabama. There, he befriended another local pastor, Martin Luther King Jr., with whom he had frequent conversations about civil rights.

In 1955 the men were urged into action by the arrest of **Rosa Parks** (1913–), a black seamstress who refused to yield her seat on a public bus to a white passenger. Following the teachings of American writer Henry David Thoreau (1817–1862) and India's spiritual leader Mahatma Gandhi (1869–1948), they agreed that nonviolent protest would be the only acceptable means of action. Through church meetings King and Abernathy led a mass boycott of Montgomery's buses that continued for more than a year. In June 1956 a federal court ruled that the bus company must end its **Jim Crow** policy (segregating the races and giving preferential treatment to whites).

In January 1957 the **Southern Christian Leadership Conference (SCLC)** was created in Atlanta, Georgia, with King as president and Abernathy as secretary-treasurer. While he attended the meeting, Abernathy's home and church were bombed in Montgomery; his family narrowly escaped physical harm. A few years later King and Abernathy moved to Atlanta, where Abernathy became the pastor of the West Hunter Street Baptist Church.

The two men led nonviolent protests in southern cities, including **Birmingham** and **Selma, Alabama.** Both were arrested many times and experienced violence and threats of violence. When King was assassinated in Memphis, Tennessee, in 1968, Abernathy was unanimously elected his successor. He resigned from the SCLC in 1977.

When Abernathy was compared to King, he was usually described as lacking the charm and poise of his friend. Some accused him of being cross or crude in his leadership style. More criticism came just a year before his death, when Abernathy published an **autobiography,** *And the Walls Came Tumbling Down* (1989). Its content and literary style were overshadowed by the book's revelations about King's extramarital affairs. Some critics accused Abernathy of betraying his long-deceased friend.

Rev. Ralph Abernathy speaking at the Poor People's Campaign on the Capitol steps (AP/Wide World Photos. Reproduced by permission)

Abolition

Abolition was an organized effort from around the late 1700s to the mid-1800s to abolish, or put an end to, **slavery** in the United States. Although different abolition groups had different methods, they achieved a common goal during the 1860s. President Abraham Lincoln (1809–1865) issued the Emancipation Proclamation in 1863, declaring all slaves held in the Southern states to be "forever free." In 1865, with the enactment of the Thirteenth Amendment to the U.S. Constitution, slavery was outlawed in the rest of the United States. Free African Americans played an important role in bringing about abolition, along with white clergymen, politicians, journalists, speakers, authors, and women's groups.

Early Steps Taken against Slavery

Ideas about equality and the rights of all people, which fueled the **American Revolution** (1775–83), were used to combat slavery in the United States. During the 1780s abolitionist societies were formed, and a national abolitionist convention met each year from 1794 to 1806. English abolitionists sent speakers, books, pamphlets, and money to antislavery groups in the United States. Members of a small religious group called the Quakers led the movement to end slavery, just as Quakers had done in England, where slavery was abolished in 1833. In 1808 the U.S. Congress ended the foreign **slave trade,** although slavery itself remained legal.

The Colonization Movement

During the 1820s a new idea attracted more people to the antislavery cause—the idea of sending freed slaves to **Africa,** the American West, or Central America. This idea appealed both to people who disliked and feared blacks and to those who saw how blacks, both slave and free, suffered because of racism. Promoting this idea was the American Colonization Society (ACS), founded in 1816. It sent a few thousand blacks to its African colony, Liberia, before 1830, but, although it had the support of many prominent leaders, it failed to get enough funding and died out in the early twentieth century.

The Immediatist Movement

Only a small number of free African Americans and whites supported the idea of colonization. Many others took a different direction, organizing an antislavery movement in the North that was against colonization and the ACS. They believed that slaves should be freed immediately and that blacks should be allowed to make their homes in the United States and enjoy the same rights as whites. This movement was coordinated by white newspaperman William Lloyd Garrison (1805–1879). His Boston-based newspaper, the *Liberator,* started in 1831, published articles condemning slavery, prejudice, and colonization. Many blacks saw the *Liberator* as their voice in American public life.

Speakers such as New York reformer and lecturer Theodore Dwight Weld (1803–1895) also joined the fight for immediate abolition. Weld focused on getting ministers and slaveholders to see slavery as a sin, appealing to their sense of right and wrong to persuade them that slavery should be abolished. Other important abolitionist leaders included brothers Lewis and Arthur Tappan (**New York City** merchants) and poet John Greenleaf Whittier (1807–1892). In 1833 the American Anti-Slavery Society (AASS) was formed. By 1838 it claimed to have nearly a quarter million members, mostly in the Northern states.

Abolitionists tried various ways to accomplish their goals. During the 1850s people like journalist Horace Greeley (1811–1872) and clergyman Henry Ward Beecher (1813–1887) used newspapers and lectures to get the message out that slave labor could take paying jobs away from workers and farmers across the North and much of the West. This threat to white economic welfare caused public antislavery opinion to grow.

African Americans Work for Abolition

In the 1840s many blacks, unhappy that they had been allowed few leadership positions in abolitionist organizations, formed their own groups. They held their own conventions and supported their own newspapers, like Samuel E. Cornish's *Colored American* and **Frederick Douglass**'s (1817–1895) *North Star.*

The African-American minister, abolition leader, and former slave Henry Highland Garnet (1815–1882) gave a speech in 1843 urging slaves to rise up against their masters and resist slavery. **Free blacks** and a few whites engaged in peaceful public protest against segregated schools and streetcars, and blacks helped **fugitive slaves** in every way they could.

The Civil War and the End of Slavery

When the American **Civil War** (1861–65) broke out, abolitionists pressured the Union (Northern) army to accept black soldiers. Before slavery was abolished, abolitionist men and women went south to work among freedmen (freed black slaves) in areas occupied by Union troops, setting a pattern for efforts to help freed slaves. Their work increased during the **Reconstruction** period following the war.

At the end of the Civil War, and with the enactment of the Thirteenth Amendment, slavery came to an end. The *Liberator* stopped publishing, and the AASS disbanded. But younger abolitionists continued to work, promoting **education** for African Americans and criticizing violations of their civil rights, long after the war was over. At the end of the nineteenth century, however, many of their victories were overturned. Some scholars condemned abolitionists as fanatics who were partly responsible for dividing the North and the South in civil war. Still, Northerners praised the abolitionists as a group that led the nation to higher ideals and practices.

Ace, Johnny

MUSICIAN, SONGWRITER
1929–December 25, 1954

Rhythm-and-blues (R&B) artist Johnny Ace was born John Marshall Alexander Jr. in Memphis, Tennessee. The sixth child in a family of ten, he displayed talent in voice, piano, composition, and painting as a young boy. He left school early to join the U.S. Navy, but was given a dishonorable discharge in 1947.

By 1949 Alexander was playing piano in **blues** great **B. B. King**'s (1925–) band, the Beale Street Blues Boys (later the Beale Streeters). In 1952 Duke Records of Memphis renamed Alexander "Johnny Ace" and released his ballad "My Song." African-American entrepreneur Don D. Robey then acquired controlling interest in Duke Records and promoted Ace's record to the top of the R&B charts.

Ace's career lasted less than two and a half years, but he produced eight R&B top ten records, including two number one hits. "Pledging My Love" (1954) was part of a trend introducing black musical sounds and cultural styles to white teenagers, a development that revolutionized American popular music. Ace died on Christmas night 1954 while playing Russian roulette (a game of chance involving a partially loaded gun) during intermission backstage at Houston, Texas's City Auditorium.

Adderley, Julian Edwin "Cannonball"

JAZZ SAXOPHONIST, EDUCATOR
September 15, 1928–August 15, 1975

Julian Edwin Adderley, better known as "Cannonball" Adderley, was a famous **jazz** musician who played the saxophone and was also a bandleader. Jazz musicians do a lot of "improvisation," making up the music as they perform, which is called "free form." Adderley was especially good at this and is considered a pioneer of the free-form style. One of the things that made Adderley's music unique was his use of silence, or pauses, in the music to create a dramatic effect. Adderley was far from silent, however, when it came to promoting black music. He gave great speeches at colleges that helped more people understand and enjoy jazz music.

Cannonball Adderley was born in 1928 in Tampa, Florida. He developed an interest in jazz while attending high school. He went to college at

"Cannonball" Adderly holding his alto saxophone (Archive Photos. Reproduced by permission)

Florida A&M University in Tallahassee and directed a high school band in Fort Lauderdale, Florida, from 1948 to 1950. Adderley then played in U.S. Army bands from 1950 to 1953 before settling in a teaching career in Florida until 1955. He later put together a band who played from 1959 to 1975 and had a big impact on the success and popularity of jazz.

Adderley worked with the famous trumpet player **Miles Davis** (1926–1991) and saxophonist **John Coltrane** (1926–1967). He later formed a very successful quintet (five-member band) with his brother, Nathaniel, in 1959. Cannonball and Nat developed a unique form of jazz that combined bebop, a peppy form of jazz, with jazz-soul, a more mellow form of jazz. Adderley's band played their unique form of jazz throughout New York City, making an important contribution to African-American culture.

Aerospace

African-American involvement in aviation dates back to 1917 and **World War I** (1914–18), when an African American named Eugene Bullard flew a plane for the French army. Although Bullard is usually identified as the first African-American pilot, an even more inspiring story is that of the first black woman pilot, **Bessie Coleman** (1892–1926), who was forced to travel to France to receive her flight training because of racial discrimination in the United States. After Coleman died in a plane accident in 1926, an

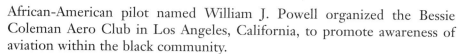

African-American pilot named William J. Powell organized the Bessie Coleman Aero Club in Los Angeles, California, to promote awareness of aviation within the black community.

Although many African Americans participated in the early years of flight, most of the activities were segregated, meaning black and white pilots were not allowed to train or serve together in the armed forces. Prior to World War II (1939–45), many African Americans completed long-distance flights. In 1932 James Herman Banning became the first black pilot fly across North America.

Throughout the 1930s a Chicago, Illinois, publisher named **Robert Abbott** tirelessly promoted aviation awareness in the black community. He also lobbied the U.S. Congress, unsuccessfully, for black inclusion in aviation training programs sponsored by the government. Perhaps the most influential African-American pilots and teachers during this time were Cornelius R. Coffey and his wife, Willia B. Brown, who founded the Coffey School of Aeronautics at Harlem Airport in Chicago. Brown, a licensed mechanic and pilot, later became a lieutenant—the first African-American officer—in the Civil Air Patrol.

The Military Opens Up

Coffey and Brown were crucial to one of the most historic advances in black aviation. The U.S. Army Air Corps (the parent organization of the U.S. Air Force) expanded greatly in the United States prior to World War II, but it remained closed to blacks. In 1941, after an intense lobbying effort led by Coffey, Brown, and a man named Enoch P. Waters, Congress agreed to let blacks into the government's Civilian Pilot Training Program (CPTP), which trained pilots who could later be called upon to serve in the **military.** The CPTP programs, which were offered at many black colleges, trained over 2,000 black pilots. Approximately 450 of them served in **World War II.**

On July 26, 1948, by executive order, President Harry S. Truman officially ended segregation in the armed forces, and African-American pilots were slowly integrated into all-white units. By the close of the **Korean War** (1950–53), blacks were participating in all activities of the U.S. Air Force and U.S. Army Air Cavalry units, with some earning the military's highest honors for pilots. Eventually, African Americans held officer rank at all levels.

Commercial Success

Following the Korean War, African Americans became active in commercial aviation as helicopter pilots, flight attendants, aircraft owners, airline operators, and executives. In 1965 a notable antidiscrimination lawsuit against Continental Airlines forced airlines to hire black pilots. Warren Wheeler, a former pilot for Piedmont Airlines, began Wheeler Flight Services, the first black-owned airline, in 1969.

U.S. aircraft manufacturers also recognized the value of black aerospace engineers. Beginning in the mid-1960s, African Americans became active in all areas of the U.S. aerospace industry. Within this group of outstanding African Americans, Wesley L. Harris was the first to obtain the rank of full professor in the Department of Aeronautics and Astronautics at the Massachusetts Institute of Technology (MIT). Woodrow Whitlow, a student

THE TUSKEGEE AIRMEN

The efforts of black lobbyists and white supporters who fought to achieve equal rights for African-American pilots led to a small—and now famous—military project. In 1941, over the opposition of many in Congress, the War Department, and the Air Corps, the U.S. Army activated the all-black 99th Pursuit (later Fighter) Squadron at Tuskegee Army Air Field in Alabama. Despite inadequate training and racist riots at training sites throughout the South and Midwest, the "Tuskegee Airmen" were sent to North Africa, attached to the white 33rd Fighter Group, and performed honorably. On July 2, 1943, Charles Hall became the first African-American pilot to shoot down an enemy fighter plane, and he later received the Distinguished Flying Cross. In 1943 the 99th Squadron merged with three others trained at Tuskegee to form the 332nd Fighter Group. The group was eventually sent to Europe, where the U.S. Army's black airmen distinguished themselves as bomber escorts. Since then, the Tuskegee Airmen have been recognized in several books and movies.

of Harris's, later became the first African-American branch chief at the National Aeronautics and Space Administration's (NASA) Langley Research Center.

African Americans in the Space Program

An outstanding group of black astronauts and scientists have supported the U.S. space program, both as mission control specialists and as astronauts. The first African American in space was **Guion S. Bluford Jr.,** a **Vietnam War** (1959–75) veteran with a Ph.D. degree in aerospace engineering. Bluford flew aboard the space shuttle *Challenger* on August 30, 1983. On April 29, 1985, Frederik Gregory took the controls of the space shuttle *Challenger/Spacelab 3* and became the first African American to pilot a space mission. Ronald E. McNair was the first African American to conduct experiments in space, aboard the *Challenger* in 1984. He was later killed when the *Challenger* exploded on January 28, 1986. Other African-American astronauts with flight experience include Charles F. Bolden, Bernard A. Harris (the first African American to walk in space), and **Mae C. Jemison,** who in September 1992 became the first African-American woman in space.

In the 1980s and 1990s the rich heritage of African-American aviation received increased attention. In 1982 "Black Wings," a special exhibit on black aviation pioneers, was featured at the Smithsonian Institution in Washington, D.C. In 1995 the film *The Tuskegee Airmen*, starring Laurence Fishburne and Cuba Gooding Jr., was released to critical acclaim.

Affirmative Action

People are sometimes treated unfairly for a number of reasons, including where they come from, what language they speak, what color their skin is, what religion they practice, whether they are male or female, or for having a disability. Affirmative action is a policy or law created by a government, institution, or business to remedy, or make up for, such unfair treatment. For African Americans, affirmative action is intended to correct inequalities that have existed in the United States since the seventeenth century.

How Affirmative Action Works

Affirmative action, or ensuring equal opportunity, in business means making an effort to hire African Americans, as well as people of other races and national origins. It usually involves a goal of hiring a certain number of such individuals within a specific time period. Employers often choose the number of individuals to hire based on what percentage of the national or local population that group represents. Another goal of equal opportunity in business is to ensure that people of all races are represented in upper-level, or management, positions.

In education, affirmative action for African Americans began with desegregation, or allowing black and white students to go to public and private schools together. Before the historic U.S. Supreme Court decision **Brown v. Board of Education of Topeka, Kansas** (1954) ended racial segregation of public schools, black students and white students in many states attended separate, or segregated, schools. Since then, schools have set goals for hiring African-American teachers and for enrolling black students. Some schools offer special scholarships, subjects, and programs for African-American students. Colleges and universities often enroll a percentage of African-American and other nonwhite students to ensure that all groups and cultures are represented in the student body.

Affirmative action is also carried out by federal government programs. These programs make public and private funds available to individuals based on race, need, and qualification. For instance, a percentage of government work contracts is awarded to African-American or other minority businesses. Scientific or cultural organizations might give a portion of their grants, awards, and prizes to African Americans and other nonwhites. Voting district boundaries might be redrawn so more African Americans can vote in districts where they were once underrepresented.

How Affirmative Action Began

President Abraham Lincoln (1809–1865; president 1860–1865) signed the Emancipation Proclamation in 1863, and the Thirteenth Amendment ended slavery in 1865, but it would be more than seventy years before the U.S. government would create an official policy to try and end discrimination. In 1941 President Franklin D. Roosevelt (1882–1945; president 1933–1945) issued Executive Order 8802, calling for "special measures" to end "discrimination in the employment of workers in the defense industries or government . . . because of race, creed, color, or national origin." As a result, violence broke out between blacks and whites in some states as black workers began competing for jobs traditionally held by whites.

The Civil Rights Act of 1964 outlawed racial discrimination in jobs, education, housing, and voting. It desegregated restaurants, hotels, stores,

Affirmative Action in business means making an effort to hire African Americans, as well as people of other races and national origins.

How Fair Is Affirmative Action?

Critics of affirmative action believe the policy creates "reverse discrimination" against whites and others who would otherwise receive job positions or be eligible for government work contracts. Those who support affirmative action believe in the policy and that quotas help remedy past discrimination and create a more representative work force or student body.

There are also critics of affirmative action within the African-American community. Most African Americans support affirmative action policies, but some say the policies discourage a "colorblind" society in which people are judged on their merits and not given special treatment because of race or other factors. These African Americns also say affirmative action benefits mostly middle-class blacks and does nothing for the poor. The same critics claim it reinforces the idea that blacks are inferior to whites and sometimes causes low self-esteem among African Americans. Others say that whites living today should not be held responsible for the wrongs done by slaveholders of the past.

Supporters of affirmative action say the issues of unemployment, poor health care, homelessness, and hunger facing many African Americans today are the result of a history of oppression, beginning with slavery and continuing with racial segregation and discrimination. They say that affirmative action helps create minority role models—such as intellectuals, artists, and civic leaders—while acknowledging society's diversity.

theaters, beaches, and transportation, such as trains and buses. It also prevented schools that were still segregated from receiving government funding. Title VII of the act created the Equal Employment Opportunity Commission (EEOC) and banned job discrimination by employers with twenty-five or more workers.

In 1965 President Lyndon B. Johnson (1908–1973; president 1963–1969) made affirmative action the center of U.S. employment policy, where it remained during the 1970s. During the 1980s and early 1990s the federal government relaxed enforcement of affirmative action because Presidents Ronald Reagan and George Bush opposed the push to meet quotas.

The Future of Affirmative Action

Between 1969 and 1993 the U.S. Supreme Court considered more than twenty major cases about affirmative action. Many of these were decided in favor of affirmative action, but several important cases related to education, voting, jobs, and minority business opportunities rejected affirmative action.

Among the most well known cases was *Regents of the University of California v. Bakke* (1978). Alan Bakke was a white student who applied for medical school at the University of California, Davis, but was denied admis-

Poster encouraging affirmative action and equal opportunity

sion. The medical school had a policy that at least 16 percent of its students must be "blacks, Chicanos, Asian Americans, and American Indians." According to Bakke, he was being discriminated against because he was white. Ultimately, the Supreme Court decided that Bakke should be admitted to the school, that his rights had been violated, and that the school's admission quota policies were unlawful.

In July 1995 the trustees of the University of California voted to end minority preferences in state college admissions. In 1996 a group led by California governor Pete Wilson and African-American businessman Ward Connerly introduced Proposition 209 to bar affirmative action programs. California voters approved the proposition, and voters in the state of Washington approved a similar measure in 1998. (*See also* **Economics; Education.**)

Africa

Most early Africans were farmers who raised crops using complex irrigation techniques based on mathematics.

Many of the ancestors of modern-day African Americans came from West and Central Africa. African Americans are proud of their heritage and their link to modern African people. They strive to show how much the continent of Africa has given to the world, beginning nearly five thousand years ago with the pharaohs and pyramids of ancient Egypt. Africa has been compared to a museum where cultural patterns from many periods in history exist at the same time.

Land and Climate

Africa has high, glacier-tipped mountains and great extinct volcanoes. It has rain forests and vast deserts. Africa also has spectacular rivers and waterfalls and some of the world's largest and deepest lakes. It is a land rich in minerals and plant and animal life. Herds of antelopes, giraffes, lions, zebras, and elephants roam the savannas (grasslands). Many animals, such as the rhinoceros, are now endangered because of excessive hunting and the growth of human populations. Although grains, fruits, and vegetables can be grown where the soil is good and rainfall is adequate, parts of Africa regularly suffer from droughts and food shortages.

Peoples, Cultures, Economies

No one knows what the earliest humans in Africa looked like, but Negro-appearing (black) people became the dominant population south of the Sahara, a desert stretching across northern Africa. Caucasian (white) peoples lived in northern Africa and parts of the Nile River valley. People with yellowish skin and wiry hair, called the Khoisan, lived in parts of southern Africa. Whites of European ancestry and people of Indian ancestry occupied southern and east-central Africa. People of Southeast Asian and South Pacific Ocean origins settled Africa's largest island, Madagascar, in the northeastern part of the country. African culture developed over centuries, through contact between the many different groups within Africa as well as through trade with neighboring civilizations of the Middle East, the Mediterranean, and Asia. As a result, about eight hundred different languages are spoken in Africa, the largest group of languages found on any continent.

People of the Nile valley began cultivating crops and raising animals for food about six thousand years ago. Most early Africans were farmers who raised crops using complex irrigation techniques based on mathematics. They also studied the sun, moon, and stars to determine when to plant and harvest crops. They raised cereal grains, rice, beans, yams, bananas, and cotton for making cloth. People living in the savannas herded cattle, sheep, goats, camels, donkeys, and horses. Some groups also hunted and fished for food.

In small farming settlements, people later made iron tools and pots, and in larger societies craftsmen worked gold, tin, copper, and silver. Weavers, carpenters, and glassmakers produced trade goods for distant cultures whose merchants crossed the Sahara in camel caravans. Beads, cloth, bracelets, shells, gold dust, and even slaves were used as money. In West Africa, the

THE ANCIENT SUPERCONTINENT

The continent of Africa, at 11.7 million square miles, is more than three times the size of the United States, including Alaska. Some geologists believe that Africa was once the core of an ancient supercontinent, which they call Gondwanaland. They believe this enormous land mass fractured into pieces around two hundred million years ago. Portions separating from what is now Africa drifted away to form South America, Australia, Antarctica, and part of India.

great kingdoms of Ghana, Mali, and Songhay grew rich during the tenth through the sixteenth centuries by trading some of their gold for other goods.

Mummies, Kings, and Medicine Men: Africans built great cities as their capitals, using mathematics to plan massive structures like the pyramids of Egypt (first built in 2780 B.C.) and great palaces. Writing developed early, and knowledge of the human body and medicine came about as Egyptians developed ways to preserve the bodies of their dead rulers by making them into mummies.

Most Africans lived in large family groups, with specific duties for men and women. African children were trained at home by parents and other family members. Older children went to schools, where they learned good manners, civic responsibilities, and religious teachings. Some great rulers used these schools to train soldiers for their armies. African kingdoms had large, complex governments and societies. Smaller farming communities depended on more primitive means to conduct their affairs and run their society, such as use of rain-making medicines in times of drought and medicine men to heal sickness and drive away evil.

"Divine" kings, whose rule was believed to be blessed by heaven and the royal ancestors, were found throughout Africa. Often ruling at their side were women called queen mothers, queen sisters, or princesses. Both male and female rulers had holy shrines, priests, and religious objects to show their great power. From elaborate courts, temples, or capital cities, they ruled over their territory. Rulers dressed in splendid, colorful clothing and were surrounded by gold and silver objects.

Religious Beliefs

Most early African religious beliefs were based on myths about a creator-god who lived in the sky and could take the form of the sun, the earth, or the moon. In Egypt the pharaohs (rulers) were considered gods; this was also true of kings in other African societies.

Ancestor veneration (showing great respect for) was an important feature in early African religions. It was believed that the ancestors appeared to people in their dreams to warn them that sickness or evil was caused by something they had done. To atone, the people were required to make sacrifices to the ancestors. Some cultures portrayed the ancestors as masked fig-

AFRICA: CRADLE OF MAN

S cientists who study fossil human bones and other remains have found human-like bones in Africa dating to about four million years ago. Named *Australopithecus africanus,* this apelike creature walked upright and is believed to be the first hominid (human). Many scientists now believe that the origins of all modern humans on earth can be traced to a woman who lived in Africa about two hundred thousand years ago.

ures who came from the land of the dead to attend trials involving the living. Christianity, Judaism, and **Islam** were introduced to Africa centuries ago. Islam has become a major **religion** in northern, western, and eastern Africa.

Arts and Music

Evidence shows that prehistoric Africans styled their hair and painted and decorated their bodies. Africans created jewelry, carvings, and masks and decorated household items like pots and spoons. They created myths, legends, poetry, riddles, parables, and proverbs. Today, the Ashanti people are still known for their proverbs and the Swahili for their poetry. Africans developed an impressive number of musical instruments, songs, and dances for religious and social purposes. Instruments ranged from simple sticks and rattles to bells, stringed instruments, horns, and flutes. Many African songs are based on the "call and response," in which one person sings a line and the group chorus responds. Music and singing most often accompany dancing.

New Interest in African Culture

After Africans were introduced to the New World as slaves, beginning in the 1500s, many of their cultural traditions died out. However, African Americans have revived many of those traditions or combined them with those of other cultures. Today, many African Americans travel to Africa to learn more about the culture of their ancestors so they can establish new African traditions in the United States for their children and grandchildren. (*See also* **Afrocentricity.**)

African-American Dance. *See* Ballet; Breakdancing; Dance Theater of Harlem; Social Dance; Tap Dance; Zydeco

African-American Literature. *See* Autobiography; Children's Literature; Comic Books; Comic Strips; Folklore; Science Fiction; Slave Narratives

African-American Magazines. *See* The Crisis; Ebony; Jet Magazine

African-American Music. *See* **Blues, The; Concert Music; Folk Music and Singers; Gospel Music; Jazz; Motown; Opera; Ragtime; Rap; Reggae; Rhythm-and-Blues**

African-American Newspapers. *See* **Liberator, The**

African-American Philosophies. *See* **Afrocentricity; Conservatism**

African Methodist Episcopal (AME) Church

The African Methodist Episcopal Church (the AME) was founded by **Richard Allen** (1760–1831), a former slave and traveling preacher who settled in Philadelphia, Pennsylvania, to preach to blacks at the St. George Methodist Episcopal Church. Some of Allen's views, especially his ideas about creating a separate African-American church, created tensions with white church leaders. Allen left St. George to build the Bethel African Methodist Episcopal Church, often called the Mother Bethel Church, in 1794. In his fight with white church leaders, Allen drew support from other black congregations in the region. After Pennsylvania's supreme court ruled in 1816 that Allen's Bethel congregation was legally an independent church, black supporters traveled from all over the eastern United States to Philadelphia to form the AME Church. At this first meeting, Allen was selected as the AME's first bishop.

Under Allen's leadership the church grew rapidly, expanding to the north, south, and west. By the time of the American Civil War (1861–65), the denomination included congregations in several slave states and throughout the Pacific Coast region. Branches of the AME also sprang up in Canada and Haiti. In 1864, thirty-three years after Allen's death, the AME Church had fifty thousand members in sixteen hundred congregations.

During the **Civil War** period many ministers and congregations were involved in the **abolition** movement (the fight to end **slavery**). Morris Brown, Allen's successor as bishop, was supposedly involved in the **Denmark Vesey Conspiracy,** a failed slave revolt in South Carolina in 1822. According to white authorities, those involved had planned the revolt during AME church services. The abolitionist views of leaders such as Allen and Brown could be heard at the 1840 AME annual conference in Pittsburgh, Pennsylvania, where it was proclaimed that "slavery pollutes the character of the church of God."

The Civil War and Reconstruction

An important church leader during the Civil War period was Daniel A. Payne, a freeborn schoolteacher in South Carolina whose school had been closed by a state law forbidding the education of blacks. In 1863 Payne, by then a bishop, convinced AME leaders that providing higher education for blacks would help them achieve power. He ultimately helped found **Wilberforce University** in Ohio, the first black college started by African

THE WOMEN OF THE AME CHURCH

In 1819, when Bishop Richard Allen authorized Jarena Lee to become an exhorter (someone who leads prayer and discussion meetings) in the AME Church, he opened the door to women in the ministry. For nearly 150 years unordained (unofficial) female evangelists played important roles as preachers, pastors, and founders of congregations. During the nineteenth and early twentieth centuries, Amanda Berry Smith, Sarah Hughes, and Lillian Thurman preached in AME pulpits. Smith evangelized (preached) widely in the United States and then abroad in the British Isles, India, and West Africa. Like many, Millie Wolfe, a female preacher in Waycross, Georgia, focused her efforts on the denomination's Women's Home and Foreign Missionary Society. Wolfe published a book of sermons titled *Scriptural Authority for Women's Work in the Christian Church*. Female evangelists in the Rocky Mountain states were crucial to AME expansion in Colorado, New Mexico, Arizona, Wyoming, and Montana in the early 1900s. Although the gifted preaching of Martha Jayne Keys, Mary Watson Stewart, and others sustained the visibility of female ministers in the first half of the twentieth century, it was not until 1960 that the denomination allowed the full ordination (authority to serve as a church minister) of women.

Americans. Wilberforce was the first of many colleges to be founded by the AME Church.

The Civil War years were also important for the church's development. Many black soldiers were recruited from AME congregations, and many AME clergymen fought on the Union (Northern) side. As Northern armies proceeded to conquer areas in the South, AME preachers were sent to those states to attract blacks into African Methodism. By 1880 church membership from Virginia to Texas had swelled to 387,566 people in 2,051 churches.

During **Reconstruction,** the period after the Civil War when Southern states struggled to recover, AME clergy had a significant influence. They served in state legislatures and even in the U.S. Congress. But not everyone in the AME was happy about the political involvement of the Southern clergymen. Bishop Payne, in particular, believed the church was being made too political in the South. But there was also increasing political involvement of AME clergy in the Northern branch of the denomination. A Milwaukee pastor named Ezekiel Gillespie, for example, initiated a state supreme court case that won voting rights for Wisconsin blacks in 1866.

Expansion Overseas and at Home

In the late nineteenth century, the church expanded to Great Britain and several African nations. Missionaries were also sent to Cuba and Mexico. The issue of overseas expansion, combined with **black nationalism**—the idea that blacks should form their own nation, separate from the United States—caused feuding within the church, however. Nationalists felt that the church should work to send all American blacks back to **Africa.** Others, such as **Benjamin T. Tanner,** believed that to abandon the fight for racial equality in the United States would be cowardly. The issue dominated church conferences for many years.

In the **Great Migration** during World War I (1914–18) and World War II (1939–41), thousands of blacks from rural communities in the South migrated to industrial centers across the country. This migration caused major growth in AME churches in cities such as New York; Chicago, Illinois; Atlanta, Georgia; and Los Angeles, California. In these cities clergy involved themselves in such issues as housing, social welfare, and unionization. When the **Civil Rights movement** began to bloom in the late 1940s and early 1950s, AME clergy lent support.

The Church Today

Since its formal founding in 1816, the AME Church's general conference (held every four years) has remained the supreme authority in church matters. Annual conferences take place at various locations around the country. At these yearly meetings church leaders assign ministers to the churches they will pastor. The AME has no central headquarters; it has a publishing house located in Nashville, Tennessee. Twenty active bishops and thirteen general officers make up the African Methodist Episcopal Church leadership. According to the latest available figures, the AME has more than two million members in approximately thirty countries. It is the second-largest Methodist denomination in the United States.

AfriCobra

The African Commune of Bad Relevant Artists (AfriCobra), established in 1968, is an organization that promotes political expression through artwork. Its founders (Jeff Donaldson, Jae Jarrell, Wadworth Jarrell, Barbara Jones-Hogu, and Gerald Williams) wanted to inspire artists to produce work that would lead people to revolt against racial inequality. Emerging during the **Civil Rights movement** of the 1950s and 1960s, AfriCobra still exists as a major sponsor of black artwork.

AfriCobra originated in Chicago, Illinois, and spread to eastern cities such as Boston, Massachusetts, and Washington, D.C. (where it is currently headquartered). One of the most impressive works of art inspired by the founders of AfriCobra is the "Wall of Respect" (1967), an enormous painting of African-American leaders such as **Frederick Douglass** (1817–1895) and **Malcolm X** (1925–1965) on the side of a building in Chicago.

AfriCobra's artistic style blends traditional African colors with political statements from black leaders. For example, one of AfriCobra's works (Wadworth Jarrell's "Revolutionary," 1971), is a picture of **Angela Davis** (a 1960s political activist, revolutionary, and author who was on the FBI's ten most-wanted list in 1970) with her face and hands made from the words of her political slogans.

AfriCobra's work often focuses on political struggles such as the South African liberation movement's fight to end apartheid (strict segregation of blacks and whites) in South Africa. AfriCobra encourages political and social change and has inspired people around the globe to reflect on the historic and current injustices done to blacks. In May 2000 AfriCobra put together a touring display called "Transatlantic Dialogue," which opened in Washington, D.C.

Afrocentricity

"Afrocentricity" refers to the idea that there is a common cultural history shared by all descendants of **Africa.** According to scholars, this shared African heritage is a way for blacks to unite and to regain the power that over the centuries has been taken away from them. Throughout history countries in Africa have been invaded, conquered, and colonized by European nations; African people have been captured and sold into **slavery.** Individuals who were sent to live in other countries were forced to take on non-African identities and to live by non-African rules. Those who remained in African countries ruled by white invaders were also forced to live by foreign rules. Such upheaval contributed to the destruction of the African culture.

Blacks struggled against the odds to gain freedom and equality. This political and cultural struggle peaked during the 1950s and 1960s in the United States. Afrocentricity, which puts Egypt and black culture at the center of all art and knowledge, was embraced as a way for blacks to combat white authority. Since then, it has grown into more than just a tool to fight white dominance. It is a way of life for all blacks who wish to recognize their common history and to better their lives, families, and communities. (*See also* **Kwanzaa.**)

AIDS (Autoimmune Deficiency Syndrome). *See* Diseases and Epidemics

Ai Ogawa, Florence

POET
October 21, 1947–

Florence Ai Ogawa is a poet and writer who has won numerous awards for her work. Born Florence Anthony on October 21, 1947, she grew up in a poor Mexican neighborhood (called a barrio) in Tucson, Arizona. She is one-half Japanese and one-quarter African American; she is also a mixture of Choctaw Indian, Irish, and Dutch. Ai Ogawa's father was a Japanese American, but she never knew him, because he was not married to her mother. At age twenty-two she adopted the pen name "Ai," a word that means "love" in Japanese. Four years later, she learned that her natural father's name was Ogawa, and she adopted that name too. Thus the woman who was born Florence Anthony became the poet Florence Ai Ogawa.

Ai Ogawa graduated from the University of Arizona in 1969 and from the University of California in 1971, where she studied Asian culture and creative writing. She then taught at many colleges and universities, including the State University of New York at Binghamton; the University of Massachusetts, Amherst; Wayne State University in Detroit, Michigan; Arizona State University (Tempe); and the University of Louisville (Kentucky).

Ai Ogawa's first book of poems, *Cruelty*, was published in 1973. It was followed by *Killing Floor*, published in 1979, *Sin* (1985), *Fate* (1991), and *Greed* (1993). In 1997 she published a novel, *Black Blood*. Her poems tell the stories of the poorest members of society. Some of her characters are criminals, even murderers and prostitutes, and some are victims of violent crimes. Because of her multiracial origins, she considers herself to be the voice of all people. According to Ai Ogawa, "Whoever wants to speak in my poems is allowed to speak, regardless of sex, race, creed [religious beliefs], or color."

Ailey, Alvin

DANCER, CHOREOGRAPHER
January 5, 1931–December 1, 1989

After a poor rural childhood, Alvin Ailey fell in love with dance and the theater as a teen and became one of the world's best-known dancers and choreographers (dance composers and arrangers).

Ailey was born in Rogers, Texas, the only child of working-class parents who separated when he was two. He moved to Los Angeles, California, with his mother, Lula Cooper, when he was eleven. There, he saw dancers on the stage for the first time. Even though he was shy, Ailey began to study with dancer Lester Horton at his Hollywood studio in 1949. He poured himself into his study and developed a powerful performance style that suited his athletic body.

Ailey moved to New York City in 1954. There, he studied with leading modern-dance and **ballet** teachers, including Martha Graham and Charles Weidman. By 1958 he had founded his own dance company, the Alvin Ailey American Dance Theater (AAADT). It began with only seven dedicated dancers who performed both modern-dance classics and new works created by Ailey and other young artists. Ailey's *Blues Suite* (1958), which is influenced by early-twentieth-century African-American **social dance**s, expresses the difficulties and joys of life on the edge of poverty in the American South. This and other early performances marked the beginning of a new era of dance devoted to African-American themes.

Performances of Ailey's *Revelations* (1960) established the AAADT as the leading dance interpreter of African-American life. Set to a series of spirituals and gospel selections, *Revelations* includes different scenes from black religious worship. It quickly became the AAADT's best-known ballet.

In 1976 the AAADT honored African-American bandleader and composer **Duke Ellington** (1899–1974) with a festival featuring fifteen new bal-

THE ALVIN AILEY AMERICAN DANCE THEATER

A lvin Ailey created the Alvin Ailey American Dance Theater (AAADT) in 1958 to feature the talents of his fellow African-American dancers, but the company has always included white dancers as well. Ailey once told the *New York Times*, "I am trying to show the world that we are all human beings and that color is not important. What is important is the quality of our work."

Ailey encouraged his dancers to contribute individual style and emotions to their performances. This helped to create the first star personalities in American modern dance. An example is **Judith Jamison,** whose performance in Ailey's dance *Cry,* created in 1971 as a birthday present to his mother, has thrilled audiences by showing a relationship between the dancing body and life as a black woman in the United States. Jamison was appointed artistic director of the AAADT after Ailey's death in 1989.

The AAADT earned its international reputation through a series of world tours begun in 1962. By 1989 performances by the AAADT had been seen by fifteen million people worldwide. Since the late 1960s, the AAADT has reached out to the community with programs and schools to teach dance and choreography and to enrich the lives of young people through dance. In 1989 Dance Foundation, which manages the activities of the AAADT, started the Ailey Camps program, designed to give inner-city youth confidence, critical-thinking skills, and creative expression through dance.

lets set to his music. In 1984 Ailey created *For "Bird"—With Love* in honor of American **jazz** saxophonist **Charlie Parker** (1920–1955), featuring AAADT dancer Gary DeLoatch.

Throughout his career Ailey won many major honors, including a United Nations Peace Medal and a Spingarn Medal from the **National Association for the Advancement of Colored People (NAACP),** its highest honor. In 1988 he was honored by U.S. president Ronald Reagan for a lifetime of achievement in the arts. He created seventy-nine dances for his own company as well as for the American Ballet Theater, the Joffrey Ballet, and several European ballet companies.

Ailey stopped dancing in 1965, and he slowed his choreographic work in the 1970s to manage his growing dance company and help with fund-raising. In 1980 he was briefly hospitalized for a stress-related condition. Ailey died in 1989 after a long illness.

Alabama

First African-American Settlers: African Americans have lived in Alabama since 1719, when the first enslaved blacks were brought in to work as laborers and domestics.

Slave Population: Alabama achieved statehood in 1819. During the mid-1800s up to 25 percent of white Alabamians owned slaves, who worked primarily in the cotton industry or as skilled laborers and tradespeople. In 1860 the census listed 435,080 enslaved Africans—nearly half of the state's population.

Free Black Population: By 1860 Alabama had a small **free black** population. Some slave masters freed their slaves, and other blacks bought their freedom.

Civil War: Alabama's economy was damaged heavily by the **Civil War** (1861–65); drafting of black slave laborers and white soldiers by the Confederate (Southern) army sparked a shortage of workers. As a result, some plantations were placed in the care of trusted slaves or black sharecroppers. When Union (Northern) troops entered parts of the state in 1862, some black slaves took advantage of their presence by escaping behind Union lines. Eventually, some ten thousand blacks served as soldiers in the Union army.

Reconstruction: The end of the Civil War brought freedom to Alabama's enslaved black population and saw the development of independent religious groups, friendship societies, literary groups, and public schools. In 1865, however, the state government began strict police supervision of African Americans. Although a new state constitution created in 1867 provided for some equal rights, laws setting up separate schools and other facilities for blacks and whites ("segregation") were later passed. Many black farmers fell into poverty at the turn of the century because of fraud by white landowners and destruction of cotton crops by boll weevils.

The Great Depression: Alabama black leaders were key in organizing numerous unions in the 1930s. White officials often responded to the efforts with violence. Segregation and legal harassment remained widespread in Alabama during the first half of the twentieth century. Black Alabamians nevertheless won important victories in the fight for equal employment opportunities and voting rights.

Civil Rights Movement: Alabama served as the front line in the **civil rights movement.** The state was the center of acts of brutality inflicted on nonviolent protesters, in some cases while law enforcement looked on. Crucial victories came in 1963, when downtown Birmingham was desegregated and black students entered the University of Alabama. These civil rights efforts were crucial to the passage of the 1964 Civil Rights Act.

Current African-American Population: According to U.S. Census Bureau estimates, the total black population in Alabama was 1,132,196 (26 percent of the state population) as of July 1, 1998.

Key Figures: Holland Thompson (c. 1840–1887), political activist; **Booker T. Washington** (1856–1915), first principal of **Tuskegee University;** musicians **Nat "King" Cole** (1919–1965) and **Dinah Washington** (1924–1963); **Jesse Owens** (1913–1980), Olympic **track** star; boxer **Joe Louis** (1914–1981); **baseball** player **Willie Mays** (1931–); writers **Margaret Walker** (1915–1998) and **Sonia Sanchez** (1934–); civil rights leaders E. D. Nixon (1899–1987), **Rosa Parks** (1913–), **Coretta Scott King** (1927–), and

Ralph Abernathy (1926–1990); Earl F. Hilliard (1942–), first black U.S. congressman from Alabama since **Reconstruction.**

(SEE ALSO **FREEDOM RIDES; TUSKEGEE UNIVERSITY; SCOTTSBORO BOYS; CONGRESS OF RACIAL EQUALITY.**)

Alaska

First African-American Settlers: Official records seldom accounted for African Americans in Alaska's early years. Personal documents, however, detail their active participation in settling the Alaskan frontier.

Slave Population: Alaska became the forty-ninth state in 1959. There was no official documentation of a population of enslaved blacks.

Free Black Population: According to U.S. census records, African Americans made up ½ to 1 percent of Alaska's population from 1890 to 1940 (from 112 to 141). They overcame social prejudice to become shop owners, miners, whalers, fishermen, laborers, and trappers.

The Great Depression: In 1943 the all-black Ninety-seventh Division of the Corps of Engineers was chosen to build the Alaskan section of the Alcan (Alaskan-Canadian) Highway. Forced to live in tents while white troops enjoyed the warmth of a newly built air base, the Ninety-seventh Division endured the worst winter in recorded Alaskan history. They finished the road ahead of schedule, however, attesting to their dedication and hard work.

Civil Rights Movement to the Present: Pete Aiken, elected to the Fairbanks North Star Borough Assembly in 1956, was the first African American in the state to be elected to public office. In 1960 Blanche Smith became the first African American to serve in the state legislature. Willard Bowman served as the first executive director of the State Commission for Human Rights, created in 1963. Civil rights organizations included the Alaska Black Caucus, the Alaska Black Leadership Conference, and the Black Business Council. Since 1959, fewer than twenty African Americans have been elected to office; only five have served in the state house of representatives, and none in the senate.

Current African-American Population: According to U.S. Census Bureau estimates, the total black population in Alaska was 23,771 (less than 4 percent of the state population) as of July 1, 1998.

Aldridge, Ira

ACTOR
July 24, 1807–August 7, 1867

Born a **free black** in New York City, Ira Aldridge won fame throughout Great Britain, Europe, and Russia as one of the greatest actors of his time. He was compared to the great English actor David Garrick (1717–1779), who was famous for his roles in both tragedy and comedy.

Aldridge traveled to England at age seventeen to pursue a career in the theater. His first London stage appearance was in 1825. During a six-year tour of England, Scotland, and Ireland, he played most of the major roles for black actors, including the great English writer William Shakespeare's (1564–1616) Othello from the play *Othello* (1604–05); English poet Edward Young's (c. 1683–1765) Zanga the Moor from this tragedy *The Revenge* (1721); and the Irish playwright Isaac Bickerstaffe's (c. 1735–c. 1812) comic slave Mungo from the play *The Padlock* (produced 1768).

During his early twenties Aldridge began to perform traditionally white roles, such as Shakespeare's Macbeth, King Lear, and Hamlet. He got his first chance to perform at a major London theater in 1833 when he took over the role of Othello at the Covent Garden theater after the leading English actor became ill.

At age forty-five Aldridge began touring Europe, performing white Shakespearean roles such as King Lear, Hamlet, the Merchant of Venice, and Macbeth, along with the black roles of Othello and Aaron the Moor. These tours brought him fame and many honors.

Aldridge was thinking of returning to the United States when he became ill and died in 1867 while on tour. Married twice, Aldridge raised four children; three became professional musicians.

Ali, Muhammad

BOXER

January 17, 1942–

Cassius Marcellus Clay, better known as Muhammad Ali, is often considered the greatest boxer of all time. He was the first heavyweight boxer to regain the world championship **boxing** title three different times. Ali was also the first superstar athlete who generated a lot of press and who had a huge following of fans. Standing six feet three inches tall and weighing two hundred pounds, Ali was an imposing figure. At one point he was even portrayed in a **comic book** defeating Superman in a boxing match.

Ali began boxing at age twelve. His success as an amateur led him to the 1960 Olympics in Rome, where he won a gold medal. In February 1964 he defeated **Sonny Liston** for the heavyweight championship. It was not just his boxing ability but also his entertaining personality and outspoken confidence that helped Ali become one of the most famous athletes in the world.

Ali was also an important political figure who inspired future generations of black athletes. He was committed to stopping racism, which led him to join a group called the **Nation of Islam (NOI)** and to become friends with civil rights leader **Malcolm X.** The NOI is a political-religious organization that was seen by many at the time as a militant antiwhite hate group. When the public found out about these associations, many whites reacted with hostility toward Ali.

In 1967, during the Vietnam War (1959–75), Ali was drafted (ordered to enroll for military service). He refused to join because war was against his religion. He was convicted of violating the Selective Service Act (the draft

Muhammad Ali fighting Joe Frazier
(AP/Wide World Photos. Reproduced by
permission)

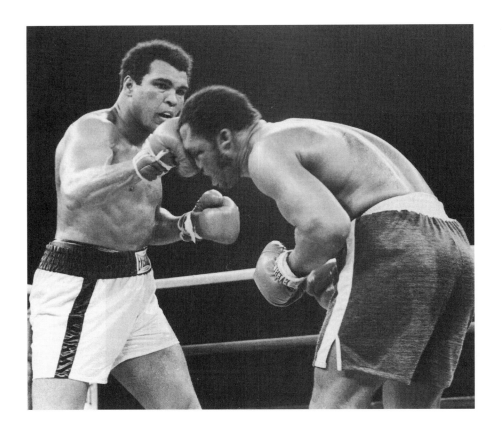

law). Ali challenged the decision before the Supreme Court and won. During this time (1967–70) he was not allowed to box.

Ali returned to boxing in 1971, defeating Jerry Quarry. The following year, he was narrowly defeated by **Joe Frazier.** After defeating **George Foreman** in 1974 and regaining the heavyweight title, he turned the tables on Frazier in 1975, winning a match against him in Manila, the Philippines, which Ali dubbed "The Thrilla in Manila." Ali distanced himself from the violent side of racial politics and regained his popularity. In 1977 Ali starred in a movie titled after his **autobiography,** *The Greatest.* He retired from boxing in 1980 after losing to Larry Holmes. Ali was voted into the Boxing Hall of Fame in 1987.

After Ali retired, his health began to deteriorate because of Parkinson's Disease. Ali still lives a full life, however, and in 1996 he lit the torch at the Olympic Games in Atlanta, Georgia. That same year, he was featured in *When We Were Kings*, a movie about his 1974 defeat of George Foreman.

Allain, Théophile

POLITICIAN
October 1, 1846–February 2, 1917

Théophile Allain was a politician in Louisiana whose career spanned almost twenty years. Allain's father, who was white, took his son on trips to the northern United States and Europe and sent Théophile to school in

New Orleans, Louisiana, and New Jersey. Allain was well educated, spoke French, and was a forceful public speaker.

Allain was elected to the Louisiana House of Representatives in 1874, served in the state senate from 1876 to 1880, and served again as a state representative until 1890. He believed that education was necessary for people to succeed, and he worked hard to provide educational opportunities for African Americans. Allain helped pass laws to establish schools for blacks and was responsible for the creation of Southern University in Baton Rouge, a college blacks could attend.

Allen, Debbie

DANCER, TELEVISION PRODUCER-DIRECTOR, ACTRESS
January 16, 1950–

Debbie Allen is a talented entertainer who has worked as a dancer, choreographer (someone who makes up and teaches dance routines), director, producer, and actress. She was born in Houston, Texas, where her father was a dentist and her mother was a writer. Her sister, Phylicia Rashad, is well known for her role on the television series *The Cosby Show*.

Allen tried to take **ballet** classes at the Houston Foundation for Ballet, but was rejected for reasons her mother thought were race related. Instead, Allen took private lessons and moved with her family to Mexico City, where she danced with the National Ballet of Mexico. Allen re-auditioned for the Houston Foundation for Ballet in 1964, was admitted, and became the company's first black dancer. After graduating from **Howard University** in Washington, D.C., Allen moved to New York City to become a professional entertainer.

Allen soon won parts in musical plays such as *Purlie* and *West Side Story*. In 1981 she made her movie debut in *Ragtime* and then appeared in the hit movie *Fame*, with a small part as the dance teacher Lydia Grant. When the movie was turned into a **television** series of the same name, Allen returned as Lydia Grant and developed the role that made her famous. She remained on the show until 1987, serving as choreographer and eventually as director and producer.

During the 1980s Allen also continued to act in the movies and in theater productions. In 1988 she became director of *A Different World* and helped turn it into a top twenty television hit. During the 1990–91 season Allen directed episodes of the television shows *Fresh Prince of Bel Air* and *Quantum Leap*. Allen was also a choreographer for the Academy Awards show from 1991 to 1994.

In 1997 Allen realized a decades-long dream by producing director Steven Spielberg's epic movie *Amistad*, about slaves who fight for their freedom in the early 1800s. The following year, she directed a musical at the Kennedy Center in Washington, D.C. In 2000 Allen publicly disagreed with the decision to eliminate dance performances from the Academy Awards show, because she believes dance is an important part of the movies.

Allen, Richard

MINISTER, COMMUNITY LEADER
February 14, 1760–March 26, 1831

Born into **slavery,** Richard Allen bought his freedom from his master, a Delaware farmer, at age twenty. He then launched his career as a traveling minister. He walked thousands of miles from North Carolina to New York, preaching to black and white audiences in villages and forest clearings. His preaching brought him to the attention of white Methodist leaders who, in 1786, asked him to preach to black Methodists in **Philadelphia, Pennsylvania.** Allen would spend the rest of his life there.

Soon after arriving in Philadelphia, Allen began pressing for an independent black church. He established one, named Mother Bethel, in a converted blacksmith's shop in 1794. However, his desire to stand apart from white society launched a twenty-year struggle with white Methodist leaders. They were determined to make Allen bow to their authority. The struggle was resolved in 1816 when the Pennsylvania Supreme Court ruled that Mother Bethel was legally an independent church. Shortly thereafter, African-American ministers from across the mid-Atlantic region gathered in Philadelphia to form the **African Methodist Episcopal (AME) Church.** The church would spread across the United States and abroad in the nineteenth and twentieth centuries. Allen served as the AME's first bishop.

Although he received no formal education, Allen became a successful businessman and property owner. He was also an accomplished writer of pamphlets and sermons attacking slavery, the **slave trade,** and white racism. Most of the African-American institutions formed in Philadelphia in the early 1800s included Allen's name in theirs. When Allen died in 1831, his funeral was attended by a vast congregation of black and white Philadelphians.

Richard Allen (Courtesy of New York Public Library Picture Collection)

Ambassadors and Diplomats

Throughout American history blacks have had tremendous difficulty obtaining positions of social and political importance. Obtaining positions with the Foreign Service Office has not been an exception. Foreign Service officers, including ambassadors and diplomats, work to help maintain good relationships between the United States and foreign countries. Ambassadors are nominated by the president and confirmed by the U.S. Senate. Only a few African Americans have been asked to represent the United States in international affairs.

Clifton R. Wharton Sr. was the first African American to break the color barrier when he was asked to serve in Africa as third secretary to Monrovia, Liberia, in 1924. However, social progress was slow; in 1961 only seventeen out of approximately thirty-seven hundred Foreign Service positions were held by blacks. In the 1960s civil rights activists pressured the U.S. government to appoint more blacks to these important posts. Politicians began to realize that U.S. relations with countries who had large black populations would benefit from appointing African-American diplomats and ambassadors. Nevertheless, from 1948 to 1992 only fifty-seven blacks served in high-ranking ambassador positions. Among them was Patricia Roberts Harris, the first black female ambassador.

In recent years there has been an increase in the number of blacks appointed to diplomatic positions. And organizations such as the Association of African American Ambassadors in Washington, D.C., have been established to help blacks gain diplomatic positions. Even so, the U.S. State Department has been criticized for racial hiring practices, and the number of black Foreign Service officers is still low.

Some African-American Ambassadors

1990
Aurelia Erskine Brazeal, Micronesia

1990
Arlene Render, Gambia

1990
Leonard O. Spearman Sr., Lesotho

1991
Charles R. Baquet III, Djibouti

1991
Johnnie Carson, Uganda

1992
Ruth A. Davis, Benin

1992
Kenton Wesley Keith, Qatar

1992
Edward J. Perkins, United Nations

1992
Joseph Monroe Segars, Cape Verde

American Indians

In a 1920 article in the *Journal of Negro History*, African-American historian **Carter G. Woodson** (1875–1950) called the relationship between

Africans and American Indians "one of the longest unwritten chapters in the history of the United States." Partly because it had its beginnings in slave resistance and involved the harboring (giving refuge to) of slaves by Indians, and sometimes the gradual merger of the two groups into biracial communities, this story remains largely unresearched and untold.

Early Contact between Africans and Indians

During the early 1500s, in Portuguese and Spanish colonies in Latin America and the West Indies, as well as in French and British settlements in North America, American Indians often helped African slaves escape to freedom. The earliest slave rebellion in America, in 1526 in what would become North Carolina, was successful because blacks and Indians worked together.

North America's white rulers feared contact between Africans and Indians and attempted to create conflict between them. British officials in Virginia and the Carolinas paid Indians deerskins, blankets, and muskets for hunting and capturing escaped slaves.

In 1830 Congress passed a law that gave the U.S. president the power to remove American Indians from their homes in the eastern states to unoccupied lands west of the Mississippi River. Because this removal took place in the era of the most significant slave uprising in U.S. history, **Nat Turner's Rebellion** (1831, in Virginia), some historians believe it might have been partly related to white fears that Indians and African slaves would join forces against whites.

Indians of the Five Civilized Tribes (the Creek, Chickasaw, Cherokee, Choctaw, and Seminole), the Iroquois Confederacy, and the Huron and Delaware nations signed treaties from the 1700s to the mid-1800s, agreeing to return runaway slaves that escaped to their villages. But historian Kenneth W. Porter says that although each of these tribes harbored slaves, none turned any of them in to white authorities.

The African-Seminole Alliance

The largest and most successful alliance between American Indians and Africans began in Florida before the American Revolution (1775–83). African slaves from Georgia had arrived in Florida first and welcomed Seminole Indians fleeing the Creek Indian federation. They taught the Seminoles West African rice-cultivation methods, and the two groups formed an agricultural and military alliance. Africans also held important positions on Seminole councils. In 1816 a U.S. officer reported prosperous African-Seminole plantations extending for fifty miles along the banks of the Appalachicola River. African-Seminole military forces kept slaveholders away and fought U.S. troops in the First and Second **Seminole Wars** (1817–18; 1835–42), which at times occupied half of the American army. The United States purchased Florida partly to stop slaves from running away to become allies with the Seminoles.

In the decades before the American Civil War (1861–65), Native American nations along the Atlantic coast became biracial communities, with mixed African and Indian families. In response, white Southerners tried to end tax exemptions for Indians and close down Indian reservations.

CHIEF JOHN HORSE, BLACK SEMINOLE LEADER

Black Seminole chief John Horse was a significant African-American Indian leader in the United States. A master marksman and diplomat, he became the black Seminole chief in Mexico and Texas by the time of the Civil War (1861–65). In 1870 he signed a treaty with the United States to bring his Seminole people from Mexico to Texas so that his skilled desert soldiers could serve as U.S. Army scouts. He made history by bringing his African people onto American soil as a free nation under the command of their own leader.

Indian Removal to the West

The Seminoles, like many other American Indian tribes, were eventually removed to Indian Territory in the West. Black Seminoles traveled with them. Thousands of black Indians joined the Cherokee Indians on the long march to Indian Territory in Oklahoma in the summer of 1838. This march, on which some two thousand people died, became known as the Trail of Tears. By 1860 black Indians made up 18 percent of the Five Civilized Tribes in Indian Territory.

After the Civil War and **emancipation** (freeing) of slaves, the Seminoles elected six black Seminoles to their governing council. Other tribes followed their example. By 1900 people of African ancestry living among American Indians enjoyed more freedom, opportunity, and equality than their fellow African Americans in white society, whether in the North or the South. Oddly enough, African Americans serving in the U.S. Cavalry, who became famous as the so-called Buffalo Soldiers, helped to end Indian resistance to white takeover of their lands. They also acted as a police unit, enforcing reservation policies.

Indian Family Roots

Many African Americans have found American Indian ancestry when researching their family roots. As a result of continuing intermarriage between African Americans and American Indians, many African-American families in the United States today—including those of such famous African Americans as authors **Alex Haley** (1921–1992) and **Alice Walker** (1944–), the Reverend Dr. **Martin Luther King Jr.** (1929–1968), and politician and civil rights activist **Jesse Jackson** (1941–)—can claim an Indian branch in their family trees.

American Revolution

The American Revolution (1775–83), a bloody struggle for "liberty and equality," was a major event in the history of the United States and the world. Not only did it win independence for the American colonies, it also spread around the world new ideas about basic human rights and the equal-

ity of all people. Thousands of African-American soldiers, sailors, cooks, guides, spies, and road builders played an important role in the Revolution. Their contributions would later be used in the fight to ban **slavery.**

African Americans in the Colonies

At the time of the American Revolution, about one out of five people in the thirteen colonies was African American. Some five percent of them were free and had some citizens' rights. The rest were the "property" of their owners. They could not vote and had no say in the government. Slavery existed in all thirteen colonies, but most slaves lived in the South, where the majority cultivated crops sold by their owners, including cotton, tobacco, rice, indigo, and sugar. Others were personal servants or worked in crafts, producing clothes and tools. In New England some also worked on boats or ships in seaport towns.

African Americans Join the Fight

The Revolution was fought to overthrow Great Britain's harsh rule of the American colonies. When Britain's Parliament (the group of representatives who create the laws of a country) passed the Stamp Act in 1765, placing a tax on publications and documents, the colonists protested, "No taxation without representation!" British rule tightened after the famous Boston Tea Party in December 1773, when colonists dumped tea from three ships into the harbor to protest a tea tax. Finally, in April 1775, war broke out.

Prior to the war, blacks had petitioned to the colonial government to end slavery. And even though their petitions were ignored, slaves and **free blacks** fought with other colonists in the first battles, at the villages of Lexington, Concord, and Bunker Hill in Massachusetts.

When General George Washington (1732–1799) took over leadership of the Continental Army (the name for the American troops fighting the British), he disapproved of blacks serving in the war. He immediately barred any more free blacks from enlisting and dismissed any soldiers who were slaves; free blacks already serving were allowed to remain.

As war intensified throughout the colonies, however, the Continental army became desperate for more soldiers. African Americans were needed to help fight the British. In January 1777 Washington agreed to let all free blacks enlist. In some states, whites who did not want to join the war even hired free blacks to join for them; others sent their slaves to fight in their place. Eventually, the need for soldiers became so great that by 1871 all of the New England states, New York, and Maryland allowed slaves to join the army.

Approximately five thousand blacks joined the American armed forces during the Revolution, most of them from the North. Several won special notice for their heroism, including Prince Whipple, who is featured in the famous painting *Washington Crossing the Delaware* (1851), by Manuel Leutze. Some blacks did serve on the British side. The most well known were the three hundred slaves of the "Ethiopian Regiment," who joined forces with Lord Dunsmore in 1775. Lord Dunsmore was the royal governor of Virginia and promised freedom to any slave who fought with the British. A few dozen blacks served in the British Royal Navy as seamen and pilots.

African Americans after the War

After the war ended in 1783, many black veterans, especially in the North, were freed by the government. Others were freed by their masters, but many were not. Slaves who had been purchased by the government to fight were resold. Blacks who fought for the British were sold into slavery or moved to colonies in the West Indies, Florida, Nova Scotia (Canada), England, or Africa.

The role that African Americans played in the Revolution had several consequences. For the first time, blacks in the American colonies were recognized and given attention for their service and loyalty. Also for the first time, the institution of slavery was seriously challenged. How could colonists who were fighting for freedom from England and who were willing to die for equality enslave African Americans? Many people, even some slaveholders, came to see slavery as evil. These early stirrings would later fuel the fight for **abolition,** or the ending of slavery.

The most important effect of the war for African Americans was that it created a larger group of free blacks who organized to make their lives and the lives of future generations better. Free blacks created their own communities, with their own churches, schools, and other organizations. They also banned together to form abolition groups in the struggle to achieve freedom and equality for all African Americans in the country that so many had fought and died for. (*See also* **Military.**)

Amistad Mutiny

In the summer of 1839 a large group of West Africans were captured in Sierra Leone, taken from their homeland aboard a Portuguese slave ship, and smuggled into Cuba, which was then a Spanish colony. Fifty-three of the captives—forty-nine men, three girls, and a boy—were sold to two Spaniards, in violation of a treaty between England and Spain that prohibited the **slave trade** (although **slavery** was still legal in Cuba). The Spaniards, José Ruiz and Pedro Montes, loaded the Africans aboard the Spanish schooner *La Amistad* and set sail for Spain.

A few days later, on July 1 and 2, the captives, led by Sengbe Pieh (later called Joseph Cinqué), rose up in revolt against their captors. They freed themselves from their chains and launched an armed assault against the ship's crew, killing the captain and the cook. Then they commanded Ruiz and Montes to sail back to **Africa.** But the Spaniards tricked them, sailing gradually northward until they reached New York State waters in late August. An American ship captured the *Amistad* and towed her to the port of New London, Connecticut. The Africans were taken to New Haven, Connecticut, and placed in jail to await a hearing in court.

The *Amistad* case attracted widespread U.S. and international attention. Ruiz and Montes told the court the Africans had already been slaves in Cuba when they purchased them. Because they were legally their property, the Spaniards insisted, the Africans should be returned to them. The Spanish government wanted the slaves tried on charges of piracy and murder. Cuban

EXCERPT FROM JOHN QUINCY ADAMS'S ARGUMENT IN THE AMISTAD CASE

I said, when I began this plea, that my final reliance for success in this case was on this Court as a court of JUSTICE; and in the confidence this fact inspired that, in the administration of justice, in a case of no less importance than the liberty and the life of a large number of persons, this Court would not decide but on a due consideration of all the rights, both natural and social, of every one of these individuals. I have endeavored to show that they are entitled to their liberty from this Court. I have avoided, purposely avoided, and this Court will do justice to the motive for which I have avoided, a recurrence to those first principles of liberty which might well have been invoked in the argument of this cause. I have shown that Ruiz and Montes, the only parties in interest here, for whose sole benefit this suit is carried on by the Government, were acting at the time in a way that is forbidden by the laws of Great Britain, of Spain, and of the United States, and that the mere signature of the Governor General of Cuba ought not to prevail over the ample evidence in the case that these Negroes were free and had a right to assert their liberty. I have shown that the papers in question are absolutely null and insufficient as passports for persons, and still more invalid to convey or prove a title to property.

authorities demanded the return of their ship and its surviving human "cargo" (only thirty-nine men and the four children remained; the others had died on the journey or in jail, and eight more would die before their release).

U.S. abolitionists (people working to end slavery) began defending the Africans, hoping to prove they had been unlawfully enslaved and must be set free. Through the press, artists' sketches, and public speaking tours, the abolitionists introduced the Africans and their cause to the American public, raising money for their defense. They also found two African-born seamen, James Covey and Charles Pratt, who could communicate with them. Eventually the Africans were taught English and instructed in Christianity.

In January 1840 Judge Andrew T. Judson of the U.S. District Court ruled that the Africans had been illegally kidnapped and sold and that they had had a right to rebel to win back their freedom. Judson ordered that they be returned to their homes in Africa.

The U.S. government, however, had expected the court to rule that the Africans be returned to Spain. The government filed an appeal, and the *Amistad* case went to the U.S. Supreme Court, where former U.S. president John Quincy Adams (1767–1848) defended the Africans. He argued for their freedom on the basis of human rights outlined in the U.S. Declaration of Independence. Although a majority of the justices were Southerners who had once owned slaves, the Supreme Court ruled in favor of the Africans in March 1841. The *Amistad* mutineers were free to set sail for home.

Traveling with protection from the British, they reached Africa in January 1842, two and a half years after their capture by the Portuguese. Little is known of Cinqué and the others after they returned home, but he remains a leading symbol of resistance to the Atlantic slave trade. This was the only known time in history that blacks captured as slaves in the New World returned home to Africa.

Tulane University in New Orleans, Louisiana, houses one of the largest collection of records on African-American history and race relations at its Amistad Research Center, named for the historic event. In 1997 American film producer Steven Spielberg released a movie about the mutiny and the trials that followed. Called *Amistad*, the film is based on the 1953 book *Slave Mutiny: The Revolt on the Schooner Amistad* (later reprinted as *Black Mutiny: The Revolt on the Schooner Amistad*), by American author William Owens (1905–1990).

Amos 'n' Andy

Amos 'n' Andy was a radio and television show that gave the twentieth-century its most popular and longest-lived comic portrayal of African-American characters. The radio series was broadcast from 1928 until 1960, and the television show from 1951 until 1966. *Amos 'n' Andy* won fans among both whites and African Americans. It also drew protests from leaders of the **National Association for the Advancement of Colored People (NAACP)** and other blacks. They said the show made fun of African Americans' struggle to build a dignified life in modern society. Beginning in the 1950s, the NAACP's protest discouraged sponsors from supporting television comedies featuring blacks for a number of years.

Two white men, Freeman Gosden (1899–1982) and Charles Correll (1890–1972), created *Amos 'n' Andy*. The daily radio show was first called *Sam 'n' Henry* and began broadcasting in Chicago, Illinois, in 1926. It featured two black characters (played by Gosden and Correll) who, like many African Americans of the time, had left the rural South to look for jobs in a northern city. These characters were renamed Amos Jones and Andy Brown in 1928, and in 1929 the National Broadcasting Company (NBC) began airing the show nationwide. It became a national craze and was played in restaurants, hotel lobbies, and cinemas, helping to launch **radio**'s "golden age."

Amos was meek and eager to please, while Andy was lazy but pretended to be superior to others. Owners of a "taxicab company" with only one old car, they were ignorant of city life and spoke in an exaggerated Southern black dialect (language). Other black characters on the show were intelligent and accomplished, especially Ruby Taylor, a young Chicago woman who eventually married Amos. A less likable character was the scheming Kingfish, leader of a club to which Amos and Andy belonged. Part of the reason for the show's popularity was that Gosden and Correll, borrowing heavily from the work of African-American **comedians,** created situations that their listeners could relate to and sympathize with.

When *Amos 'n' Andy* came to **television** on the Columbia Broadcasting System (CBS) network in 1951, well-known African-American performers played the main characters. Harry R. "Tim" Moore (1888–1958), a former stage performer, played the Kingfish; Alvin Childress (1908–1986), a classically trained actor, played Amos; and Spencer Williams Jr. (1893–1969), a

retired film director, writer, and actor, played Andy. The show was a hit among blacks and whites in its first season on television. It was canceled after a second season because of low ratings, but local stations continued to run the episodes until 1966. Gosden and Correll continued to broadcast new radio episodes of *Amos 'n' Andy* until 1960. When their show ended, the hundred-year-old American tradition of white men playing black comic characters ended with it.

Anderson, Eddie "Rochester"

ACTOR
September 18, 1905–February 28, 1977

Film and **television** actor Eddie Anderson is best known as comedian Jack Benny's (1894–1974) sidekick, "Rochester." Anderson was born in Oakland, California, to a family of vaudevillians and began performing at age fourteen. (Vaudeville theater shows were popular at the beginning of the twentieth century and featured a variety of short acts.) He also appeared in black movies but in the early 1930s crossed over to the white studios, playing small parts in Hollywood movies.

A 1936 comic film role eventually led Anderson to star as the train porter (baggage carrier) Rochester on the *Jack Benny Program* **radio** show. Rochester became the most popular character on the show, aside from Benny. With masterful sarcasm, characterized by his famous line "What's that, boss?" Anderson regularly punctured Benny's inflated ego. The friendship between them went beyond the standard portrayal of white and black master-servant relationships, and they continued to entertain audiences for over two decades.

Anderson's easy familiarity with white characters was featured in later films, including *Brewster's Millions* (1945). That film was banned in Memphis, Tennessee, because it portrayed "too much social equality and racial mixture."

In 1962 Anderson was listed by *Ebony* magazine as one of the one hundred wealthiest African Americans in the United States. He died in Los Angeles, California, at the Motion Picture Country Home and Hospital in 1977.

Anderson, Marian

OPERA SINGER
February 17, 1897–May 19, 1993

Marian Anderson was an **opera** singer whose voice was so beautiful that people cried when they heard her sing. She performed in the greatest concert halls of Europe, but she was denied access to many places in the United States because of the color of her skin. Eventually, however, she became the first African American to perform at the Metropolitan Opera in New York City.

Anderson was born on May 19, 1897. As a young girl she sang at the Union Baptist Church in her hometown of Philadelphia, Pennsylvania. Because of her voice range, called contralto, she was able to sing many different styles of songs in many keys. In 1921 she received a scholarship from the National Association of Negro Musicians.

When Anderson was a young woman, many states had laws that prevented entertainers from performing to integrated (mixed black and white) audiences. As a result, she performed mostly in Europe for many years. In 1935 a prominent theatrical agent named Sol Hurok heard her sing in Paris, France. He became her manager, and Anderson's fame spread rapidly. She performed before royalty and other dignitaries around the world.

In the spring of 1939, Marian Anderson was not allowed to sing at Constitution Hall in Washington, D.C., because she was African American. The disturbing situation turned into a joyous event when the U.S. secretary of the interior arranged instead for Anderson to perform a concert on Easter

Eddie Anderson: Selected Movies and Television Shows

Jezebel
(1938)

Gone with the Wind
(1939)

Man About Town
(1939)

Buck Benny Rides Again
(1940)

Love Thy Neighbor
(1940)

Birth of the Blues
(1941)

Cabin in the Sky
(1943)

Stormy Weather
(1943)

Brewster's Millions
(1945)

The Jack Benny Show
(1960–65; television)

Bachelor Father
(1962; television)

It's a Mad, Mad, Mad, Mad World
(1963)

Dick Powell's Theatre
(1963; television)

Love American Style
(1969; television)

Marian Anderson singing at the Lincoln Memorial (Corbis Corporation. Reproduced by permission)

Sunday at the Lincoln Memorial. Over 75,000 people turned out to see her. Some of the spectators broke into tears as she sang "My country 'tis of thee, sweet land of liberty...."

Also because of racial discrimination, Anderson was not invited to sing at the famous Metropolitan Opera in New York City until 1955. She was nearly sixty years old by then, which made the situation odd, because many opera singers retire long before they reach their fiftieth birthday.

People everywhere admired Marian Anderson because she was dignified and quiet-spoken. She never complained about the treatment she received because of her skin color. She believed that most people felt happy to live together as one, regardless of race, religious beliefs, or skin color. In 1938 First Lady Eleanor Roosevelt presented the Spingarn Award, the highest honor bestowed by the **National Association for the Advancement of Colored People (NAACP),** to Anderson. In 1941 Anderson received the Edward Bok Award, given annually to the most outstanding Philadelphian of the year. She used part of the money to establish a scholarship fund for future singers.

In 1958 Marian Anderson represented the United States as a delegate to the United Nations. She performed her final public concert at New York's Carnegie Hall on Easter Sunday of 1965. She died on May 19, 1993.

Andrews, Benny

ARTIST, ART ACTIVIST, EDUCATOR
November 13, 1930–

Benny Andrews has worked as an artist in New York City for forty years, a glamorous-sounding career that actually included many obstacles. Andrews grew up in Madison, Georgia, where his family worked as share-croppers (farmers who rent land, paying with part of their crops). He drew cartoons as a child and, after four years in the U.S. Air Force, received his bachelor of fine arts degree from the Art Institute of Chicago in 1958.

Andrews's artwork includes collage (combining different materials on a surface), **painting,** and pen-and-ink drawings. His compositions show scenes of black life in America based on personal experiences. During the 1960s Andrews had difficulty finding galleries that would exhibit his works. In 1969 he helped found the Black Emergency Cultural Coalition, with the goal of opening museums to black artists in the United States.

Andrews does not think of his art as political but admits that his contemporary themes occasionally take a political turn. *Did the Bear Sit Under the Tree?* (1969) shows a black man raising his fists at the American flag, angered at its failure to protect him. During the 1970s Andrews began using photocopies, spray paint and stencils, and folded paper to add texture to his compositions.

Andrews exhibited in museums and galleries through the 1990s. He has also illustrated books and organized art education programs for local prisons. He has taught art at Queens College in New York since the 1970s.

JANITORS AT REST

One of Andrews's best-known early works is *Janitors at Rest* (1957), which depicts workers at the Art Institute of Chicago who reminded him of characters from his childhood. The collage is made from paper towels and toilet paper, the same materials the janitors worked with on a daily basis.

Angelou, Maya

WRITER
April 4, 1928–

Maya Angelou's autobiographies, poetry, plays, and essays have been nominated for numerous awards, including a Pulitzer Prize for poetry. Her works are especially known for providing insight into the life of an African-American woman.

Angelou was born Marguerite Annie Johnson and was raised in Stamps, Arkansas, by her grandmother. Her popular **autobiography** *I Know Why the Caged Bird Sings* (1970) draws on her experiences in Stamps and is the story of her life growing up black and female in the American South. One of the incidents Angelou writes about is how as a young girl she was raped by her mother's boyfriend. Until that time, rape and incest were taboo subjects (not acceptable to talk about) in African-American literature; *Caged Bird* helped to break that silence.

Angelou sees herself as not only an individual but also a representative of all black people. Her many writings address the issues that African Americans face in their lives, such as marriage, child rearing, and pursuing a career. Her own experiences include living in the harsh urban world of Los Angeles, California, working with the leaders **Martin Luther King Jr.** (1929–1968) and **Malcolm X** (1925–1965) during the **Civil Rights movement** (1954–65), and traveling to Africa, where she experienced the complexity of an African American trying to relate to Africans.

Angelou's poetry is based on the African-American oral tradition, or passing down stories from one generation to the next by word of mouth. When she reads her poetry to audiences, her strong, melodious voice resonates. She has also written and acted for television, written plays, and acted in the theater. In 1998 she directed the movie *Down in the Delta*. In 1993 she composed and read a poem for the inauguration of U.S. president Bill Clinton, titled "On the Pulse of Morning." Says Angelou, "All my work is meant to say 'You may encounter many defeats but you must not be defeated.'"

Maya Angelou: Selected Writings

I Know Why the Caged Bird Sings
(autobiography; 1970)

Just Give Me a Cool Drink of Water 'fore I Diiie
(poetry; 1971)

Gather Together In My Name
(autobiography; 1974)

Oh Pray My Wings Are Gonna Fit Me Well
(poetry; 1975)

Singin' & Swinging & Getting Merry Like Christmas
(autobiography; 1976)

The Heart of A Woman
(autobiography; 1981)

Shaker Why Don't You Sing?
(poetry; 1983)

All God's Children Need Traveling Shoes
(autobiography; 1986)

Now Sheba Sings the Song
(poetry; 1987)

I Shall Not Be Moved
(poetry; 1990)

Wouldn't Take Nothing For My Journey Now
(essays; 1993)

Phenomenal Woman
(poetry; 1995)

Even the Stars Look Lonesome
(essays; 1997)

Antelope Case

The African **slave trade** (taking Africans from their homeland to be sold into slavery in other countries) was declared illegal in the United States in 1808. The *Antelope* case, heard by the U.S. Supreme Court in 1825, allowed for the punishment of American slave traders. At the same time, it protected the slave-trading rights of people of other countries where the trade was considered legal.

The *Antelope* was a Spanish ship seized by pirates. A U.S. revenue cutter (a ship that enforces the collection of tolls charged for imported and exported goods) captured the *Antelope* off the U.S. coast and took it to the port of Savannah, Georgia. Officials found 280 slaves on board, who were owned by Spanish, Portuguese, and U.S. citizens. The Supreme Court ruled

that the slaves belonging to the Spaniards should be returned to them. The 120 Africans who were owned by Americans, however, were kept by the U.S. government because it was considered illegal to trade slaves in the United States. Approximately 30 were sent to slavery in Spanish Florida.

Supreme Court Chief Justice John Marshall (1755–1835) offered the most important interpretation of the slave trade law: that although slave trading was against the law of nature, if other nations allowed the slave trade, the United States could not judge foreign citizens for participating in it.

Apollo Theater

The Apollo Theater, in the heart of **Harlem, New York,** is one of the most important African-American theaters in the country. Now a National Historic Landmark, the Apollo, at 253 West 125th Street, is famous for its weekly Amateur Hour, when audiences cheer the best new performers but boo less-talented ones off the stage. Many famous African-American singers, dancers, actors, and **comedians** started their careers at the Apollo, and the theater has hosted top performers, both black and white, for decades.

The Apollo opened in 1913 as Hurtig and Seamon's Music Hall, playing to white audiences. Businessman Sidney Cohen bought it in 1933 and renamed it the Apollo Theater. The Apollo was opened to black audiences in 1936. In the years that followed, it held thirty shows each week and hosted the greatest **jazz** musicians of the time, including the **Duke Ellington** (1899–1974) Orchestra and **Lionel Hampton**'s (1908–) band. The shows were broadcast live on twenty-one **radio** stations across the United States.

The Amateur Hour began in 1934, and some winners became world famous, such as the singing legends **Ella Fitzgerald** (1918–1996), **Sarah Vaughan** (1924–1990), and **Pearl Bailey** (1918–1990). Concerts at the Apollo during the mid-1940s included jazz artists like the **Count Basie** (1904–1984) Orchestra.

By the mid-1950s the Apollo featured **rhythm-and-blues** singers, **gospel music** stars, and comedians such as **Jackie "Moms" Mabley** (1897–1975) and **"Pigmeat" Markham** (1906–1981). When soul music became popular in the 1960s and early 1970s, stars like **James Brown, Sam Cooke, Gladys Knight,** and the Jackson Five (with budding superstar **Michael Jackson**) performed at the Apollo.

When black artists found better-paying performance locations during the mid-1970s, the Apollo went bankrupt and closed its doors. In 1981 an investment group headed by businessman **Percy Sutton** bought the theater and renovated it, adding a television studio and a black-entertainment museum. It reopened in 1985 with a fiftieth anniversary celebration featuring celebrities from several decades. In 1991 a nonprofit group led by Leon Denmark and New York congressman **Charles Rangel** took over the theater.

Famed black comedian **Bill Cosby** hosted the Apollo Theater's Hall of Fame event in 1993, which was also filmed for television. Among those inducted into the theater's hall of fame were singers Ella Fitzgerald and

The historic Apollo Theater on 125th St. in New York's Harlem (Courtesy of the National Archives and Records Administration)

Billie Holiday (1915–1959), **blues** guitarist **B. B. King** (1925–), and comedians Redd Foxx (1922–1991) and **Richard Pryor** (1940–).

During the late 1990s the Apollo continued to draw both live and **television** audiences, with new African-American performers like the singing group TLC, singer-actress Brandy, and comedian-actor Chris Rock. The TV series *It's Showtime at the Apollo* has been filmed live from the theater since 1987.

In 1999 a state investigation of the theater's financial management ended with Sutton and Rangel cleared of any wrongdoing. In February 2000 Al Gore and Bill Bradley, candidates for the Democratic presidential nomination, held a debate at the Apollo Theater, addressing concerns of African Americans. In June 2000 the Apollo held a concert featuring black superstars to help launch the opening of the new Harlem USA shopping and entertainment complex, with money from the concert going to Harlem-based charities.

Architecture

African Americans have been involved in building and architecture since colonial times (1700s). The colonial plantation system relied heavily on slave craftsmen imported from Africa, who were skilled in ironworking, woodcarving, and the use of earth and stone to produce buildings, furniture, and tools. Slaves were especially involved in early plantation construction throughout Louisiana.

Some **free blacks** also designed and built in the South prior to the Civil War (1861–65), including Louis Metoyer, the child of a former slave.

Metoyer studied architecture in Paris, France, and designed several buildings in Isle Breville, Louisiana, a settlement of "free people of color." Central African influences are noticeable in most of his work, especially the African House (c. 1800), now designated a landmark as the only structure of its type still standing in the United States.

Architecture During Reconstruction

This period of African-American activity in building and construction ended abruptly after the **Civil War.** Industrialization, unions in the North that excluded blacks, and an economic depression largely eliminated the free-black planter class, and with it the independent artisan and craftsman. Many free-black landowners either lost their property or had their holdings greatly reduced.

In 1868, not long after the Massachusetts Institute of Technology (MIT) launched the nation's first formal architecture program, the U.S. government helped establish the **Hampton Institute** (now Hamptom University) in Virginia to train black men and women to "go out and teach and lead their people." From the start, Hampton offered a full building-skills program, and several campus buildings were designed and built by faculty and students. **Booker T. Washington,** founder of the **Tuskegee Institute** (now Tuskegee University) in Alabama, modeled his school after Hampton, and by 1893 Tuskegee offered a complete architectural drawing program. Tuskegee's early buildings were designed by faculty members and built by students.

A goal of Washington's Tuskegee program was to bring African Americans back to skilled trades. Speaking in 1901, Washington said, "We must have not only carpenters, but also architects; we must not only have people who do the work with the hand but persons who at the same time plan the work with the brain." According to the 1890 census, there were only forty-three black architects in the United States.

The First African-American Architects

Through determination and persistence, blacks slowly began to enter the architectural arena. Paul Revere Williams (1894–1980), discouraged by his high school teacher from pursuing a career in architecture because of his race, ignored this advice and worked his way through the University of Southern California's School of Architecture, graduating in 1915. He went on to become famous and is now best known for designing houses for such Hollywood celebrities as singer Frank Sinatra and actor Cary Grant. In 1926 he became the first black member of the American Institute of Architects (AIA) and was also named by President Calvin Coolidge to the National Monument Commission. Over the years, Williams received numerous awards for his residential designs.

The Postwar Years

Industry in the United States was booming during **World War II** (1939–45) because of the need for war materials. This industrial expansion had a major effect on the progress of African Americans in architecture. In

WILLIAM SYDNEY PITTMAN: EARLY ARCHITECT

One of the first African-American architects in the United States, William Sidney Pittman (1875–1958), was born and raised in Montgomery, Alabama. He attended Tuskegee Institute in 1892, where he was assigned to make alterations in the home of Tuskegee's president, Booker T. Washington. Pittman graduated from Tuskegee's department of mechanical and architectural drawing in 1897 and entered Drexel Institute in Philadelphia, Pennsylvania, on an architectural scholarship. After graduating in 1900, he spent five years teaching architecture at Tuskegee.

In 1905 Pittman established an architectural office in Washington, D.C., and two years later married Portia Washington, Booker T. Washington's daughter. Pittman designed and built a home for his family in Fairmont Heights, Maryland. His professional accomplishments included designs for schools, libraries, lodges, and other public buildings from 1907 to 1913, which established his reputation as one of the nation's most promising black architects.

The frequent "Negro Exhibits" held at national expositions (fairs) following the World's Columbian Exposition at Chicago, Illinois, in 1893 gave Pittman and many other black architects a chance to display their skills. Pittman won the national competition for the design of the Negro Building for the Jamestown Exposition in Virginia in 1907, a building that was erected by an all-black team of contractors and workmen. The building made Pittman the first African American to be given a federal government architectural contract. The building's two-story structure was a major engineering feat for its time because, despite the classical design of its exterior, the interior auditorium was free of columns.

a milestone decision for black architects, the U.S. War Department awarded a $4.2 million contract in 1941 to McKissack & McKissack, a black architecture and construction firm, for the construction of Tuskegee Air Force Base, Alabama. In 1943 Allied Engineers, a California firm organized by architect Paul Williams, received a $39 million contract for the design and construction of the U.S. Navy base in Long Beach.

With funds available through the GI Bill of 1944, African-American veterans returning from World War II were eligible for educational opportunities far better than those of previous generations. In 1949 **Howard University**'s School of Architecture became the first predominantly black architecture school to be accredited. A series of U.S. Supreme Court cases, resulting in the 1954 *Brown v. Board of Education of Topeka, Kansas,* opened the doors of white architectural schools to black students. By 2000 eight institutions identified as historically black colleges and universities offered professional architecture degrees, and two offered degrees in architectural engineering.

In 1968, at the urging of civil rights leader Whitney M. Young Jr., the AIA and the Ford Foundation established a minority scholarship program. To honor Young's contribution, the Whitney M. Young Jr. Citation Award was established in 1970 by the AIA. It is awarded to an architect or an architectural organization in recognition of a contribution to social responsibility. Robert Nash was the first recipient of the citation, and he became the AIA's first African-American vice president in 1970. The status of black architects is also promoted by the National Organization of Minority Architects (NOMA), founded in 1971 by twelve black architects. By the year 2000, NOMA's membership exceeded six hundred.

Despite the many successes of African-American individuals and groups, professional status as an architect remains an uphill climb for many. In 2000 the directory of African-American registered architects identified approximately thirteen hundred black architects in the United States. Of these, only about 1 percent were women. Several African-American women have risen to significant prominence in the field, however: Norma Merrick Sklarek became the first African-American woman to join the American Institute of Architects in 1966; Cheryl McAfee-Mitchell is an Atlanta-based architect who is the president of the Charles F. McAfee firm; Sharon E. Sutton is a noted professor of architecture at the University of Michigan. In 1997 black architects made up only about 1.7 percent of the profession as a whole—the smallest fifteen-year increase of any minority group in architecture. In addition, most black architects work on government projects because business and professional prejudice continue to restrict their access to private contracts.

Arizona

First African-American Settlers: The first African to visit the land that later became Arizona was Estevanico de Dorantes, a Spanish Moor who took part in an expedition to the territory in 1539. The first African Americans to settle in the area arrived in the 1860s; the 1870 census listed 26 blacks in Arizona.

Reconstruction: In the years following the American **Civil War** (1861–65), many black troops were sent west; some were stationed at Fort Huachuca, Arizona, in the 1880s. Known as "the Buffalo Soldiers," they fought **American Indians** and policed the territory. African-American cowboys also settled in Arizona and were a significant part of the territory's labor force. Other blacks came as a result of a failed scheme intended to relocate freed slaves to Mexico. Arizona became a state in 1912, and its first constitution legalized segregation and imposed laws against racial intermarriage. By 1916 a **Ku Klux Klan** unit had been organized in the state, and in Phoenix an all-white Pioneers Association was created to protect "native-born" Arizonians. African Americans responded by creating similar all-black organizations, such as the Colored Pioneers Association (1917).

The Great Depression: During the **Great Depression** in the 1930s, the Colored Businessman's Council and the Phoenix Protection League organized mass meetings and demonstrations by unemployed blacks. After **World War II** (1939–45), however, the Fair Employment Practices Committee forced military contractors to hire large numbers of black employees. The *Arizona Sun* newspaper, started in 1942, was a powerful force for equality during its twenty-year existence. In 1950 Phoenix businessman Carl Sims and lawyer H. B. Daniels (Arizona's only black attorney at the time) became the first African Americans elected to the state legislature.

Civil Rights Movement: In 1952 H. B. Daniels and a group of white lawyers successfully brought suit against segregated schools. This set a "legal precedent," making it easier the next year for the Supreme Court to support its ruling in a landmark case known as ***Brown v. Board of Education of Topeka, Kansas.*** In that ruling, the Court sought to end segregation, declaring that separate schools for blacks and whites were unequal and thus unconstitutional. In the late 1950s the state supreme court declared the law against intermarriage unconstitutional. In 1964 three hundred protesters from the Arizona chapters of the **Congress of Racial Equality (CORE)** and the **National Association for the Advancement of Colored People (NAACP)** marched on the state capitol. A statewide Civil Rights and Fair Employment law was passed in 1965.

Current African-American Population: According to U.S. Census Bureau estimates, the total black population in Arizona was 169,191 (less than 4 percent of the state population) as of July 1, 1998.

Key Figures: Henry O. Flipper (1856–1940), the first African American to graduate from West Point Military Academy; cowboy **Nat "Deadwood Dick" Love** (1854–1921); poet **Jayne Cortez** (1936–).

(SEE ALSO **BLACK TOWNS; WEST, BLACKS IN THE.**)

Arkansas

First African-American Settlers: The Post (a settlement or camp) of Arkansas was granted to financier John Law by France's King Louis XV. It was colonized with 2,000 white German immigrants and 200 enslaved Africans. When the United States acquired Arkansas as part of the Louisiana Purchase (1803), the post had 874 residents, including 107 black slaves and 2 **free blacks.**

Slave Population: Arkansas became the twenty-fifth state in June 1836. By 1840 there were 19,935 slaves in Arkansas, most working on small farms or clearing frontier land for the planting of cotton. The slave population reached 111,115 by 1860, one-fourth of the state's total population.

Free Black Population: Despite efforts by Arkansas lawmakers to solidify the slave trade, a small free black community grew. In a setback for African Americans, however, the Supreme Court ruled in its 1859 *Dred Scott v. Sandford* decision that no former slave or descendant of a slave could be a citizen. After that ruling, Arkansas expelled its free black population.

Civil War: After Arkansas seceded (left) from the Union in 1861, many enslaved blacks liberated themselves by going behind Union lines, working as cooks or laborers. In 1864 the Union army began forming brigades of Arkansas blacks, and some five thousand joined up.

Reconstruction: Under **Reconstruction,** blacks were able to vote and to attend school for the first time. The majority of Arkansas's African-American population, however, remained poor. Black laborers did not have legal and economic protection and were vulnerable to being cheated by dishonest planters. The last years of the nineteenth century saw a drop in the political and social status of African Americans in Arkansas as white supremacist sentiment spread. Segregation was widespread, and blacks were restricted to sharecropping, low-wage factory jobs, and domestic service work.

The Great Depression: In 1933, after the Federal Agriculture Adjustment Administration set production quotas for cotton, thousands of sharecroppers were removed from the land they worked. The interracial Southern Tenant Farmers' Union (STFU) publicized the plight of farmworkers and won victories in improving their conditions. The 1950s saw the integration of public schools, including Little Rock's Central High School (which required the troops of the 101st Airborne Division to ensure the safe enrollment of nine African-American students).

Civil Rights Movement: The Arkansas civil rights battlefield remained relatively quiet during the 1960s. Thousands of African Americans were registered as voters through the **Student Nonviolent Coordinating Committee**'s Arkansas Project, led by Rev. Ben Grinage.

Current African-American Population: According to U.S. Census Bureau estimates, the total black population in Arkansas was 407,618 (16 percent of the state population) as of July 1, 1998.

Key Figures: Rev. Elias Morris (1855–1922), founder and president of the **National Baptist Convention**; Mifflin Gibbs (1823–1915), the first U.S. African-American municipal judge; composers **Florence Price** (1887–1953) and **William Grant Still** (1895–1978); **jazz** musician Louis Jordan (1908–1975); **"Sister" Rosetta Tharpe** (1915–1973), **gospel** singer and guitarist; publisher **John Johnson** (1918–); Daisy Bates (1920–), co-founder of the *State Gazette*; **baseball** player **Lou Brock** (1939–); **Maya Angelou** (1928–), writer and poet; Dr. **Joycelyn Elders**, U.S. surgeon general.

(SEE ALSO **NATIONAL BAPTIST CONVENTION; EXODUSTERS**.)

Armstrong, Henry Jr. "Homicide Hank"

BOXER
December 12, 1912–October 22, 1988

Henry Armstrong was a boxer born in Columbus, Mississippi, on December 12, 1912. He earned the nickname "Homicide Hank" because he knocked out many of his opponents.

Armstrong's given name was Henry Jackson Jr. When he took up **boxing** after graduating high school in St. Louis, Missouri, he changed his name to Armstrong, which was his mother's family name. When he became a professional boxer in 1931, his fight record was fifty-eight wins and four losses. He stood five feet five and a half inches tall.

Armstrong was the only boxer ever to hold three world championships at the same time. In October 1937 he won the world featherweight (very light) title. Just a few months later, in May 1938, he won the welterweight (middleweight) championship. In August 1938 he won the lightweight title

Armstrong was the only boxer ever to hold three world championships at the same time.

by defeating Lou Ambers. After he became the featherweight champion in 1937, no one came forward to challenge him in that division. He retired from his title, undefeated, in November 1938. The following year, he lost a rematch with Ambers for the lightweight title. Armstrong continued to fight in the welterweight division until his retirement in 1945.

Armstrong's professional fight record at retirement was 144 wins and 21 losses. He knocked out a total of ninety-seven opponents, and during the peak of his career he scored twenty-seven knockouts in a row. He won forty-seven consecutive fights and collected over $1 million in prize money. Armstrong was elected to the Boxing Hall of Fame in 1954.

In 1951, after he retired, Armstrong became an ordained **Baptist** minister. He operated the Henry Armstrong Youth Foundation to fight juvenile delinquency and was the director of the Herbert Hoover Boys Club in St. Louis. Armstrong's **autobiography**, *Gloves, Glory and God*, was published in 1956. The movie *King Punching* tells the story of his life. He died on October 22, 1988.

Armstrong, Louis "Satchmo"

JAZZ TRUMPETER, SINGER
August 4, 1901–July 6, 1971

Louis Armstrong was one of the twentieth century's most beloved entertainers. He was famous as both a musician and a singer. His trumpet playing was so innovative and different that he is considered the first great improviser (somebody who makes things up offhand) of **jazz.**

Raised in terrible poverty in New Orleans, Louisiana, Armstrong contributed to the family income from his earliest years. In 1912 or 1913, according to legend, he celebrated the Fourth of July by firing a pistol; he was arrested and sent to the Colored Waifs' Home, where he remained for about two years. It was there that his interest in music was first encouraged. He was given instruction on cornet and made a member of the band. Later, he worked in local bands, where he met many jazz musicians. He soon developed a reputation as one of the best young musicians in the city. In 1919 he began playing on riverboats on the Mississippi, where he learned to read music.

In 1923 Armstrong joined the Creole Jazz Band in Chicago, Illinois, and made his first recordings. The following year, he joined the jazz orchestra of **Fletcher Henderson** in New York City. His big-band experience helped Armstrong create a new type of jazz featuring long solos. It was during this time that Armstrong met his first wife, pianist Lil Hardin, who would play an important role in supervising her husband's career.

In 1929 Armstrong became leader of his own orchestra. He also developed a style of singing called *scat* (singing random syllables, such as "BEE-bity BEE bop," to a rhythmic tune). Scat influenced all later jazz singers. During the next several years, his recordings, including "Body and Soul," "Memories of You" (both 1930), and "Stardust" (1931), introduced dramatic changes in jazz music.

Legendary jazz entertainer Louis Armstrong (AP/Wide World Photos. Reproduced by permission)

While on his first tour of Europe in 1932, Armstrong got the nickname he was so famous for—"Satchmo." "Satchmo" was short for "Satchelmouth," because his mouth looked as big as a suitcase when he blew his horn. Armstrong became so popular that, in addition to his musical accomplishments, he also became an entertainment celebrity. He was the first African American to appear regularly on network **radio** programs; he was also featured in movies, including *Pennies from Heaven* (1936) and *Going Places* (1938).

In 1947 Armstrong formed a small band called Louis Armstrong and the All-Stars, which he continued to lead for the remainder of his life. In his later years Armstrong made many tours of Europe, Asia, and Africa. In 1960 the U.S. government made him a special "ambassador of goodwill." Although Armstrong learned early in his career not to discuss racial matters in performance, he cared deeply about racial injustice. In 1957 he made public comments that supported racial equality in schools.

Armstrong was perhaps best known to the general public through popular recordings featuring his singing, including "Blueberry Hill" (1949), "Mack the Knife" (1955), and "Hello, Dolly!" (1967). In 1988 his 1968 recording of "It's a Wonderful World" appeared on the popular charts after it was used in the film *Good Morning, Vietnam*. Louis Armstrong, whose career had slowed after a 1959 heart attack, died in Corona, Queens, New York, in 1971.

Artis, William Ellisworth

SCULPTOR, POTTER, TEACHER
February 2, 1914–1977

Sculptor William Ellisworth Artis's work received recognition and awards throughout his life. It was described by critics as capturing a "sense of the divine in human character" and as "a statement of pride and beauty of subject, a fitting tribute to his people."

Artis was born in Washington, North Carolina, and raised by a great-grandmother and, later, by his mother. His talent was recognized early, and a 1933 award enabled him to study sculpture in the evenings while attending high school. After graduating from high school, he became the protégé (special student) of Augusta Savage (1892–1962), a leading sculptor in the **Harlem Renaissance,** an exciting period of cultural development in **Harlem, New York,** during the 1920s. Artis's work with Savage also brought him into contact with other prominent artists. Artis later showed his work in both black and white art shows nationwide and served as artist-in-residence at historically black colleges.

Drafted into the U.S. Army in 1941, Artis served through 1945 and received several outstanding awards for two heads he sculpted while in service, entitled *Negro Children* (1942) and *Portraits of a Brother and Sister* (1944). He also received an award for *Negro Boy* in 1944 and won other annual awards from Atlanta University (now Clark-Atlanta University, part of the **Atlanta University Center**) in Georgia.

After completing bachelor's and master's degrees, Artis dedicated the last twenty years of his life to teaching and researching at Nebraska State College (1956–66) and Makato State College (1966–77). He died in 1977. In May of that year, Artis was awarded an honorary doctorate in fine arts. His work is featured in permanent collections at Clark-Atlanta University and **Howard University** in Washington, D.C.

Ashe, Arthur

TENNIS PLAYER, POLITICAL ACTIVIST
July 10, 1943–February 6, 1993

Arthur Ashe was one of the best **tennis** players of all time. He was the first African American to win a Grand Slam event (one of the four major professional tennis tournaments)—the US Open, in 1968. Ashe later won two other Grand Slam events, paving the way for black participation in what had been an all-white sport.

Ashe took up tennis as a young boy in Lynchburg, Virginia. He became so good at it that Dr. Walter Johnson decided to coach him. Johnson had a keen eye for talent; he also discovered **Althea Gibson,** who was the first black woman to win England's Wimbledon tournament. Ashe went to the University of California at Los Angeles (UCLA) on a tennis scholarship in 1960. After graduating he began his outstanding professional tennis career. Ashe stayed with tennis after retiring, coaching the U.S. Davis Cup team (1981–85). He then became a journalist and television commentator and wrote a book, *A Hard Road to Glory* (1988).

Ashe was also a leader in the fight against racism, participating in the all-white South African Open in 1973. This caused a stir because apartheid, or a strict separation of the races, was practiced in South Africa at that time.

Ashe was forced to retire from tennis in 1979 after having a heart attack. He later contracted the AIDS virus through a blood transfusion he had received during heart surgery. After he became ill, Ashe continued to work for several foundations, including the American Heart Association, the

An African-American F I R S T

Arthur Ashe was the first African American to win a Grand Slam title. "Grand Slam" refers to the four biggest professional tennis tournaments: the US Open, the Australian Open, Wimbledon, and the French Open. Ashe won the US Open in 1968, the Australian Open in 1970, and his crowning achievement, Wimbledon, in 1975.

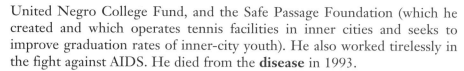

United Negro College Fund, and the Safe Passage Foundation (which he created and which operates tennis facilities in inner cities and seeks to improve graduation rates of inner-city youth). He also worked tirelessly in the fight against AIDS. He died from the **disease** in 1993.

In 1996 a statue was created in Ashe's honor in Richmond, Virginia (his birthplace), in tribute to his many achievements. The Flushing Meadows (New York) Tennis Stadium, home of the US Open, was rededicated as the Arthur Ashe Stadium in 1997.

Ashford, Evelyn

TRACK-AND-FIELD ATHLETE
April 19, 1957–

Four-time Olympic gold medal winner Evelyn Ashford did not start running in competition until she was a senior in high school. Her California

Evelyn Ashford crossing the finish line of the women's 100-meter-dash (AP/Wide World Photos. Reproduced by permission)

high school did not have a girls' **track** team, so Ashford had to run on the boys' team. In 1975 she won a track scholarship to the University of California at Los Angeles (UCLA).

Ashford first competed in the Olympics at age nineteen in Montreal, Canada (1976). She won the 100-meter dash at the 1979 World Cup competition, becoming the top woman sprinter (a fast short-distance runner). She was prepared to compete in the 1980 Olympics in Moscow, Russia, but the United States decided to withdraw its athletes from the Olympics to protest the Soviet Union's invasion of Afghanistan.

Ashford was so disappointed that she considered quitting running, but her husband and coach, Ray Washington, encouraged her to continue in her sport. She went on to win the women's 100-meter dash at the 1981 World Cup. She then won two gold medals at the 1984 Olympics in Los Angeles—in the 100-meter dash and the 400-meter relay.

In 1986 Ashford again won the World Cup. She competed in her third Olympics, in Seoul, South Korea, in 1988, winning a silver medal in the 100-meter competition and a gold in the 400-meter relay. In 1992, at age thirty-five, she competed in the Olympics in Barcelona, Spain, where she won her fourth gold medal as the lead-off runner on her 400-meter relay team. She retired from competition in 1993 but has continued to support other athletes training for the Olympics.

Atkins, Cholly

CHOREOGRAPHER, TAP DANCER, DIRECTOR, TEACHER
1913—

Dancer and choreographer (someone who creates and arranges dance numbers) Cholly Atkins was born in Birmingham, Alabama, but grew up in Buffalo, New York. At age ten he won a Charleston (a dance popular during the 1920s) contest, and in high school he alternated basketball practice with rehearsals for musicals.

In 1929 Atkins became a singing waiter at a club, where he met dancer William Porter. From 1933 to 1939 the two performed as the Rhythm Pals, doing a song-and-dance act. During 1941 and 1942 Atkins performed with his future wife, dancer and singer Dottie Saulter, appearing with the **Mills Brothers,** the **Earl Hines** Orchestra, the **Louis Armstrong** Orchestra, and the **Cab Calloway** Revue.

After three years in the U.S. Army during World War II (1939–45), Atkins formed a **tap-dancing** team with **Charles "Honi" Coles** (1911–1992). From 1946 to 1949 they appeared with big bands, including those led by **Count Basie** (1904–84) and **Billy Eckstine** (1914–1993). In 1949 Coles and Atkins were cast in the Broadway musical *Gentlemen Prefer Blondes.* However, when the musical closed in 1952, the popularity of tap was declining. Atkins started teaching dance at the Katherine Dunham School of Arts and Research in New York City. Coles and Atkins reunited in 1955 to work in Las Vegas, Nevada, but parted again in 1961.

Atkins then became a dance coach for vocal groups. This second career spanned almost forty years and included work with Frankie Lymon & the Teenagers, the **Supremes,** the **Temptations, Gladys Knight** & The Pips, and the **O'Jays.** He worked as staff choreographer for **Motown** Records of Detroit, Michigan, from 1965 to 1971 and choreographed for Broadway shows.

In 1989 Atkins shared a Tony Award for the choreography in *Black and Blue.* The National Endowment for the Arts awarded him a three-year Choreographer's Fellowship in 1993 to write his memoirs and take teaching tours of colleges and universities. In March 2000 Atkins participated in a program entitled "Jazz Music in Motion: Dancers and Big Bands" at Columbia University in New York.

Atlanta Compromise

African-American educator **Booker T. Washington** (1856–1915), founder and president of the Tuskegee Institute (now **Tuskegee University**) in Tuskegee, Alabama, gave a speech at the Cotton States and International Exposition in Atlanta, Georgia, on September 18, 1895, that made him the leading spokesman for African Americans of his day. His speech became known as the Atlanta Compromise because he called on black southerners to peacefully but temporarily accept segregation (the separation of blacks and whites) so they could concentrate on improving their economic and social status.

The most famous statement from the speech is "In all things that are purely social we can be as separate as the fingers, yet one as the hand in all things essential to mutual progress." Washington thought that southern blacks should be willing to remain socially separate for the time being but work together as a race alongside whites to improve the American economy.

Washington encouraged southern blacks to "cast down your bucket where you are," meaning they should make the most of the opportunities they had in the South by getting an education and learning job skills that would make them valuable to society. In this way, blacks could make social, economic, and political gains through their own efforts rather than protest unfair treatment by whites.

Washington's idea that blacks should live peacefully with whites in spite of unequal rights was later criticized by many blacks. Many also disagreed with Washington's plan for using technical and industrial job programs for blacks, because these plans often disregarded intellectual and artistic values.

Atlanta, Georgia

Atlanta Beginnings

The origins and early growth of Atlanta can be directly traced to the railroads. In 1837 a small settlement, aptly named Terminus, arose at the spot the Western and Atlantic Railroad selected as the southern end point for their railroad line. While work was progressing on the Western and Atlantic, Terminus grew, changed its name twice (to Marthasville in 1843 and finally to Atlanta two years later), and linked up with two other Georgia railroads. The joining of these three railroads made Atlanta the center of a growing transportation network and hastened the city's development as a commercial center of the Southeast. By the eve of the **Civil War** (1861–65), Atlanta, with a population of more than 9,000, was the fourth largest city in Georgia.

Fewer African Americans, either free or enslaved, were present in Atlanta during the pre-war period than in the older, more-established cities of the South. One Atlanta resident noted in 1847 that "there are not 100 Negroes in the place, and white men black their own shoes, and dust their own clothes, as independently as in the north." Between 1850 and 1860 the number of slaves in Atlanta increased from 493 to 1,914, and "free persons of color" grew slightly in number from 19 to 25. (By way of contrast, Savannah's 1850 slave population of 6,231 was about 40 percent of that city's population, and 686 free blacks resided in the city.)

The Civil War Years

Whatever biracial residential patterns had been established in Atlanta were disrupted by the siege and destruction of the city during the Civil War and the tremendous inflow of blacks and whites following the war. In the intense competition for living space that followed, race and class were the major determinants of residential location. The resulting patterns resembled those found in many cities of the time, with the upper class living near the center of the city and the poor (both black and white) on the edges of town. Emerging black settlements in Atlanta, as in many other southern cities, were further confined to the most undesirable areas of the city: back alleys; low-lying, flood-prone ground; industrial sites; and tracts of land adjacent to railroads, cemeteries, city dumps, and slaughter houses. These locations not only tended to separate black settlements from surrounding white neighborhoods, but also contributed in some cases to very high black mortality rates.

For African Americans in Atlanta after the Civil War, employment opportunities were largely confined to unskilled labor, domestic service, or to jobs that whites did not want. Rural blacks migrating to the city tended to swell the ranks (increase the number) of unskilled workers, and even those freedmen who enjoyed positions as craftsmen or artisans before the war were often denied the opportunity to use those skills by white prejudice and an increasingly specialized job market (a market filled with jobs requiring special skills as opposed to unskilled jobs). As a result, the vast majority of the city's unskilled labor positions were filled by African Americans.

Despite the considerable obstacles facing them, some black Atlantans did succeed during this period in establishing thriving businesses and accumulating wealth and property. These businessmen made their mark in a hostile economic environment in part by catering to black clients or by providing services to whites that were not in direct competition with white businesses.

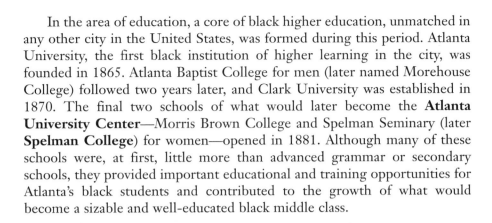

In the area of education, a core of black higher education, unmatched in any other city in the United States, was formed during this period. Atlanta University, the first black institution of higher learning in the city, was founded in 1865. Atlanta Baptist College for men (later named Morehouse College) followed two years later, and Clark University was established in 1870. The final two schools of what would later become the **Atlanta University Center**—Morris Brown College and Spelman Seminary (later **Spelman College**) for women—opened in 1881. Although many of these schools were, at first, little more than advanced grammar or secondary schools, they provided important educational and training opportunities for Atlanta's black students and contributed to the growth of what would become a sizable and well-educated black middle class.

The Early Twentieth Century

Efforts in Atlanta to segregate African Americans and restrict their political rights increased in the period from 1890 to 1920 as the city's black population more than doubled. In 1892 local Democratic officials passed a "white primary" law, effectively limiting voting in primary elections to white males. That same year, the city passed its first segregation ordinance, which ordered the separation of black and white passengers on streetcars. In 1913 Atlanta became the first city in Georgia to try to extend segregation to housing patterns through use of a residential segregation ordinance. Although this law was struck down by the state supreme court two years later, the city council passed a similar statute in 1917 and in 1922 tried to formalize segregated housing through use of a broad zoning ordinance.

Violence or threats of violence often accompanied attempts in the South during this period to segregate African Americans. A dramatic example of the ever-present potential for racial violence occurred in the Atlanta Riot of 1906. Racial tensions that year were aggravated by a long and bitter campaign for governor in which both candidates called for the complete exclusion of blacks from the political process. Following a series of unconfirmed reports in the local newspapers about wanton black attacks on white females, a race riot erupted in the city. Spurred on by lurid newspaper accounts of black rapists and rumors of black rebellion, roving gangs of white males attacked African Americans wherever they could find them in the downtown area and in nearby black neighborhoods.

The riot hastened the city's move toward the economic exclusion and residential segregation of African Americans. Following the riot, African Americans were more likely to settle in established black communities, particularly those located on the eastern fringe of downtown or on the west side of the city near Atlanta University. And black businesses, which had once been mixed among white stores on Peachtree Street, were now increasingly located to the east on Auburn Avenue, where a thriving but separate black business district soon developed.

Ironically, the economic exclusion of Atlanta's African Americans from white business dealings also contributed to the growth of the city's middle class and the development of a black business and cultural center on Auburn Avenue that *Fortune* magazine would later describe as "the richest black street in the world." By 1920 Auburn Avenue was already home to a wide range of black-owned and operated businesses, such as insurance companies, banks, a newspaper, barber and beauty shops, restaurants, grocery stores, photo studios, and funeral homes that provided African Americans the services denied them in the larger urban community. Freed from competition with white businessmen and assured the patronage of Atlanta's black community, many black businesses prospered under **Jim Crow.**

The Civil Rights Era

By 1930 Jim Crow and the color line had been firmly established in the city. In the period from 1940 to 1960, however, black leaders began negotiating with city hall and white business leaders to weaken Jim Crow's hold. That city hall and the white business elite were even willing to discuss the issue with black leaders was a reflection of two important post-**World War II** developments: increased black voting strength and a rapidly deteriorating housing situation.

This increased black voting power and the severe housing shortage facing black Atlantans brought city hall, black leaders, and the white business elite together in behind-the-scenes meetings to discuss such issues as the range and location of black residential expansion, redevelopment of the central business district, and city plans for annexation and growth. Each side succeeded in taking something away from the table. Black leaders got land for expansion and the construction of new housing and commitments from the city to build additional low-income housing. They also got promises from Mayor Hartsfield for a gradual phase-out of Jim Crow and increased protection against white violence. The agreements on black housing were important for African Americans of all income levels, as dwelling units in most of the city's black neighborhoods were overcrowded and in poor condition.

The peaceful biracial negotiations of this era contributed to Atlanta's emerging image as the most racially progressive city in the South. In 1961 this national reputation was further enhanced by the peaceful desegregation of four of the city's white high schools. Atlanta, always aware of the value of a good image, promoted itself during this decade as "the city too busy to hate."

Signs were already appearing, however, that suggested that the era of backstage biracial negotiations and gentlemen's agreements was fast coming to a close. **Sit-ins** in 1961 by black students to desegregate Atlanta's downtown restaurants threatened to upset relationships created between black leaders and the white business elite and exposed generational splits within the black community. **Martin Luther King, Jr.**, who had personally led one of the sit-in demonstrations, soon found himself in the tricky position of mediating between the more radical college students and older black leaders like his father, "Daddy" King.

One year later, changes in black leadership and tactics became even more obvious in the response of African Americans to the so-called "Peyton Road barricades." In that year, as blacks moved into a new white-only subdivision in southwest Atlanta, the city responded much as it had in the past by creating obstacles to slow and contain further black expansion (in this instance, by putting up street barricades). The resulting uproar in the black community and the accompanying national press coverage embarrassed the city and forced city hall to recognize that the days of a tightly segregated

housing market in Atlanta, kept in place by open discrimination and racial barriers, was over. While segregation practices would continue in more discreet forms—through the use of real estate tactics like blockbusting, racial steering, and discriminatory loan and mortgage policies—the right of African Americans to housing on an equal opportunity basis was now officially recognized.

This acknowledgment and the increasing movement of African Americans into formerly all-white communities in south and east Atlanta contributed to a dramatic migration of white Atlantans in the 1960s. During this decade, the city's white population declined by 60,000 while its black population increased by 70,000. The result, as documented in the 1970 census, was that Atlanta had a black majority for the first time in its history.

This dramatic population change was reflected in black political gains in the city's 1973 elections. Not only was the city council evenly divided between whites and blacks for the first time, but the school board now had a slim African-American majority and Maynard Jackson was elected the city's first black mayor. One hundred and twenty-five years of white rule in Atlanta had come to an end.

Atlanta Today

In the years following Jackson's 1973 victory, significant gains have been made in minority participation in city government and business. **Andrew Young** and, most recently, Bill Campbell have continued Atlanta's black mayoral presence. Atlanta's population base has also changed dramatically in the last few decades with the growing cultural and ethnic diversity in what has traditionally been a biracial society. Both the city and the larger metropolitan area, however, retain a high degree of racial segregation as the city remains over two-thirds black while the surrounding suburbs are over two-thirds white. The increasing movement of new jobs and businesses to the suburbs has also left Atlanta, like many other cities, with a declining economic base and decreased job opportunities for those other than white-collar workers.

The growing multicultural nature of Atlanta's population, the presence of internationally recognized businesses (for example, CNN and Coca-Cola) and the city's selection as the site for the 1996 Olympics underlie Atlanta's current claims to being "the next great international city." How well the city succeeds at this task may be determined by Atlanta's success in overcoming the racial divisions, both social and geographical, that have historically divided the city.

(SEE ALSO ATLANTA UNIVERSITY; CLARK ATLANTA UNIVERSITY; JIM CROW; ATLANTA COMPROMISE.)

Atlanta University Center

The Atlanta University Center (AUC) is a partnership that includes six historic black colleges and universities (HBCUs) located in the Atlanta, Georgia, area. This partnership is known as a consortium. The six schools include **Clark Atlanta University, Morehouse College, Spelman**

College, Morris Brown College, Morehouse School of Medicine, and the Interdenominational Theological Center. The partnership helps the individual schools to divide costs and share resources.

Each of the colleges was formed in the last half of the nineteenth century but struggled to stay in existence. By the end of World War I (1914–18), economic difficulties became even worse. Another problem was that the Atlanta General Education Board felt there were too many HBCUs in and around Atlanta. Instead of waiting to be closed down, representatives from three of the colleges (Atlanta University, founded 1865; Spelman University, a four-year women's college, founded 1881; and Morehouse College, a four-year men's college, founded 1867) met and signed a partnership agreement in 1929. As a result of the agreement, Atlanta University became exclusively a graduate school, and several student services were combined for all three schools.

The partnership proved to be very successful, and in 1953 three other institutions near Atlanta University were invited to join. They were Morris Brown College (founded 1881), the Gammon Theological Seminary (founded 1869), and Clark University (founded 1869). By 1957 negotiations were completed and the Atlanta University Center was established, with each of the individual schools considered an equal partner. The Interdenominational Center (which absorbed the Gammon Theological Seminary), became a member in 1958, and Morehouse School of Medicine joined in 1982.

Because the schools carefully plan and coordinate their resources, the center offers students much more than any one of the members could provide on its own. Two of the most important joint projects are the Robert W. Woodruff Library and the Science Research Institute. The Robert W. Woodruff Library, founded in 1982, was designed to hold over one million volumes. It is home to one of the largest collections of African-American documents in the United States. The Dolphus E. Milligan Science Research Institute (SRI), named for the black Atlanta University graduate and scientist, also opened in 1982. The institute receives federal research grants, plays a large role in the training of future African-American scientists, and offers an internship program that gives students experience in laboratories across the nation.

Since 1948 the AUC has also hosted numerous meetings and civil rights conferences. These have included meetings of the board of directors of the United Negro College Fund, the Association of Social Science Teachers, the American Association for the Advancement of Science, and a Conference on Discrimination in Higher Education. An annual art exhibit (begun in 1942) was founded to develop art appreciation in the Atlanta region.

Atlanta University. *See* Clark Atlanta University

Attaway, William Alexander

NOVELIST
November 19, 1911–June 17, 1986

Born in Greenville, Mississippi, and raised in Chicago, Illinois, novelist William Attaway attended local public schools and the University of Illinois.

His father died during his second year in college, and young Attaway left school to work his way west, taking jobs along the way as a cabin boy, dock-worker, and migrant laborer. He returned to Chicago and the university in 1933, where he published his first literary efforts. During this period Attaway became involved with the Illinois branch of the Federal Writers' Project (one of several government programs during the **Great Depression** of the 1930s that funded the arts).

After graduating from the university in 1936, Attaway moved to New York City, determined to earn his living as a writer. His first novel, *Let Me Breathe Thunder*, about the experiences of two white migrant farmworkers, was accepted for publication in 1939. *Blood on the Forge* (1941), Attaway's second and most important novel, narrates the mass migration of southern blacks to northern cities in search of jobs. The book traces the experiences of three half-brothers in the steel mills of Pennsylvania. Although *Blood on the Forge* received favorable critical reviews, the novel was not a commercial success. In his later years Attaway wrote for radio, film, and television; developed a deep interest in Caribbean and U.S. **folk music;** and published two works, *The Calypso Song Book* (1957) and *Hear America Singing* (1967). He spent the last years of his life in Los Angeles, California, where he died relatively unknown.

Attucks, Crispus

PATRIOT

1723–March 5, 1770

Crispus Attucks is famous as the first hero of the **American Revolution** (1775–83). Attucks, a tall, muscular man of African and American Indian ancestry, was a slave until he ran away in November 1750. For the next twenty years he worked on whaling ships operating out of many New England ports. On the night of March 5, 1770, he was a leader of a crowd of twenty to thirty workers and sailors who confronted a group of British soldiers in Boston, Massachusetts. Attucks struck one of the soldiers with a club, and then several soldiers fired into the crowd. Attucks fell instantly, becoming the first of five to die in the so-called Boston Massacre. He and the other victims of the massacre were given a public funeral, and ten thousand people marched in their funeral parade. During the soldiers' trial their defense attorney, John Adams (1735–1826), who would become the second president of the United States in 1796, said Attucks was to blame for the massacre, and the soldiers were let go without being punished.

The Boston Massacre was used by patriots (American colonists who supported independence from Great Britain) as another example of British misuse of power, and Attucks became known as a hero who stood up for American freedom. By the middle of the nineteenth century, many African-American schools and other institutions were named for Crispus Attucks. In 1888 Boston authorities erected a monument to him in Boston Common.

Monument dedicated to Crispus Attucks in
Boston (AP/Wide World Photos.
Reproduced by permission)

Autobiography

Autobiography—the writing of one's own life story—has held an important place in African-American literature since the mid-1700s, when most autobiographies were stories told by former slaves. These narratives were often published with the help of abolitionists, Americans who worked to end **slavery.** They believed that personal accounts of slaves who had made their way to freedom would influence whites to support the antislavery movement. African-American writers have used autobiography not only as a means of self-expression but also as a method for bringing about social and political change that will benefit all blacks.

Early Autobiographies

An early slave account that sold tens of thousands of copies was *The Interesting Narrative of the Life of Olaudah Equinao, or Gustavus Vassa, the African* (1789). Slave narratives that are considered classic works (perfect examples or masterpieces) include *The Narrative of **William Wells Brown**, a Fugitive Slave* (1842), by abolitionist-author William Wells Brown (1815–1884), and *Incidents in the Life of a Slave Girl, Written by Herself* (1861), by writer **Harriet Jacobs** (1813–1897).

From the end of the American Civil War (1861–65) to the beginning of the 1930s national economic diaster known as the **Great Depression** (1929–39), at least fifty former slaves came out with their autobiography. One best-selling autobiography was African-American educator **Booker T. Washington**'s (1856–1915) *Up from Slavery* (1901), in which Washington tells how he rose from slavery to become an educated and successful American. Leaders such as **Frederick Douglass** (1817–1895) and **W. E. B. Du Bois** (1868–1963) also wrote their autobiographies, giving readers an understanding of the hopes and ambitions of African Americans in their ongoing struggle for freedom and equality.

Some African-American ministers, such as Bishop Daniel Payne (1811–1893) with his *Recollections of Seventy Years* (1888), told readers that black survival depended on building strong black churches and schools through which African Americans could stand together against white supremacy (the belief that the white race is superior to the black race).

Early-Twentieth-Century Accounts

Some of the most important African-American works of the first half of the twentieth century were autobiographies, such as *Black Boy* (1945), by novelist **Richard Wright** (1908–1960), which was widely read and discussed during the post–World War II (1939–45) period. During this period African-American writers became more blunt about how they perceived the lives of black people in the United States. Other important black autobiographies of the period were *The Big Sea* (1940), by the poet and playwright **Langston Hughes** (1902–1967), and *Dust Tracks on a Road* (1942) by the novelist and short story writer Zora Neale Hurston (1903–1960).

Narratives from the Civil Rights Era

With the 1960s came a new generation of black autobiographers whose focus on the oppressed masses of blacks in the United States accompanied

Selected Autobiographies by African Americans

Gwendolyn Brooks
Report from Part One (1972)

Frederick Douglass
Life and Times of Frederick Douglass, Written by Himself (1845; 1892).

W. E. B. Du Bois
The Autobiography of W. E. B. Du Bois: A Soliloquy on Viewing My Life from the Last Decade of Its First Century (1968).

Nikki Giovanni
Gemini: An Extended Autobiographical Statement on My First Twenty-Five Years of Being a Black Poet (1971).

Marita Golden
Migrations of the Heart (1983).

Audre Lorde
A Burst of Light (1988).

William Pickens
Bursting Bonds: The Heir of Slaves (1923).

Ida B. Wells-Barnett
Crusade for Justice: The Autobiography of Ida B. Wells (1970).

the Civil Rights and Black Power movements. The most important of these was the orator (speech maker) Malcolm Little (1925–1965), who was better known as Malcolm X and who cowrote the African-American classic *The Autobiography of Malcolm X* (1965). He wrote the book with African-American author Alex Haley (1921–1992), who later wrote *Roots: The Saga of an American Family* (1976). *Roots*, an autobiographical account of Haley's search for his ancestors, became a phenomenal best-seller, won a Pulitzer Prize, and was turned into a miniseries that captured one of the largest television audiences ever.

When the African-American poet-novelist **Maya Angelou**'s (1928–) *I Know Why the Caged Bird Sings* was published in 1970, it began a new era of personal narratives by black women. These women included poet the Audre Lorde (1934–1992) and the writer Marita Golden (1950–). Their narratives tell about the African-American experience from the viewpoint of women artists and activists. The political activist and writer Angela Davis (1944–) is best known for *Angela Davis: An Autobiography* (1974), which tells of her childhood, education, career, and early public life.

The poet, dramatist, and literary critic **Amiri Baraka** (1934–), who also wrote under his birth name LeRoi Jones, was a key figure in the Black Muslim and "Beat" movements of the mid-1900s. The *Autobiography of LeRoi Jones* was published in 1984. African-American essayist and critic Henry Louis Gates Jr. (1950–), best known for his writings about African-American culture, published an autobiography, *Colored People: A Memoir*, in 1994.

Late-Twentieth-Century Stories

As African Americans made their mark in entertainment and sports during the latter part of the twentieth century, black celebrities also wrote autobiographies. Among them are the boxer **Muhammad Ali**'s (1942–) *The Greatest: My Own Story* (1974); *Secrets of a Sparrow: Memoirs* (1993), by the singer **Diana Ross** (1944–); the actress **Whoopi Goldberg**'s (1955–) *Book* (1997); and *The Uncommon Wisdom of Oprah Winfrey: A Portrait in Her Own Words* (1997), by the talk-show hostess and actress **Oprah Winfrey** (1954–). The autobiography of Dr. **Martin Luther King Jr.** (1929–1968) was published in 1998.

Bailey, Pearl

SINGER, ACTRESS
March 29, 1918–August 17, 1990

Pearl Bailey was a beloved singer and actress who began her career as an entertainer after winning a talent contest in Philadelphia, Pennsylvania, when she was fifteen. As Bailey toured the United States performing with many popular bands, she developed her trademark style—a warm singing voice accompanied by an easy smile—which charmed audiences. In the 1940s she made her theater debut and appeared in the motion picture *Variety Girl*, in which she sang one of her most popular songs, "Tired." In the years

that followed she made numerous stage, screen, and television appearances. Her most famous performance came in 1967, when she appeared in the all-black production of the play *Hello, Dolly!* This brought her a special Tony Award in 1968 for distinguished achievement in the New York theater.

In 1969 Bailey received the Woman of the Year award from the United Service Organization (USO; a nonprofit organization that entertains U.S. military personnel), which Bailey had toured with since 1941. The following year, U.S. president Richard Nixon appointed her "Ambassador of Love," and in 1975 she was appointed special representative to the United Nations. During this period Bailey returned to school, studying religion at Georgetown University in Washington, D.C. She received an honorary degree in 1978 and her bachelor's degree in 1985, at age sixty-seven.

Bailey also wrote several books, including the autobiographical *The Raw Pearl* (1968) and *Talking to Myself* (1971). *Between You and Me: A Heartfelt Memoir on Learning, Loving, and Living* was published in 1989, shortly before she died of heart disease on August 17, 1990. Two years before her death,

Ella Baker speaking at a news conference (AP/Wide World Photos. Reproduced by permission)

Bailey was presented with the Medal of Freedom (the highest honor that can be given to an American who has not served in the military) by U.S. president Ronald Reagan.

Baker, Ella J.
ACTIVIST
December 13, 1903–December 13, 1986

Ella Baker was a leading figure in the struggle of African Americans for equality, and she dedicated her life to helping others. Baker lived with her extended family, including aunts, uncles, and cousins, on land her grandfather had purchased from the owners of the plantation where his family were slaves. Baker's large family taught her the importance of community, the need for sharing, and the importance of continuing the struggle for social justice.

After graduating from college in North Carolina, Baker moved to New York City. She worked at several jobs, including waitressing and newspaper reporting. She also attended political meetings to continue her education. In the 1930s she taught consumer- and labor-education classes to people struggling with economic hard times.

In 1940 Baker accepted a job with the **National Association for the Advancement of Colored People (NAACP),** a group that works for equality for African Americans. She traveled throughout the United States and convinced people to join the NAACP by focusing on local issues that concerned African Americans.

After Baker left the NAACP in 1946, she became active in New York City social work organizations and political causes. In 1957 advisers to Dr. **Martin Luther King Jr.** (1929–1968) asked her to work for the **Southern Christian Leadership Conference (SCLC),** a civil rights group. Baker agreed to work for the SCLC for six weeks to organize a large voter registration drive but ended up staying for over two years. During her time at the SCLC, Baker worked to bring together student **sit-in** protest groups to draw attention to racial inequalities.

Throughout the 1960s Baker devoted her talents to many civil rights groups, such as the **Student Nonviolent Coordinating Committee,** the Southern Conference Educational Fund, and the Mississippi Freedom Democratic Party. Baker developed a belief that people who belonged to organizations should determine their own actions rather than always following a single leader. She shared this belief with every civil rights organization she worked with and helped inspire other groups, including the antiwar movement and the women's rights movement.

Eventually, Baker returned to New York, where she remained active in human rights affairs to the end of her life. In her later years she worked with such varied groups as the Puerto Rican Solidarity Committee, the Episcopal Church Center, and the Third World Women's Coordinating Committee. Baker's motto was "A life that is important is a life of service."

Baker, Josephine

ENTERTAINER
June 6, 1906–April 14, 1975

Josephine Baker was a highly original singer, dancer, and actress who refused to accept racial prejudice in the United States—by becoming a celebrity in France. Baker got her start in a small traveling production when she was sixteen. She quickly advanced to more important roles and was invited to perform in Paris, France, in 1925.

Baker became an overnight sensation in France, and her style and flair soon made her more famous than her singing talents. People began to copy her hairdo and her style of dancing, and clothing designers created clothes especially for her. Baker's performances became more and more outrageous, and in 1927 she opened her show wearing her famous costume of bananas decorated with rhinestones. She toured Europe and South America and then returned to Paris to continue her musical performances as well as acting in movies.

In 1939 Baker became a French citizen after a disastrous trip to the United States, where she learned that white audiences would not accept her. During World War II (1939–45) Baker worked for France against the Germans by spying and passing information to those fighting the Nazis. Eventually, she was sent to Morocco, where she drove an ambulance and entertained military troops. For her work she received two of France's highest honors.

After the war, Baker adopted four children of different races, calling them her "Rainbow Tribe," and turned her home into an ideal multiracial community. Baker continued to be an outspoken supporter of civil rights and refused to perform before all-white audiences in the United States. Instead, Baker continued to tour and perform in other countries. Despite her continuing popularity and performances, as her Rainbow Tribe grew to twelve she spent more money than she could earn.

Baker's health grew steadily worse after a heart attack in 1963, and she eventually lost her home and most of her money. She continued, however, to perform whenever possible and had just begun a new show when she died in 1975. Her funeral was televised and she was given full state honors in France, including a twenty-one-gun salute.

Baldwin, James

WRITER, CIVIL RIGHTS LEADER
August 2, 1924–November 30, 1987

"If we—and now I mean the relatively conscious whites and the relatively conscious blacks . . . do not falter in our duty now, we may be able to end the racial nightmare, and achieve our country, and change the history of the world."

(Source: James Baldwin. "The Fire Next Time," 1963.)

Born in New York City's Harlem district in 1924, James Baldwin began his writing career in the late 1940s. He rose to international fame after the publication of his most famous essay, "The Fire Next Time," in 1963. Nearly two decades before its publication, however, he had already captured the attention of many writers, literary critics, and intellectuals in the United States and abroad.

Much of Baldwin's writing has been autobiographical. The story of John Grimes, the main character of his first novel, *Go Tell It on the Mountain* (1953), closely resembles Baldwin's own childhood. Raised in a strict Pentecostal household, Baldwin became a preacher at age fourteen, and his sermons drew larger crowds than his father's, which aggravated tensions between them. The problems between father and son became a central theme in much of Baldwin's writing.

In 1948 Baldwin won a fellowship that allowed him to move to Paris, France, and complete *Go Tell It on the Mountain.* Although he spoke little French at the time, Baldwin bought a one-way ticket and later achieved success and fame as an **expatriate** (someone who settles in a foreign country). Writing about race and sexuality, he published twenty-two books, among them six novels, a collection of short stories, two plays, several collections of essays, a children's book, a movie scenario, and *Jimmy's Blues* (1985), a book of poems.

Around the time of "The Fire Next Time"'s publication, Baldwin became known as a spokesperson for civil rights. He was a prominent participant in the March on Washington in 1963, and he frequently appeared on television and delivered speeches on college campuses. But it was the powerful message of love and understanding delivered in the best-selling "The Fire Next Time," published on the one hundredth anniversary of the **Emancipation** Proclamation (1863), that landed him on the cover of *Time* magazine. Some black nationalists (people in favor of a separate nation for blacks), however, including leader **Eldridge Cleaver,** questioned whether that message would do much to change race relations in the United States.

Later in his life, Baldwin's essays and interviews discussed homosexuality and homophobia (fear or hatred of gays). Thus, just as he had been the leading literary voice of the **Civil Rights movement,** he became an inspirational figure for the emerging gay rights movement.

During the final decade of his life, Baldwin taught at a number of American colleges and universities, frequently commuting back and forth between the United States and his home in St. Paul de Vence in the south of France. After his death in France on November 30, 1987, the *New York Times* reported on its front page for the following day, "James Baldwin, Eloquent Essayist in Behalf of Civil Rights, Is Dead."

Ball, James Presley

PHOTOGRAPHER

1825–1905

A freeborn man from Virginia, J. P. Ball was an early photographer who was active in the abolitionist (ending **slavery**) and civil rights movements.

Ball started making daguerreotypes (an early form of photography) in his own Cincinnati, Ohio, studio in 1845. The business failed, but he continued to make portraits after taking a job in a Richmond, Virginia, hotel. He rented a furnished room, where he made portraits of local residents from all economic classes, both black and white, enslaved and free.

Ball worked as a traveling photographer in Ohio from 1847 until 1849, when he returned to Cincinnati. Among a series of studios that Ball operated there, the Ball & Thomas Photographic Art Gallery earned $100 a day and attracted such famous sitters as black abolitionist **Frederick Douglass** (1817–1895) and Ulysses S. Grant (a Union general and U.S. president, 1869–1877).

In 1887 Ball became the official photographer of the twenty-fifth anniversary celebration of the Emancipation Proclamation, which had declared all slaves in the South to be free. He then moved to Helena, Montana, where his son was an editor for a local newspaper, the *Colored Citizen.* In Helena, Ball photographed the construction of the state capital, newly arrived immigrants, civic celebrations, individuals in the African-American community, and public hangings.

1855 Antislavery Panorama

Ball's most famous work, created in 1855, was a 2,400-square-foot series, or panorama, of antislavery photos and illustrations. The series was accompanied by a pamphlet called *Ball's Splendid Mammoth Pictorial Tour of the United States Comprising Views of the African Slave Trade; of Northern and Southern Cities; of Cotton and Sugar Plantations; of the Mississippi, Ohio and Susquehanna Rivers, Niagara Falls, & C.* With the help of painter and daguerreotypist Robert S. Duncanson, Ball captured the slave experience, from life in Africa, to the horrors of the ocean passage, to daily routines in America. The panorama included portraits, cityscapes, and events in the history of American slavery. It was seen by thousands of viewers at Ball's studio and in an 1855 exhibit at Boston's Armory Hall.

Ball also began a political career. He served as a delegate to an 1887 civil rights convention and the 1894 Republican Party convention. Also in 1894, he became president of Montana's Afro-American Club.

Around 1900, Ball moved to Seattle, Washington, and opened the Globe Photo Studios. Seeking relief from rheumatism (stiff and painful joints or muscles), Ball moved to Hawaii in 1904, where he died the following year.

Ballet

Although African Americans were slow to be accepted in classical ballet in the United States, black dancers made their mark in this dance form beginning in the early 1920s and 1930s. At first, black dancers were believed to lack the culture and temperament—as well as the feet, joints, and knees—for ballet. Most black dancers were barred from all-white ballet schools and turned to modern and **jazz** dance, but because ballet training was the basis of many types of dance, African Americans continued to work at this form. Individual teachers greatly affected early black dancers.

Early Black Dance Companies

Racial division led to the formation of several all-black dance companies, including the New Negro Art Theater Dance Group, whose performances at the Roxy Theater in New York City in the 1930s proved that white audiences would accept black dancers. The American Negro Ballet first performed in 1937 in New York, but by 1939 the company had broken up because the audiences were too small to support it. The Negro Dance Company, founded in 1940, struggled for five years to get dancers and an audience.

In 1948 a truly classical black ballet company, the First Negro Classic Ballet, was formed in Los Angeles, California. In 1956 this successful company combined with the New York Negro Ballet Company, founded in 1955 by black dancer Edward Flemyng. Flemyng raised the money for his dance

JANET COLLINS: AFRICAN-AMERICAN PRIMA BALLERINA

Janet Collins (1917–) was the most famous African-American classical ballet dancer of the post–World War II (1939–45) era. Born in New Orleans, Louisiana, she was a member of dancer **Katherine Dunham**'s original ballet troupe in the 1920s. In 1948 Collins won a Rosenwald Fellowship to tour parts of the United States performing her own dances. She won a Donaldson Award for her Broadway performance in composer Cole Porter's *Out of This World* (1951). Collins's greatest fame as prima (leading) ballerina came during the early 1950s at the Metropolitan Opera in New York, where she danced in *Aida* (1951), *La Gioconda* (1952), and *Samson and Delilah* (1953). Collins's style was said to be a combination of modern and technical ballet with a personal approach. According to one critic, she "dances with something of the speed of light, seeming to touch the floor only occasionally with affectionate feet." Collins also choreographed dances, taught dancing, and painted.

company to tour England, Scotland, and Wales in 1957, but by 1960 the company had disbanded because of lack of funding.

The First African-American Dancers

Individual black dancers had been performing toe dances (dancing on the tips of the toes by means of a ballet slipper with a reinforced toe) since Helena Justa-De Arms performed in 1910 and Mary Richards danced on toe on Broadway in 1923. The New York Ballet (now the American Ballet) Theater School had a "Negro Wing" during the 1930s and 1940s.

After World War II (1939–45) African-American and white ballet dancers began to appear together on the stage. Among the first black dancers to appear with the New York Ballet Society were Talley Beatty, Arthur Bell, and Betty Nichols. African-American choreographer (dance composer and arranger) Louis Johnson (1931–) had a significant career in New York ballet; an integrated (both black and white) cast danced in his first story ballet, *Lament* (1953). Throughout the 1960s mostly white ballet companies, including New York's Harkness Ballet, the Joffrey Ballet, and the American Ballet Theater, recruited black dancers.

Modern African-American Ballet

The founding of the **Dance Theater of Harlem (DTH)** and its school in 1969 by dancer **Arthur Mitchell** (1934–) provided new opportunities for black dancers and choreographers. Within its first fifteen years, it became famous as a major ballet company, setting the standard for classical black ballet and documenting African-American influences on ballet as a dance form.

Black musicians and choreographers, including the American Ballet Theater's **Alvin Ailey** (1931–1989), composer **Duke Ellington** (1899–1974), musician **Wynton Marsalis** (1961–), choreographer Peter Martin, pop musician **Prince** (1958–), dancer and choreographer Paul Russell, and choreographer **Ulysses Dove** (1947–1996), inspired several important ballets from the 1970s through the 1990s. The DTH and black dancers around the world created ballet that is undeniably African American. Different from classical ballet's strict body lines and silent, motionless audiences, African-American ballet values invention, audience participation, and an overwhelming sense of the physical dancer that continues to attract audiences.

Baltimore, Maryland

Baltimore Beginnings

When Baltimore was established as a town in 1729, many African Americans already lived in the area which, like most of Maryland, was rural. As the town grew during the eighteenth century, its African-American population increased gradually. Both slaves and free blacks worked as house servants, laborers, and craftsmen. Trades such as barbering, blacksmithing, and coach driving came to be almost exclusively black.

In Baltimore, as elsewhere, African Americans fought on both sides of the **American Revolution** (1775–83). Many enslaved blacks emancipated during the Revolutionary era settled in Baltimore. In 1789 a group of prominent Baltimoreans formed the Society for the **Abolition** of **Slavery** and the Relief of Poor Negroes and Others Unlawfully Held in Bondage. Although these abolitionists did not win a legal end to slavery, by 1810 free blacks, their numbers increased by free black and mulatto (part black and part white) refugees from Haiti, outnumbered slaves in the city.

The African-American experience in Baltimore during the pre-**Civil War** era was unique. Although Maryland was a slave state, slavery declined rapidly in urban areas. By 1820 Baltimore had the largest free black population of any city in the United States. Slavery continued in Baltimore, though on a small scale, throughout the prewar period. Most slave owners owned one or two slaves, who served as domestic servants.

There was a clear social difference between slaves and free blacks, although free blacks suffered the same discrimination the slaves did. Blacks were excluded from the inside of streetcars (until 1871 they could only ride on the outside platforms), theaters, and schools in the city, and most housing was segregated. Their always uncertain social position was increasingly attacked in the years before the Civil War (1861–65). Maryland slave owners disliked the example of freedom Baltimore's black community offered their slaves. Also, the city's economy underwent several upheavals. Job competition between black laborers and immigrant white laborers was intense, and violent conflicts often ensued.

The Civil War Years

During the Civil War pro-Confederate sentiment ran high in Baltimore. In March 1861, a white mob stoned Union troops. Following the end of slavery in 1864, African-American progress was dramatic, despite continued discrimination. In 1865 the **Frederick Douglass** Institute, a cultural center created to "promote the intellectual advancement of the colored portion of the community," opened. The building contained a concert/meeting hall, dining room, and offices of an African-American newspaper, the *Communicator.* In 1867 Centenary Biblical Institute (later Morgan State University) opened, and in 1871 "colored" public schools opened for the first time. The great lasting legacy of late nineteenth-century black Baltimore is the *Baltimore Afro-American* newspaper, founded in 1892, the oldest major black journal still in publication. The era's most famous black Baltimorean was explorer Matthew Henson, codiscoverer of the North Pole.

The Early Twentieth Century

Black political influence in the city waned after 1900, and conditions for blacks worsened. In 1904 railroads and ships (but not trolley cars) were segregated. Soon, further ordinances followed, as Baltimore's racial lines hardened and the city sought to imitate other southern cities. For a short time after 1912, the city ordered separate black and white city blocks.

In 1935 the Baltimore **National Association for the Advancement of Colored People (NAACP),** largely inactive since its founding in 1913, was revived by Lillie Mae Carroll Jackson, who built it into the largest NAACP chapter outside **New York City.** During the 1930s the NAACP organized a "Don't Buy Where You Can't Work" campaign that opened up job opportunities for blacks throughout Baltimore, arranged the hiring of black police officers, registered large numbers of new voters, and, with the aid of Baltimore-born NAACP counsel **Thurgood Marshall,** pushed successfully for equalization of black and white teachers' salaries.

The Civil Rights Era

World War II (1939–45) brought 33,000 new black migrants to Baltimore in two years, sparking racial tension. In April 1942, after a white policeman shot an African American in the back, thousands marched on Baltimore in protest. The first victory over black exclusion from public facilities occurred in 1946, when Willie Adams, a millionaire gambler and liquor industry tycoon, led a successful protest over segregated city golf courses. However, while Ford's Theater and downtown department stores began admitting blacks in the early 1950s, most of the city remained segregated until 1954, when the Supreme Court's ***Brown* v. *Board of Education of Topeka, Kansas*** ruling led to the integration of public schools. Further integration was slow. In 1956 the city passed an equal employment ordinance but without enforcement powers. In early 1960 students from Morgan State began lunch counter sit-ins aimed at desegregating city facilities. However, city authorities did not pass a civil rights statute until 1962.

Baltimore's economy worsened during the 1960s. Police brutality was a chronic problem, and job and union discrimination remained rampant. On April 6, 1968, following the assassination of the Rev. Dr. **Martin Luther King, Jr.,** rioting erupted in Baltimore. Looting broke out on Gay Street, then spread as blacks started fires and broke windows. The next day, as rioting grew more intense, Maryland Governor Spiro Agnew declared the riot

AFRICAN-AMERICAN CULTURE IN BALTIMORE

However bleak the political situation for blacks in Baltimore in the early part of the twentieth century, the cultural picture was impressive. Baltimore natives such as Eubie Blake had long played a part in black theater and music. During the 1920s and 1930s Pennsylvania Avenue in West Baltimore emerged as the center of local African-American business and social life. Baltimore native Cab Calloway and other important musicians were featured in clubs, while the city gave birth to performers such as Billie Holiday, Chick Webb, John Kirby, and Joe Turner.

an insurrection and called in National Guard troops. Violence continued for two more days. Altogether there were six deaths, dozens of injuries, 5,512 arrests, and 1,208 major fires. On Wednesday, April 10, Agnew met with a hundred moderate black leaders, but instead of promising to deal with conditions causing the riot, he blamed the disturbance on black radicals and denounced the moderates as "cowards" for not opposing them. Most of the group walked out, and Agnew refused to listen to the remaining leaders. Agnew's inflexible stance soon led to his nomination and subsequent election as vice president of the United States.

Baltimore Today

Since 1968 Baltimore has followed the pattern of many urban areas in the United States. During the mid-1970s, Baltimore became a black majority city. The city's economy has declined in the face of the loss of industries and middle-class migration to nearby suburbs. Unemployment and crime have been recurring problems. In 1992 a Maryland Commission report found that over half of Baltimore's black men between eighteen and thirty-five were in trouble with the law.

At the same time, blacks have established political control of the city. In 1970 in a close election, Parren Mitchell became Baltimore's first African-American congressman from a district that had a white majority at the time. After retiring in 1986, he was succeeded by **Kweisi Mfume.** That same year, in tribute to the city's civil rights past, the NAACP relocated to Baltimore. In 1996 Mfume retired from Congress and returned to Baltimore as executive secretary of the NAACP.

In 1987 **Kurt Schmoke,** a former Rhodes scholar and state's attorney, became the city's first black mayor. Schmoke has adopted various reforms to deal with the housing, health, and safety problems of the city's African Americans and has focused his attention on improving education. He has also gained national attention through his controversial advocacy of drug legalization.

In 1991 Baltimore became the home of the Great Blacks in Wax museum, the nation's first wax museum devoted to African Americans, a fitting tribute to the important place blacks have occupied in the city's history.

(SEE ALSO **CABELL CALLOWAY; BILLIE HOLIDAY.**)

Bambara, Toni Cade

WRITER
March 25, 1939–December 29, 1995

Born Toni Cade in New York City, Bambara adopted her last name in 1970. She grew up in New York as well as in Jersey City, New Jersey. She graduated from Queens College in 1959—the year in which she published her first short story, "Sweet Town." Bambara earned a master's degree in English from City College of New York in 1965. At the same time, she served as a community organizer and activist, and as an occupational therapist for the psychiatric division of Metropolitan Hospital.

Bambara grew up quickly in her urban neighborhoods, acquiring early in life the flexibility and strength that would be needed for a poor, black female to survive. The skills and attitudes needed to endure an often violent urban environment, or "street smarts," are seen in two collections of writings by black women that Bambara edited, *The Black Woman* (1970) and *Tales and Stories for Black Folks* (1971).

In 1972 Bambara's first solo work, *Gorilla, My Love*, a collection of fifteen stories that focus on family, community, and self-love, was published. Her second collection of stories, *The Sea Birds Are Still Alive* (1977), revolves around the theme of community healing. The theme of healing is further explored in Bambara's novel *Salt Eaters* (1980), which won the American Book Award, presented annually by the National Book Foundation for the best work of fiction in the United States.

Bambara taught at several universities, including Rutgers University (New Brunswick, New Jersey), Duke University (Durham, North Carolina), and **Spelman College** (Atlanta, Georgia). She died of colon cancer on December 29, 1995.

Banks, Ernest "Ernie"

BASEBALL PLAYER
January 31, 1931–

Ernest "Ernie" Banks is one of **baseball**'s greats. He played shortstop and later first base for the Chicago Cubs for nineteen years. Banks made it to the big leagues during an era of racial inequality; in fact, he was only the second African American to play for the Cubs. Banks loved the game of baseball and is known for saying, "Let's play two," meaning one game was not enough for him; he would rather play a "doubleheader."

Born in Texas, Banks proved himself in the Negro Leagues in 1950. He played for the Cubs from 1953 until his retirement in 1971. Banks made his mark on the game of baseball by setting a record for the most home runs by a shortstop (47) and being the first player to have his number (14) retired by the Cubs. He was voted to the Baseball Hall of Fame in 1978. Since retiring, Banks travels the United States giving motivational speeches and supports youth programs in Chicago (see http://www.letsplaytwo.com).

Banneker, Benjamin

MATHEMATICIAN, ASTRONOMER
November 9, 1731–October 9, 1806

Benjamin Banneker is considered the first African-American man of **science**. In 1781 he helped U.S. president George Washington (1732–1799) survey (determine the form, extent, and geographical position of) ten square miles of land in Virginia and Maryland to help build the nation's capital. This was very difficult to do because there was not a lot of advanced surveying technology at the time. In fact, Banneker used the stars (astronomy) and math formulas as his guide. He created mathematical tables based on where the stars are at a given point in time to construct a layout of the land. This kind of table is called an "ephemeris," which was Banneker's area of expertise.

Banneker was born in a log cabin in Maryland. As a young boy he could attend school for only a few months. Taught to read by his grandmother, Banneker spent most of his time with his nose buried in all kinds of books. He enjoyed solving complex math problems just for fun. When he was twenty-two years old, he built a clock, carving all of the pieces out of wood.

Banneker was a self-sufficient man who lived on a farm. It was not until he retired that he finally discovered his passion for studying the stars. Banneker taught himself enough math and astronomy to be able to make an ephemeris (a star and planet chart) for an almanac (a book with charts, tables, and general information about a region). It was around this time

Benjamin Banneker's **PENNSYLVANIA, DELAWARE, MARYLAND, AND VIRGINIA ALMANAC,** FOR THE YEAR of our LORD 1795; Being the Third after Leap-Year.

BANNAKER.

—PRINTED FOR— And Sold by JOHN FISHER, Stationer. BALTIMORE.

(1781) that Banneker did his survey, along with the help of Andrew Ellicott, for George Washington. They studied the land for three months, living in a tent the entire time. Experts have studied Banneker's almanac with modern technology and found out that he was extremely accurate. Banneker's almanac was published in Baltimore, Maryland, in 1792.

Bannister, Edward Mitchell

PAINTER
c. 1826–January 9, 1901

Landscape painter Edward Mitchell Bannister became known in New England art circles during the American Civil War (1861–65), despite a lack of formal training. Born about 1827 in New Brunswick, Canada, Bannister was raised by his widowed mother, who supported his interest in art. As a boy, Bannister won a local reputation for clever crayon portraits.

By 1850 Bannister had moved to Boston, Massachusetts, with the hope of becoming a painter, but he was unable to find an established artist who would accept a black student. By 1853 he was working as a barber in the shop of the African-American businesswoman Madame Christiana Carteaux, whom he married in 1857.

Bannister continued to paint, finding support in Boston's African American community. In 1854 he received his first commission (paid assignment) for an oil painting, entitled *The Ship Outward Bound*. By 1863 Bannister was featured in **William Wells Brown**'s book celebrating prominent African Americans. His earliest surviving portrait, *Prudence Nelson Bell*, was completed the next year.

About 1864 Bannister received his only formal art training, at the Lowell Institute in Boston. He also learned about the realistic landscapes of the French Barbizon painters (active in the mid-1800s), who would strongly influence his style. At this time Bannister's **painting**s began receiving favorable notices from Boston critics. His growing confidence as an artist is reflected in *Herdsman with Cows* and *Untitled* [Man with Two Oxen] (both 1869).

In 1869 the Bannisters moved to Providence, Rhode Island, where he was immediately recognized by its growing art community. His first exhibit included *Newspaper Boy* (1869), one of the earliest depictions of working-class African Americans by an African-American artist, and a portrait of abolitionist (antislavery advocate) William Lloyd Garrison (1805–79).

Bannister's prominence in the art community continued to grow. By 1878 he sat on the board of the newly created Rhode Island School of Design, and he helped found the influential Providence Art Club. His Saturday art classes were well attended, and he won numerous awards for his work.

Although he experienced heart trouble in his later years, Bannister continued to paint. His later works show an interest in experimentation, with a more abstract use of form and color. On January 9, 1901, Bannister collapsed at an evening prayer meeting and died shortly thereafter. That same year, the Providence Art Club organized a memorial exhibition, and a stone monument was erected on his grave.

Baptists

Baptists follow the Christian religion and emphasize "baptising," a ceremony involving immersing (dunking) new members in water to proclaim faith in the church. The practice stems from the biblical account of the prophet John the Baptist, who, according to Matthew 3:13-15, baptised Jesus in the Jordan River. African-American Baptists are the largest and most diverse group of the many African-American religious groups in the United States. African-American Baptists are particularly known for their emphasis on emotional preaching and worship, the importance of music in their worship services, community leadership, and social and political activism.

The Early Church

In early America only a few white Baptists shared their religion with African slaves, but as the Baptist religion spread throughout the South between 1750 and 1850, the numbers of African-American Baptists increased. Some Baptist churches accepted both black and white members, and in some churches in the South there were more slaves than whites. No matter how many African-American members there were in a white Baptist church, however, they were still limited in their privileges and responsibilities, either because they were slaves or, if they were free, because they were discriminated against.

Slave preachers, some of whom had served as religious leaders in **Africa,** were the first to call for a separation from white Baptists. In 1775 David George organized the first black Baptist church in North America, at Silver Bluff, South Carolina. Soon after, slaves and **free blacks** in other parts of the country, including the North, began similar movements.

When several congregations or smaller groups of African-American Baptists join together, they form what is called a "cooperative." The roots of the African-American Baptist cooperative movement go back to the early 1830s. Local churches began to join together to better support their causes, which included promoting education and establishing foreign missions, especially in **Africa.** As early as 1840, black Baptists of New England and the Middle Atlantic states gathered to organize the American Baptist Missionary Convention, their first cooperative movement to include members from several states. On September 28, 1895, William W. Colley, a missionary just back from Africa, helped establish the **National Baptist Convention,** which became the central organization that oversees the individual Baptist congregations.

Divisions in the Church

In the early part of the 1900s, members were divided over several issues. Some African-American Baptists were opposed to sending missionaries to Africa because they believed in predestination, meaning that God has a purpose for the way things are and determines beforehand the fate of all individuals. Therefore, if someone lived in Africa, he or she was probably not "predestined" to be (meant to be) converted to Christianity by Baptists from the United States. Baptists who opposed the missionary movement formed their own group, the African-American Primitive Baptists. By 1907 Primitive Baptist churches had gained enough followers to organize into a national convention, but their rate of growth was far slower than that of the National Baptists.

Other debates concerned how much the church depended on funding that came from white sources and the level of control the national convention had over local churches. A great rift occurred in 1915 over the level of control the national convention should have, and a separate, smaller denomination, the National Baptist Convention of America, was formed as a result.

A major crisis occurred within the National Baptists in 1961 relating to the **Civil Rights movement.** Joseph H. Jackson, president of the National Baptist Convention, was opposed to the civil rights strategies used by groups such as the **Southern Christian Leadership Council (SCLC).** The civil rights leaders in the church, including Rev. **Martin Luther King Jr.,** wanted the church to adopt a more progressive stance toward civil rights. These leaders organized a new denomination, the Progressive National Baptist Convention of America, which promoted King's civil rights agenda and launched an era of cooperation with the largely white American Baptist Churches.

The Modern Church

Education for African Americans has always been an important goal of the Baptist cooperatives and national conventions, and the development of higher education for African Americans has been among the lasting contributions of African-American Baptists. Several historically black colleges and universities were founded with Baptist support.

African-American Baptists have also continued to stress the importance of reaching out to the local community. This commitment has grown even more since the 1960s. Many black Baptist pastors work directly with troubled teenagers and prison populations and promote programs to discourage drug use.

One of the important developments in the black Baptist church in recent decades has been the changing status of women. For the most part, until the late 1900s women were not allowed to be ministers or to hold leadership positions within the church. Black women were not ordained until the 1970s, and even then in small numbers. The bias against promoting women to positions of prominence in the Baptist church is changing, although too slowly for many.

The various African-American Baptist congregations in the United States vary in size, political and community involvement, and religious practice. Some of the larger urban churches are established centers of community activity and serve as political bases for their pastors. And small rural Baptist churches, while their numbers declined somewhat in the 1990s, remain the backbone of numerous communities. (*See also* **Abyssinian Baptist Church**)

Baraka, Amiri

FICTION WRITER, ESSAYIST, PROFESSOR OF AFRICAN STUDIES
October 7, 1934–

Fiction writer and essayist Amiri Baraka (born Everett LeRoi Jones in 1934) is the most prominent figure of the **Black Arts movement.** He has

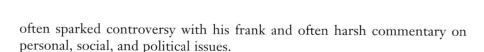

often sparked controversy with his frank and often harsh commentary on personal, social, and political issues.

Raised in Newark, New Jersey, Baraka attended **Howard University** in Washington, D.C., and served briefly in the U.S. Air Force. After moving to Greenwich Village (an area of New York City famous for attracting artists and writers), Jones met and married writer Hettie Cohen. He became part of the Village literary scene, alongside Allen Ginsberg (1926–1997) and Jack Kerouac (1923–1969), writers who led the anti-establishment "Beatnik generation" of the 1950s and 1960s. Jones and Cohen edited *Yugen*, an avant-garde (dealing with new ideas) literary magazine. Jones's book *Preface to a Twenty Volume Suicide Note* (1961) established him as an important new poet.

Jones, however, soon severed all of his Village ties. After the assassination of black activist **Malcolm X** (1925–1965), he abandoned his family, moved to Harlem, and changed his name to Imamu Amiri Baraka (Blessed Priest and Warrior). Embracing an intense black cultural nationalism, his new poems and plays attacked whites and urged blacks to discover their authentic identity in order to gain political freedom.

Baraka is probably best known for his 1964 play *Dutchman*, which explores the tense attraction between a black man and a white woman riding in the New York subway. The play reflects the racial anxieties that eventually transformed his life. Baraka's long poems, such as "In the Tradition," written later in his life, present triumphant visions of African-American culture. These poems blend references to sports, jazz, and politics. In 1984 Baraka published the ***Autobiography*** *of LeRoi Jones/Amiri Baraka*. The short novel *6 Persons*, an autobiographical account of his life before the death of Malcolm X, was published in 2000 as part of *The Fiction of Leroi Jones/Amiri Baraka Reader*.

Baraka lives in Newark, New Jersey, and is a professor of African Studies at the State University of New York-Stony Brook.

Amiri Baraka: Selected Writings

Preface to a Twenty Volume Suicide Note (1961)

Dutchman (play, 1964)

The Dead Lecturer (1964)

Slave Ship (play, 1967)

Black Magic (1969)

Hard Facts (1976)

AM/TRAK (poetry, 1979)

Spring Song (1979)

Reggae or Not (prose, 1981)

Autobiography of LeRoi Jones/Amiri Baraka (1984)

Fiction of LeRoi Jones/Amiri Baraka (2000)

Barboza, Anthony

PHOTOGRAPHER
May 10, 1944–

A widely published fashion and portrait photographer, Anthony Barboza is known for photographing his subjects in motion, giving his photographs a blurred, mystical quality. He often uses offbeat background elements such as tilted horizons, dramatic lighting, and metallic spray paint in his portraits. His photographs have appeared in such top magazines as ***Ebony***, *Esquire*, *Essence*, and *Vogue*.

Born in New Bedford, Massachusetts, in 1944, Barboza moved to New York City in 1963, at age nineteen, to study **photography**. He joined the U.S. Navy in 1965, working part-time as base photographer. In 1970 he opened his own studio, quickly building a successful business in fashion photography. In the mid-1970s he began experimenting with portraiture, taking pictures of close friends and artists, athletes, and models. The National Endowment for the Arts awarded Barboza a grant in 1980, allowing him to publish his first book, *Black Borders*.

Marion Barry (AP/Wide World Photos. Reproduced by permission)

During the 1980s Barboza turned increasingly to teaching, lecturing at such institutions as the International Center of Photography in New York City. Barboza, who also writes poetry and short stories, is a founder of International Black Photographers, an organization dedicated to recognizing the work of living black photographers. He also collects photographs by black photographers of the 1800s.

Barry, Marion

POLITICIAN
March 6, 1936–

Marion Barry has been at the center of local politics in Washington, D.C., for more than twenty years. He is considered by some to be one of the great modern-day African-American political leaders. Barry led a fight against the unequal treatment of blacks and reformed the nation's capital. Unfortunately, his accomplishments as mayor have been overshadowed by political corruption and a conviction for possession of the illegal drug cocaine in 1990.

Barry was born in Itta Bena, Mississippi. He got involved in **politics** at LeMoyne College (now LeMoyne-Owen College) in Memphis, Tennessee, where he became president of the campus branch of the **National Association for the Advancement of Colored People (NAACP).** Barry graduated from LeMoyne with a degree in chemistry and then earned a master's degree from **Fisk University** (Nashville, Tennessee).

In 1965, while working for the **Student Nonviolent Coordinating Committee** (a group that fights racism), Barry was transferred to Washington, D.C. Thus began his love affair with D.C. politics. Barry started the "Free D.C. Movement," a goal of which was to bring control of the district's government to blacks. Barry served three terms as mayor (1979–91), making important improvements in the district, such as reducing group conflicts, balancing the budget, and improving the condition of the city.

Although Barry's 1990 arrest nearly ruined his career, he was reelected to a fourth term as mayor in 1994. The term was troubled by scandal, and the city became nearly bankrupt. Barry retired in 1998 but remains active in Washington politics.

Barthé, Richmond

SCULPTOR
January 28, 1901–March 6, 1989

A sculptor who became famous in the field of modern American art, Richmond Barthé was born in Bay Saint Louis, Mississippi. His widowed mother nurtured his desire to become an artist, and at age twelve Barthé showed his work at a county fair. After a move to New Orleans, Louisiana, he won a blue ribbon for drawing in a parish (county) competition when he was eighteen.

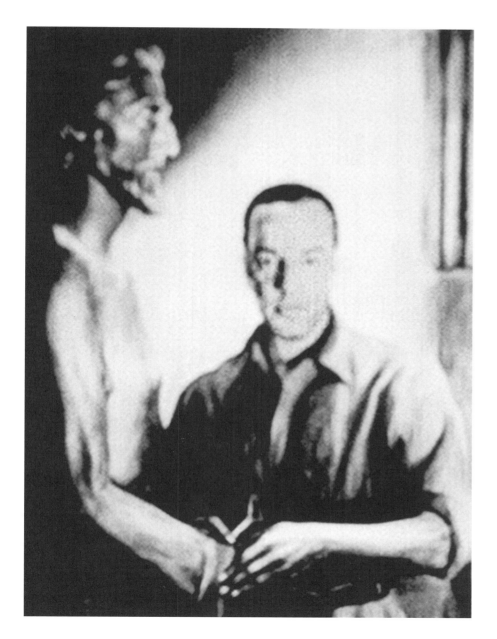

Artist Richmond Barthé with one of his sculptures (Courtesy of the National Archives and Records Administration)

With the encouragement of a reporter for the *Times-Picayune* newspaper, Barthé tried to register at a New Orleans art school. Refused because of his color, he only became more determined to succeed as an artist. In 1924 Barthé was admitted to the Art Institute of Chicago, where he studied **painting** for four years. During his senior year, however, he was introduced to **sculpture** by an anatomy teacher. This was the beginning of Barthé's long career as a sculptor.

Barthé moved to New York City in 1929 and proceeded to impress both critics and collectors. By 1934 he had his first solo show at the Caz Delbo Galleries. His works would be added to important collections, such as the Whitney Museum of American Art, the Metropolitan Museum of Art, and the Museum of the Art Institute of Chicago.

Among his works are an eight-by-eighty-foot sculpture called *Green Pastures: The Walls of Jericho*, commissioned for the Harlem River Housing Project; a garden sculpture for the famous Falling Water house in Pennsylvania, designed by architect Frank Lloyd Wright (1869–1959); and a **Booker T. Washington** (1856–1915) portrait bust for the Hall of Fame of New York University.

In 1947 Barthé moved to Jamaica, West Indies, to escape big-city life. By then he was considered one of the leading names in modern American art, but he preferred peaceful surroundings over celebrity status. Barthé later spent some time in Europe, studying the Italian Renaissance sculptors Donatello (1386–1466) and Michelangelo (1475–1564).

In 1976 Barthé returned to the United States and ultimately settled in Altadena, California. He lived there until his death in 1989.

Baseball

Because of its role in the desegregation of America, baseball has been an important element of African-American culture. Indeed, the early history of blacks and baseball mirrors the country at large, dating roughly to 1850 when middle-class populations in eastern cities adopted the sport as a favorite. Amateur clubs developed devoted followings in those days of non-professional play. The **Civil War** (1861–65) spread baseball throughout the existing United States, but whereas in the North the sport stayed primarily a game among whites, in the rural South it became established equally among blacks. Later, black semipro and college teams transformed baseball games into popular community events.

Before the sport became wholly professionalized, it was not uncommon for blacks to play on mostly white teams or for black teams to play against white teams in sanctioned (officially approved) contests. After the onset of **Jim Crow** laws, however, separation of black and white athletes became the rule. Though written policies never formally excluded blacks from professional baseball, so-called gentlemen's agreements prevented black players from competing on an equal footing with white players. As black teams were left out of organized baseball, they were forced to barnstorm the country seeking opponents. The Cuban X Giants of **Harlem, New York,** founded in 1885, was the first truly successful black professional team. Occasional efforts to establish black leagues were attempted but without lasting success. For decades, countless players went to play in Cuba, Mexico, and other Central American countries, where they were treated as equals on and off the diamond.

The Negro Leagues

In 1920 Andrew "Rube" Foster founded the Negro National League with teams in six midwestern cities. It became the first of several successful black major leagues that existed for various periods between 1920 and 1960, including the Eastern Colored League, the Southern League and the Negro American League. The Colored World Series appeared intermittently throughout the history of the Negro leagues, generally pitting the champions of two competing regional leagues against each other at season's end.

Among the most successful franchises during the Negro leagues era were the Chicago American Giants, Pittsburgh Crawfords, Homestead Grays, and Kansas City Monarchs. The caliber of play was high, but the schedules were grueling. To keep solvent, teams routinely played exhibition games with minor league and local teams as they barnstormed their way from league city to league city. The season's biggest event was not the World Series, but the annual East-West All-Star Game, which was introduced in 1933 and played regularly in Chicago. Crowds rivaling those of major league baseball's All-Star Game attended these popular events, which continued through the 1950 season. Stars of the period included **James "Cool Papa" Bell**, Oscar Charleston, **Josh Gibson, William "Judy" Johnson,** John Henry Lloyd, **Leroy "Satchel" Paige,** and "Smokey Joe" Williams.

Breaking the Color Barrier

The color barrier was finally crossed in 1947 when **Jackie Robinson** suited up for the Brooklyn Dodgers. A very good—but not great—player, Robinson was handpicked by Dodgers owner Branch Rickey to be the first black player in major league baseball history because of his personal background and even temperament. Robinson proved a good choice, as he fought his way through constant discrimination (even from teammates) to win the inaugural Rookie of the Year award. Other black players followed Robinson into the big leagues, though integration was a slow process. Every team in the majors did not have a black player on its roster until 1959. The infusion of Negro leagues talent proved a boon for several teams, as such traditionally cellar-dwelling teams as the Dodgers began winning pennants, while gate receipts jumped as black fans quickly switched allegiance from Negro league teams to major league teams with black players on their rosters. That movement of fans spelled doom for all of black baseball, major and minor, and the last black leagues ceased operation in 1960.

In the half century since integration, hundreds of black players have donned major league uniforms. Literally dozens of those players have stamped their names on league record books, earning a disproportionate share of records. Three of the top four career home run hitters are black, with **Henry "Hank" Aaron** the all-time career leader in homers, with 755, and in runs batted in (RBIs), with 2,297. Many of the top stars of baseball's so-called "golden era" of the 1950s and 1960s were black players; in addition to Aaron, they include **Ernie Banks, Roy Campanella, Bob Gibson, Willie Mays,** and **Frank Robinson.**

Black Achievements since the 1960s

The 1970s and 1980s saw an additional group of black sluggers make their marks, including **Reggie Jackson,** Eddie Murray, and Jim Rice, but black players were really making speed and baserunning a bigger part of the game. First, **Lou Brock** topped Ty Cobb's single-season and career base-stealing records, then Rickey Henderson topped Brock's marks a few years later. In fact, four of the top six career leaders in steals are black players who spent a major portion of their careers playing during those decades. There was no shortage of great hitters during that era either, as Brock, Rod Carew, Murray, and Dave Winfield all joined the exalted 3,000-hit club. Although few black pitchers have recorded outstanding career numbers, Lee Smith demolished the career saves record, retiring in 1997 with 478, which is over 60 more than the runner-up.

Starting in the late1980s, there came a new melding of speed and power in the sport. The player most often cited as the best of the 1990s, Barry Bonds, is the epitome of that combination. Bonds became the first player in major league history to record 400 steals and 400 home runs in a career in 1998, and will likely reach the 500 plateaus before he is through. Tony Gwynn, who collected his 3,000th hit in 1999, has proven himself to be one of the best pure hitters in the game's history by earning eight seasonal batting titles, tying him for the second-best total in major league history. Other top stars of the decade include Albert Belle, Ken Griffey Jr., and Frank Thomas.

In 1997, major league baseball took the unprecedented step of retiring Jackie Robinson's uniform number, 42, across both leagues in recognition of the 50th anniversary of his breaking the color barrier. Currently, black players account for approximately 20 percent of major-leaguers, well above the 12 percent found in the general population. Nevertheless, baseball has increasingly lost black fans to other spectator sports, particularly football and basketball, which have even higher percentages of black athletes. Over 50 years after integration, major league baseball has yet to welcome its first black owner into the sport.

Basie, William James "Count"

BANDLEADER, JAZZ PIANIST
August 21, 1904–April 26, 1984

Pianist and bandleader "Count" Basie was born in Red Bank, New Jersey, in 1904. As a child he played drums and piano, and in high school he formed a band with drummer **Sonny Greer.**

In 1924 Basie moved to New York City, where he was befriended by two famous stride piano players, **Fats Waller** and James P. Johnson. Basie also became a fine stride pianist (a style in which the left hand "strides" up and down the keys) and an accomplished organist. Soon he began touring with bands and variety acts, settling in 1929 with a band led by Bennie Moten in Kansas City, Missouri.

After Moten's death in 1935, Basie reorganized the group as Count Basie and the Barons of Rhythm. Producer John Hammond moved the band to **New York City** in 1936, and before long it became one of the country's best-known swing bands. Basie and his band played in such famous landmarks as the **Savoy Ballroom** and featured some of the most famous musicians and singers of the day, including saxophonist **Lester Young** and vocalist **Billie Holiday.** In 1943 the band appeared in two films, *Stage Door Canteen* and *Hit Parade of 1943.*

As swing music began to lose its popularity, Basie had trouble finding work and finally dissolved his band in 1949. After touring for a year with a bebop-style octet (a musical group of eight), he formed another big band, one that featured more complex arrangements and rhythmic accuracy.

Basie and his band toured around the world from the 1950s through the 1970s. In 1955 he had his first national hit with "Every Day I Have the Blues." The band's popularity came to eclipse even that of **Duke Ellington.** It played at inaugural balls for two U.S. presidents and appeared in the films *Cinderfella* (1959), *Sex and the Single Girl* (1964), and *Blazing Saddles* (1974).

In the 1980s Basie was still recording as a solo artist and in small-group and big-band settings. He died in 1984 in Hollywood, Florida. His **autobiography,** *Good Morning Blues,* appeared the next year. Since then, Basie's band has continued performing under new leaders.

Basketball

African Americans have made significant contributions to the sport of basketball. It would be difficult to imagine the game without names like **Wilt Chamberlain, Julius Erving, Kareem Abdul-Jabbar, Earvin "Magic" Johnson,** and **Michael Jordan.** Although at one time American courts were closed to blacks, legends such as these have afforded both male and female African Americans the opportunity to participate in every aspect of the game, including college and professional coaching, managing, and playing in the Olympics.

Basketball's Early Years

After Canadian-American physical education instructor James Naismith created the game of basketball in 1891, very few blacks played the game in its early years. The entrance of African Americans into the sport began with the efforts of Edwin B. Henderson, who helped develop youth basketball programs in Washington, D.C., in the early 1900s. He also introduced a basketball program at **Howard University** in D.C., and other black universities followed suit.

In 1916, because college associations did not allow black and white players to mix, Howard, Lincoln, Shaw, and Virginia Union Universities (all black schools) developed the Central Interscholastic Athletic Association. It was followed by the formation of the Southeastern Athletic Conference, which represented schools from the Deep South.

College Basketball

Between **World War I** (1914–18) and **World War II** (1939–45), some African-American athletes did play on a few teams at integrated universities. One of these was John Howard Johnson, the first black basketball player at Columbia University in New York, who graduated in 1921.

After World War II, blacks flooded into the college basketball scene as American society began warming up to racial integration policies. The City College of New York, which featured black players, became the only team ever to win the National Collegiate Athletic Association (NCAA) tournament and the National Invitational Tournament (NIT) in the same year, which caught the attention of many college recruiters. Certain schools developed a reputation for black recruitment, such as the University of California in Los Angeles, which won ten national championships between 1964 and 1975 and cultivated such professional greats as **Kareem Abdul-Jabbar.**

Although college basketball has grown to be dominated by black athletes, there has been growing concern about recruitment methods and academic performance. According to some, a few schools recruit African Americans merely for their athletic skills without thinking about their educational needs. Blacks often drop out if they have no chance of playing professionally; between 1985 and 1991 the graduation rate among black athletes was around 27 percent, while 46 percent of white athletes graduated.

Professional Basketball Opens Up

Although basketball began to open up to African Americans at the high school and college levels in the 1920s and 1930s, blacks were still prohibited from playing professionally. As a substitute, African Americans began developing all-black independent teams. The Renaissance Big Five (later called the Harlem Rens) and the **Harlem Globetrotters** played in games against professional teams such as the Boston Celtics. The Harlem Rens were fearless warriors who challenged any team (black or white) to defeat them. They were an unstoppable force on the court, winning eighty-eight consecutive games in 1932-33. In 1939 they won the first "world tournament" of professional basketball. Every player from the Rens has been inducted into the Basketball Hall of Fame.

By 1948 professional basketball was opening up to African Americans. Players such as **Charles "Chuck" Cooper, Early Lloyd,** and Nat

BILL RUSSELL AND K. C. JONES

Willliam "Bill" Russell (1934–) was the first African American to make a big impact in the NBA. During his college years at the University of San Francisco, he teamed up with K. C. Jones (1932–) to begin one of the greatest dynamic duos basketball has ever known. When Russell and Jones joined forces, the results were immediate: they led San Francisco to fifty-five straight wins and a championship. The two then went on to play in the 1956 Summer Olympics in Australia, where they brought home the gold medal.

Upon their return they parted ways briefly as Jones served in the military while Russell helped lead the Boston Celtics to an NBA championship his first year in the league. In 1958 the two resumed their magical connection to participate in something that the league had never seen—Russell and Jones helped lead the Celtics to nine consecutive NBA titles.

"Sweetwater" Clifton (who played for the Globetrotters and the Knicks) were the earliest black representatives of the Basketball Association of America, which later became the National Basketball Association (NBA). In the 1950s a set of rule changes sped up the game and allowed for the more fast-paced, spontaneous style of play many young African Americans had mastered on inner-city playgrounds. The changes set the stage for players such as the duo of William "Bill" Russell and K. C. Jones, Wilton **"Wilt" Chamberlain, Elgin Baylor,** and **Oscar Robertson.** A unique African-American style began to emerge on the basketball court—and fans wanted to see more of it.

Women Pick Up the Game

Although African-American men broke into basketball during the first half of the twentieth century, organized women's basketball matured much later. The 1984 women's Olympic basketball team included **Cheryl Miller,** who had led the University of Southern California to two NCAA championships, and Lynette Woodard, who later became the first black woman to play for the Harlem Globetrotters. C. Vivian Stringer made a mark for black female coaching by leading the University of Iowa to the NCAA championship game seven straight years in the 1980s. In 1996 Nikki McCray played in the 1996 Olympics and later starred in both the American Basketball League and the Women's National Basketball League (WNBA), both of which formed in the mid-1990s.

African-American Dominance

Black players who were brought up on inner-city playground courts injected a freestyle instinctive element to the game, improvisation and speed became a hallmark of this style of play. This became most evident when players such as **Walt Frazier, Julius "Dr. J" Erving, Kareem**

Abdul-Jabbar, Magic Johnson, and Michael Jordan entered the game. Chamberlain and Dr. J played record-scoring games, Abdul-Jabbar perfected the "skyhook" and Johnson and Jordan became two of the most exciting players in the history of the game. Perhaps equally important, Johnson and Jordan became ambassadors of the game, known for their winning personalities. Both received enormous amounts of press and publicity and have become spokespersons for a number of advertising campaigns.

In 1992 the NBA's elite had an opportunity to join forces in the Summer Olympics in Barcelona, Spain. Eight of the twelve-member "Dream Team" were African Americans, including Johnson, Jordan, and Shaquille O'Neal. The team took home the gold medal in Globetrotter-like fashion, outscoring their opponents by significant margins.

Basquiat, Jean-Michel

ARTIST
December 22, 1960–August 12, 1988

Artist Jean-Michel Basquiat gained worldwide recognition in the 1980s for his innovative graffiti-like artwork. Born in Brooklyn, New York, of Haitian and Puerto Rican-American parents, he left home at seventeen, determined to become a star in the downtown art and club scene of the late 1970s.

Basquiat's writings and drawings (signed "SAMO©") were first exhibited in the 1980 Times Square Show in New York City. Critical acclaim and other group shows followed. His first one-man show in New York City was held at the Annina Nosei Gallery in the SoHo district in 1982.

Soon Basquiat's work was being exhibited at prominent galleries worldwide. In 1982 he was the youngest artist to participate in the Documenta 7 show in Kassel, Germany, widely considered to be "the Olympics of contemporary art." He was also one of the youngest-ever exhibitors in the Whitney Museum of American Art's 1983 Whitney Biennial (held every two years) in New York City, held by many to be the most important art exhibition in the country. During this time he became close friends with the famous pop artist Andy Warhol (1928–1987).

Fame was not a cure for Basquiat's troubled life. A growing drug problem hurt his already difficult relationships with art dealers, family, and friends. Basquiat died of a heroin overdose in August 1988 at age twenty-seven.

Interest in Basquiat's work increased after his death. During his short career, his art developed quickly to include a complex blend of African-American and European cultural traditions using painting, collage, and sculpture. He created a kind of visual poetry that is a highly original contribution to twentieth-century **painting.** In 1998, a year after the release of the film biography *Basquiat*, one of his paintings was sold for more than $3 million.

Peg Leg Bates (Corbis Corporation.
Reproduced by permission)

Bates, Clayton "Peg Leg"

TAP DANCER
October 11, 1907–December 6, 1998

Famed tap dancer "Peg Leg" Bates danced his way into the hearts of millions. Bates lost his left leg in a cotton-seed mill accident at age twelve but went on to perform throughout America and Europe, even performing twice for the king and queen of England.

Born in Fountain Inn, South Carolina, Bates began dancing when he was five. After losing his leg he was determined to continue dancing. He left home at fifteen with a wooden leg his uncle had made for him and embarked on a career as a dancer. He quickly worked his way up from minstrel shows (performances of black American songs and jokes) and carnivals to vaudeville circuits (traveling variety shows). In France in 1929 he joined a group called the Blackbirds in Paris.

Returning to the United States in the 1930s, Bates became a featured tapper at such top nightclubs as the **Cotton Club** in New York's Harlem district. He was one of the few black tap dancers able to cross the color barrier, performing in the prestigious white vaudeville circuits, where he appeared with dance greats **Bill "Bojangles" Robinson,** Fred Astaire, and Gene Kelly. From the 1930s to the 1950s Bates was a frequent guest on the popular Ed Sullivan television show.

Because of his peg leg, Bates had to reinvent each tap step, adding his own unique interpretation to such classic tap steps as the "Shim Sham Shimmy." He was excellent at acrobatics, legomania (dancing as if he had "rubber legs"), flash (spectacularly difficult steps usually involving aerial maneuvers), and novelty dancing (dancing with the use of special props).

In 1952 Bates bought a resort in the Catskill Mountains of New York, where he and other dancers and musicians performed until he sold it in 1989. Bates was the subject of an hour-long film, *The Dancing Man: Peg Leg Bates*, released in 1992. He died at age ninety-one in South Carolina.

Battle, Kathleen

OPERA SINGER

August 13, 1948–

An **opera** singer noted for her small, sweet soprano voice (the highest singing voice), Kathleen Battle was hailed by *Time* magazine in 1985 as "the best lyric coloratura (very "colorful" or embellished vocal music) in the world."

Battle was born in Portsmouth, Ohio, and first sang at the Portsmouth **African Methodist Episcopal (AME) Church.** A National Merit Scholar in mathematics, Battle majored in music education at the University of Cincinnati College-Conservatory. She taught music for two years in Cincinnati elementary schools before embarking on her professional career.

Battle made her professional singing debut in the German composer and pianist Johannes Brahms's *German Requiem* (1868) with the Cincinnati orchestra at the 1972 Spoleto Festival in Italy. Her opera debut came soon after as Rosina in the Italian composer Antonio Rossini's *The Barber of Seville* (1816) with the Michigan Opera Theater. In 1974 she met James Levine, later to become artistic director of the Metropolitan Opera, who became her mentor. She made her Metropolitan Opera debut in 1978, singing the role of the shepherd in the composer Richard Wagner's *Tannhäuser* (1845). Since then, she has sung many leading roles.

In 1991 Battle and soprano **Jessye Norman** gave a concert of spirituals at New York's Carnegie Hall that was shown on national television and prompted a best-selling recording. Battle has won three Grammy Awards, the record industry's most prestigious award, including one for her album *Kathleen Battle at Carnegie Hall* (1992). In 1993 she premiered a song written for her by African-American writer **Toni Morrison** and composer André Previn.

Battle left the Metropolitan Opera in February 1994 and has pursued other avenues. In 1995 her voice was featured on four albums, and she appeared on a television special, *An Evening with Kathleen Battle and Thomas Hampson*. Battle opened the Lincoln Center's 1995-96 **jazz** season and in 1996 released *Angels Glory*, a collection of Christmas songs with famed guitarist Christopher Parkening. She has also performed extensively throughout Europe and Japan.

Baylor, Elgin Gay

BASKETBALL PLAYER
September 16, 1934–

Few **basketball** players could jump higher than Elgin Gay Baylor. Baylor's specialty was snatching the ball after missed shots, and his high-flying rebounding brought attention and excitement to the National Basketball League (NBA) during its early years.

Born in Washington, D.C., Baylor did not pick up a basketball until he was in high school. At Spartan High he made the All-American team. He then played at the College of Idaho and Seattle University in Washington State, where he led the country in rebounding. In 1958 he signed with the NBA's Minneapolis Lakers. He won Rookie of the Year his first season, averaging 15 rebounds and 24.9 points per game. In one game he scored 71 points against the New York Knickerbockers, a record at the time.

Baylor was short for a basketball player (six feet five inches), but he made up for it with his incredible jumping ability. In 1972 he retired from the Lakers (who had moved to Los Angeles) with 23,149 points, ten trips to the All-NBA team, and an election to the NBA Hall of Fame in 1976. Baylor coached the New Orleans Jazz in 1978 and in 1986 became vice president of basketball operations for the Los Angeles Clippers.

Bearden, Romare

ARTIST
September 2, 1912–March 12, 1988

Romare Bearden was fifty years old and a successful painter when he became a nationally renowned artist for his work in collage (a form of art that combines different materials on a surface). Born in Charlotte, North Carolina, in 1912, Bearden and his family soon moved to Harlem, New York. He grew up during the surge of black artistic development known as the **Harlem Renaissance,** which lasted through the 1920s. His mother frequently hosted prominent writers, painters, musicians, and composers in their home.

Bearden became an artist during the **Great Depression** of the 1930s, a time of great economic hardship. From 1931 to 1935 he drew editorial cartoons and illustrations for magazines, including *Collier's* and the *Saturday*

Evening Post. In 1935 he received a bachelor of science degree in education from New York University.

Time spent at New York's Art Students League was to be Bearden's only formal art training. His real art education took place in Harlem's thriving community of visual artists. From 1937 to 1940 Bearden produced his first **painting**s, realistic watercolors on brown paper, and held his first solo show. The scenes were of black life in Charlotte, Pittsburgh, Pennsylvania (where he had spent summers as a child), and Harlem.

During **World War II** (1939–45) Bearden enlisted in the U.S. Army and began to exhibit in Washington, D.C. From 1945 until 1948 he produced vibrantly colored oil paintings filled with abstract figures (figures represented by shapes, lines, and color, not by their real outer appearance as would be seen in a photograph). Despite this measure of success, Bearden grew restless. In 1950 he studied at the Sorbonne in Paris, France, but after his return suffered a nervous breakdown. He recovered with the help of Nanette Rohan, whom he married in 1954.

Bearden painted large abstract oils before experimenting with collage. While searching for a group project to celebrate the **Civil Rights movement,** he began creating collages based on childhood memories. Bearden filled his collages with trains, guitar players, birds, masked figures, and scenes involving baptisms, families eating together, funerals, and nightclubs. His collages use bold color, creating lush landscapes with layers upon layers of cut paper, photographs, and paint.

Bearden's collage work put him on the cover of the leading art magazines and earned him numerous awards. Before his death in 1988, he had received many honorary degrees and the U.S. Medal of Honor.

Beavers, Louise

ACTRESS
March 18, 1902–October 26, 1962

Louise Beavers was an actress who started out in roles that were typical for black actresses at the time, but she went on to gain fame for portraying more meaningful characters. Beavers began her acting career in theater in the 1920s and sang in the Ladies Minstrel Troupe in 1926. Her first screen role was in the 1927 silent screen version of **Uncle Tom's Cabin.** Because of her size and her southern accent, she continued to be cast in the part of "the maid." Beavers received her first important role in 1934, as a mother in the movie *Imitation of Life.* In the movie the mother's light-skinned daughter "passes" as white, but in the process she shuns her mother, even denying that she is her mother at one point. Many critics considered Beavers's performance worthy of an Oscar.

Beavers's other notable performances were as actor Cary Grant's maid in *Mr. Bandings Builds His Dream House* (1948) and as baseball great **Jackie Robinson**'s mother in *The Jackie Robinson Story* (1950). When actress **Hattie McDaniel** died suddenly in 1952, Beavers replaced her in the 1952–53 season of the television series *Beulah.* Beavers died in 1962 of diabetes and heart disease. In 1976 she was inducted into the Black Filmmakers Hall of Fame.

Bechet, Sidney Joseph

JAZZ MUSICIAN, SAXOPHONIST
May 14, 1897–May 14, 1959

Jazz musician and saxophonist Sidney Bechet was instrumental in spreading New Orleans **jazz** throughout the United States and the world. He also helped change jazz from ensemble music (music played by a small group) to a soloist's art. Known as "the king of the soprano saxophone," Bechet had a unique style marked by a passionate, commanding spirit.

Born in New Orleans, Louisiana, Bechet first borrowed his brother's clarinet at age six and within a few years was performing with the city's most established musicians. In 1914 he began a lifetime of touring, making Chicago, Illinois, his home base in 1917. In Chicago he purchased a soprano saxophone, which would become his favorite instrument. In 1919 he joined **Will Marion Cook**'s Southern Syncopated Orchestra and toured Europe.

Bechet made his first recording in 1923, establishing himself as one of jazz's premier soloists. He went back to Europe in 1925 with jazz great **Josephine Baker**'s *La Revue Nègre* (The Negro Revue) and in 1928 began a ten-year association with **Noble Sissle**'s orchestra. By the end of the 1930s Bechet was based in New York, where he performed and recorded regularly for the next decade. His 1939 interpretation of "Summertime," from composer George Gershwin's (1897–1937) **opera** *Porgy and Bess* (1935), became his best-known work. After three European tours Bechet permanently settled in France in 1951 and achieved a measure of celebrity reached by few jazz musicians. He died of cancer in 1959.

Bechet's **autobiography,** *Treat It Gentle* (1960), is a vivid portrait of his Louisiana Creole (of French or European descent) background and the formative period of New Orleans jazz.

Belafonte, Harold George "Harry"

SINGER, ACTOR, ACTIVIST
March 1, 1927–

Harry Belafonte is an amazing singer, a powerful actor, and a dedicated activist who works tirelessly for human rights causes. Born in New York City, Belafonte spent his early years in Jamaica. The island culture has influenced Belafonte's work throughout his career.

After returning to New York for high school and serving in the U.S. Navy, Belafonte began his career with small theater roles. Disappointed with the limited parts for black men, he began to develop his singing voice. His good looks and rich voice soon made him a star. He won a Tony Award in 1952 and began acting in movies. His dynamic and passionate performance in the film *Carmen Jones* (1954), an all-black version of a famous **opera** *Carmen*, brought Belafonte nationwide fame.

Singer, actor, and activist Harry Belafonte during a concert performance (© Jack Vartoogian. Reproduced by permission)

In the mid-1950s Belafonte began singing calypso, a folk song style popular in Jamaica. His emotional and humorous singing style made hits of songs like "Matilda" and "The Banana Boat Song." Belafonte's album *Calypso* became the first solo album in history to sell a million copies. Over the next decade he recorded eleven more albums.

Belafonte has always combined performing with activism. In 1956 he helped raise money for the Montgomery bus boycott and became good friends with **Martin Luther King Jr.** (1929–1968). By 1960 Belafonte was a major fund-raiser and speaker for black civil rights.

In the 1970s Belafonte resumed making **film**s, including *Uptown Saturday Night* and *Buck and the Preacher.* He also began to sing in clubs again and went on concert tours.

Throughout the 1980s and 1990s Belafonte became increasingly involved in human rights causes. Most notable was his commitment to humanitarian efforts in Ethiopia. In 1985 he came up with an idea that resulted in the recording "We Are the World," written by Lionel Richie and **Michael Jackson,** which raised over $70 million to aid victims of famine in Africa. For his humanitarian work he was awarded the position of goodwill ambassador for the United Nations Children's Fund (UNICEF) in 1986. In 1990 Belafonte served as chair of the committee that welcomed African National Congress leader Nelson Mandela to the United States. The same year, New York governor Mario Cuomo appointed Belafonte to lead the Martin Luther King Jr. Commission to promote knowledge of nonviolence.

During the 1990s Belafonte continued both his performing and movie-producing career. He starred in the television special "Harry Belafonte and Friends" (1996) and the films *Kansas City* (1995) and *White Man's Burden* (1995), which he also produced. Belafonte remained dedicated to raising funds and awareness for causes such as AIDS research and domestic violence shelters. After being diagnosed and successfully treated for prostate cancer in 1997, Belafonte became a spokesperson to encourage men to be tested for the disease. In 1999 Belafonte realized a longtime dream and published a children's book, *Island in the Sun*, about the people and beauty of Jamaica.

Bell, James Thomas "Cool Papa"

BASEBALL PLAYER
May 17, 1903–March 17, 1991

James Thomas Bell, known by his teammates as "Cool Papa," was one of the fastest **baseball** players in history. They called him "Cool Papa" because he was calm under pressure. He was so fast, it was said, that he could click the light switch off and be in bed before the lights went out.

Born in Starkville, Mississippi, Bell began playing in the Negro National League in 1922. He played for several different teams, including the St. Louis Stars, the Kansas City Monarchs, and the Pittsburgh Crawfords. Bell started out pitching but was moved to the outfield to take advantage of his lightning-fast speed. Bell's specialty, however, was stealing bases. He took up coaching when he retired in 1970. In 1974 Bell was named to the National Baseball Hall of Fame.

Berea College

Founded: Berea was founded in 1855 by Rev. John G. Fee, an abolitionist and scholar who believed in excellence in education for men and women of all races.

History Highlights:

- 1853: Prominent Kentucky businessmen Cassius Clay gives a ten-acre homestead to Rev. John Fee. Clay, a leader in the antislavery movement, believes Fee will take a strong stand against **slavery.**

- 1855: Fee builds a one-room school that also serves as a church. Named Berea, Fee envisions that one day the school will grow into a college that will provide education "to all colors [and] classes."

- 1859: Fee and Berea teachers are driven from their land by local Southerners who support slavery.

- 1869: Fee eventually returns to Berea with funds raised during the **Civil War** (1861–65) and the college is officially established. Among the first students are ninety-six blacks and ninety-one whites.

- 1883: Berea's Fireside Industries is established to preserve the tradition of Appalachian craftsmanship and to develop a market to sell Appalachian crafts.

- 1904: When Kentucky passes the Day Law forbidding black and white students to be educated together, Berea is forced to establish

Lincoln Institute, a nearby school that African-American students will attend.

- 1950: The Day Law is changed to allow integration of schools above the high school level. Berea is the first college in Kentucky to reopen its doors to African Americans.

- 1998: The *U.S. News & World Report* names Berea the number one regional college in the South.

Location: Berea, Kentucky

Known For: Berea College is a unique institution that charges no tuition but does require each student to work to earn his or her education. Its students come primarily from the southern Appalachia region in the eastern United States.

Religious Affiliation: Berea is considered to be a Christian college.

Number of Students (1999–2000): 1,500

Grade Average of Incoming Freshman: 3.0

Admission Requirements: SAT or ACT scores; Berea application for admission and for financial aid.

Mailing Address:
Berea College
Office of Admission
CPO 2344
Berea, KY 40404

Telephone: (800) 326-5948

E-mail: admissions@berea.edu

URL: http://www.berea.edu

Campus: Berea's 140-acre campus is located approximately forty miles south of Lexington, Kentucky. Buildings include a geology museum, nursery school lab, language labs, 1,100-acre farm, planetarium, and the Seabury Center, which is Berea's athletics complex. The library contains over 300,000 volumes and houses an extensive Appalachian collection of over 9,000 items. The Boone Tavern Hotel, which is owned by Berea and operated by Berea students, first opened as a guesthouse in 1909. It attracts visitors from across the United States and is known for its fine southern cuisine.

Special Programs: Each Berea student receives a four-year scholarship (equivalent to $60,000) and is required to participate in the campus work program. Each student must work ten to fifteen hours per week. Students are employed in over 140 different departments on campus. Some positions allow students to pursue academic or career interests. Many students are involved in producing regional crafts, which Berea offers for sale to the general public. The five craft areas are broomcraft, ceramics, weaving, woodcraft, and wrought iron.

Extracurricular Activities: Student government; student publications, including the campus newspaper, *The Pinnacle*; over forty-seven clubs and organizations, including the Black Music Ensemble, the Berea College

Country Dancers, and the Black Cultural Center; athletics (men's basketball, cross-country, soccer, softball, swimming, tennis, track-and-field, and volleyball); community service programs, including Students for Appalachia and People Who Care.

(SEE ALSO COLLEGES AND UNIVERSITIES.)

Berry, Charles Edward Anderson "Chuck"

ROCK-AND-ROLL SINGER
October 18, 1926–

Chuck Berry is one of the original rock and rollers whose singing and wild guitar playing helped create a new kind of music. He was inspired to become a performer and guitarist after an enthusiastic reception of his rendition of "Confessin' the Blues" at Sumner High School in St. Louis, Missouri, where he was a student. Berry began performing at clubs around St. Louis with several groups in the early 1950s. He became popular with both white and black audiences because he sang country songs and **blues** with equal talent.

In 1955 Berry moved to Chicago, Illinois, and signed a recording contract with Chess Records. His first recording, and his first hit tune, was "Maybelline" (1955), a version of the country song "Ida Red" named for the Maybelline line of hair creams. He performed the song with crisp rapid-fire delivery and introduced new lyrics on the subjects of teenage love and car racing.

Berry helped make rock and roll popular, and his greatest success was in the late 1950s with songs that expressed teenage rebelliousness and celebrated youthful vitality. His best-known recordings include "Roll Over, Beethoven" (1956), "Rock-and-Roll Music" (1957), "Sweet Little Sixteen" (1958), "Memphis" (1958), and "Johnny B. Goode" (1958).

After his heyday in the 1950s, Berry never reached his former level of popularity. He did, however, become active in the rock-and-roll revival of the 1980s and early 1990s and continues to perform across the United States.

"If I have a legacy to leave my people, it is my philosophy of living and serving. As I face tomorrow, I am content, for I think I have spent my life well. I pray now that my philosophy may be helpful to those who share my vision of a world of peace, progress, brotherhood, and love."

(Source: Mary McLeod Bethune. "My Last Will and Testament." *Ebony,* August 1955.)

Bethune, Mary McLeod

TEACHER, CIVIL RIGHTS ACTIVIST
July 10, 1875–May 18, 1955

Famous as the founder of **Bethune-Cookman College** in Daytona Beach, Florida, Mary McLeod Bethune is also known for her work with African-American women's organizations and youth organizations. In 1935 she founded the National Council of Negro Women, which helped coordinate the activities of many black women's organizations. Bethune was the first black woman to hold a high-ranking U.S. government position—director of the National Youth Administration's Division of Negro Affairs.

One of the founding fathers of rock and roll, Chuck Berry (Courtesy of the Library of Congress)

Mary McLeod was born in 1875 into a large farming family in Mayesville, South Carolina. She began teaching in 1896, after she gave up her dream of becoming a missionary to Africa. At that time, her church would not send African-American missionaries to Africa.

In 1904 Mary McLeod Bethune settled in Daytona, Florida, with her husband, Albertus Bethune, and their only child, Albert. She opened a school for African-American girls, called the Daytona Educational and Industrial Institute. At first the school was very small, with only a tiny group of students. The girls studied basic subjects like math and reading, worked on their homemaking skills, and received religious instruction.

In 1923 the school joined with the Cookman Institute of Jacksonville, Florida, and began offering classes to girls and boys. In 1929 it took the name Bethune-Cookman College, and by 1935 it had become an accredited (recognized as good enough to prepare students for more advanced education) junior college. That same year Bethune won the Spingarn Medal, the highest award given by the **National Association for the Advancement of Colored People (NAACP).** By 1943 Bethune-Cookman College was a fully accredited college awarding four-year degrees.

During Franklin D. Roosevelt's presidency (1933–1945), Bethune worked closely with his administration on behalf of African Americans. In 1936 she organized the Federal Council on Negro Affairs, also known as the Black Cabinet. This was a group of black advisers who worked to create government programs to help African Americans.

Bethune began serving as director of the National Youth Administration's Division of Negro Affairs in 1936. In 1939 this was made an official government position; Bethune continued to serve as director until 1943. Her appointment as director made Bethune the highest-ranking black woman in U.S. government up to that time.

Throughout her life Bethune continued to push for justice and equality for African Americans. Her involvement in countless organizations and the establishment of the Mary McLeod Bethune Foundation are lasting legacies to her commitment.

Bethune-Cookman College

Founded: Bethune-Cookman College was founded in 1923 when Cookman Institute for Boys (founded 1872) and Daytona Normal and Industrial Institute for Girls (founded 1904) merged.

History Highlights:

- 1904: African-American educator and activist **Mary McLeod Bethune** (1875–1955) establishes a school in Daytona Beach, Florida, for African-American girls. Although the school begins with only 5 students, within two years 250 pupils are attending.
- 1916: The school eventually grows into the Daytona Normal and Industrial Institute and is affiliated with the United Methodist Church.
- 1923: The school officially becomes Bethune-Cookman College after the Daytona Institute merges with the Cookman Institute for Boys, previously located in Jacksonville. It is originally a high school that offers some junior college courses.
- 1939: Bethune-Cookman becomes a two-year junior college, and shortly after, a four-year college.
- 1947: Mary McLeod Bethune, who has been president since the school's founding, steps down.

Location: Daytona Beach, Florida

Known For: Bethune-Cookman is the only historically black college founded by a woman.

Religious Affiliation: United Methodist Church

Number of Students (1999–2000): 2,481

Grade Average of Incoming Freshman: 3.0

Admission Requirements: At least a 2.25 GPA; at least four years of English, three years of math, three years of science, five years of social studies, recommended two years of foreign language; SAT or ACT scores; one letter of recommendation.

Mailing Address:
Bethune-Cookman College
Office of Admission
640 Dr. Mary McLeod Bethune Blvd.
Daytona Beach, FL 32114-3099

Telephone: (800) 448-0228

URL: http://www.bethune.cookman.edu

Campus: Bethune-Cookman's sixty-acre campus is located near downtown Daytona Beach. The thirty-three buildings that make up the campus include the Mary McLeod Bethune Fine Arts Center, which houses art galleries and an art studio; an outreach center; a telecommunications satellite network; a recording studio; and an observatory. An important feature is founder Mary McLeod Bethune's home and grave site, which are considered historic landmarks. The campus library contains over 150,000 documents and houses an Afro-American collection.

Special Programs: The college has a joint venture (JOVE) program with the National Aeronautics and Space Administration (NASA), where students are involved in research and receive instruction and training in the field of space science.

Extracurricular Activities: Student government; student newspaper, the *Voice*; radio station; five fraternities and six sororities; over forty-five organizations, including honor societies, religious groups, and the Bethune-Cookman Concert Chorale; athletics (men's baseball, basketball, cheerleading, cross-country, football, golf, tennis, track and field; women's basketball, cheerleading, cross-country, golf, softball, tennis, track and field, volleyball).

Bethune-Cookman Alumni: Dr. Oswald P. Bronson, educator; James Bush III, state representative; religious leader Henry Lions.

(SEE ALSO **COLLEGES AND UNIVERSITIES.**)

Bevel, James

CIVIL RIGHTS ACTIVIST
October 19, 1936–

Best known as a civil rights leader, James Bevel has worked on a broad range of social and political issues, including education and human rights abuses.

James Luther Bevel (Courtesy of the Library of Congress)

James Luther Bevel (Courtesy of the Library of Congress)

Born in Itta Bena, Mississippi, Bevel experienced a religious awakening in his early teens and became well known throughout his town as an inspiring preacher. He was ordained a **Baptist** minister in 1959 and received a bachelor of arts degree from American Baptist Theological Seminary in Nashville, Tennessee, two years later.

Bevel's childhood experiences had exposed him to the ugliness and hopelessness of rural poverty and left him determined to work for racial justice. In 1958 he attended the Highlander Folk School, an interracial adult-education center in Tennessee that focused on improving conditions for minorities and the poor. One year later, Bevel attended a Vanderbilt University training workshop for student activists in Nashville sponsored by the Fellowship of Reconciliation, a nonviolent activist group. He became a leader in the Nashville student movement and played a central role in organizing and staging **sit-ins** to force Nashville businesses to desegregate.

A dynamic and dedicated civil rights leader, Bevel composed several freedom songs that inspired many in the **Civil Rights movement.** In 1960 he became one of the founding members of the **Student Nonviolent Coordinating Committee (SNCC),** a grassroots civil rights organization. The following year, he married **Diane Nash,** an SNCC activist. In 1962 they moved to Albany, Georgia, where he became a prominent leader in the Albany movement to fight racism and segregation. He also became involved in the **Southern Christian Leadership Conference,** playing a key role in the fight for fair housing in Chicago, Illinois.

In the 1980s Bevel centered his attention on education—founding Students for Education and Economic Development in Chicago—and international issues, such as human rights abuses in foreign countries. In 1989 he formed the National Committee Against Religious Bigotry and Racism, and in the early 1990s he gained prominence as an opponent of the death penalty. (*See also* **Citizenship Schools; Highlander Citizenship School.**)

Bibb, Henry Walton

AUTHOR, EDITOR, ABOLITIONIST
May 10, 1815–1854

Famous for his autobiography and founder of the first black newspaper in Canada, Henry Bibb was born on a Kentucky plantation, the oldest son of a slave, Milldred Jackson. It was rumored that his father was James Bibb, a Kentucky state senator. Bibb's desire to obtain freedom for himself and his family (a wife and daughter) motivated him to escape from **slavery.** In 1842 he fled to Detroit, Michigan, where he joined in the fight for **abolition,** or outlawing slavery.

In 1850 he published his **autobiography,** *Narrative of the Life and Adventures of Henry Bibb, an American Slave.* It became one of the best-known slave narratives and includes detailed accounts of Bibb's life as a slave and runaway. Soon after it was published, Congress passed the **Fugitive Slave** Act of 1850, which gave Southern slave owners the right to reclaim runaways, who were considered their "property." In response, Bibb fled with his second wife, Mary Miles Bibb, to Canada.

In 1851 Bibb established the first black newspaper in Canada. Called *The Voice of the Fugitive*, it became an important newspaper for abolitionists who advocated that slaves and **free blacks** should immigrate (move) to **Canada.** The Bibbs also became leaders of the large African-Canadian community.

Two years before he died, Bibb was reunited with three of his brothers who had escaped from slavery and moved to Canada. He interviewed them and published their stories in the *Voice*. Bibb died in the summer of 1854, at age thirty-nine.

Bing, David "Dave"

BASKETBALL PLAYER, BUSINESSMAN
November 29, 1943–

David "Dave" Bing has a flair for both **basketball** and business and is just as successful off the court as he was on it. He spent most of his basketball career with the Detroit Pistons (1967–75).

Former basketball all-star and current businessman Dave Bing, pictured in his college days at Syracuse

Born in Washington, D.C., Bing played basketball in high school and went on to set a career scoring record at Syracuse (New York) University. A first-round draft pick by Detroit, Bing lived up to expectations and was named Rookie of the Year in 1967. In 1978 he retired with 18,327 points and seven trips to the National Basketball Association (NBA) All-Star Game. In 1990 he was voted to the Basketball Hall of Fame.

After retiring from basketball, Bing established Bing Steel, a successful Detroit steelworks, and later the Bing Group, a collection of his steel and other manufacturing enterprises. In 1999 the Bing Group became the fifth-largest business owned by an African American, with $300 million in sales. Bing has also been active in community affairs, helping to fund Detroit public school sports programs in 1989. In 2000 Bing also helped with Democratic presidential candidate Bill Bradley's unsuccessful campaign. Bing continues to grow his business and provides community service through his membership in the National Association of Black Automotive Suppliers.

Birmingham, Alabama

Birmingham Beginnings

Birmingham's African-American community came into existence with the founding of the city in 1871. Its initial growth was rapid, but in 1873, the outbreak of cholera and a national economic panic greatly reduced both black and white populations. Recovery was slow.

In the early 1880s, with the start of the coal and iron industry, came a revitalized economy and a renewal of population growth. Thousands of African Americans flocked to the Birmingham area to mine coal or work in the iron mills. Most African-American immigrants in Birmingham came from cotton farms in south Alabama and from the virtual enslavement of the sharecropper system. The city's lure was the promise of regular wages paid in cash, but what these migrants found available were generally the most menial jobs or those that were lowest paying. For African-American males, who worked in the mines and mills, the jobs they received were always the most dangerous. For females, job opportunities meant domestic work as maids or cooks or employment as dishwashers, laundresses, seamstresses, waitresses, or in the kitchens.

Despite the hard work, low pay, and discrimination that African Americans experienced, however, life in Birmingham was generally an improvement over what they had known on the farm. They had more money, a more active social life, more freedom from white domination, and better education for their children. The best evidence of Birmingham's attractiveness to blacks exists in the census, which shows a generally steady growth of the city's black population.

Most African Americans lived in the areas that were generally, but not strictly, segregated. New arrivals often moved into a "company house": a three- or four-room rental building owned by a coal or steel company. Usually identical in design, company houses stood in rows; several rows

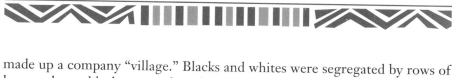

made up a company "village." Blacks and whites were segregated by rows of houses, but a black row and a white row often stood back to back. Thus, company villages respected segregation in principal, but in reality they did not keep the races very far apart.

Birmingham's African Americans encountered both prejudice and discrimination from the time the city was first established, but they especially suffered in the years just before the turn of the twentieth century. The rapid growth of the black population in Birmingham frightened local whites at a time when racist fears were on the rise nationally. In 1901, all but a few blacks lost the right to vote when a new state constitution established a poll tax, literacy tests, and "good character"—as defined by whites—as requirements for voting.

The Early Twentieth Century

In 1911 the city of Birmingham began passing segregation ordinances, outlawing saloons in black neighborhoods and making ones owned by whites divide black and white customers by using partitions. Other laws followed, including a broad **Jim Crow** statute in the 1920s.

Most African-American businesses provided services to other black Americans not provided by white businessmen. For example, A. G. Gaston, Birmingham's wealthiest black businessman, began his career with the Smith and Gaston Funeral Homes in 1923; he then added the **Booker T. Washington** Insurance Company and, subsequently, a business college, a drug store, a motel, a radio station, and a bank—Citizen's Federal Savings and Loan. All of these businesses originally filled the needs of the black community in a way that whites either refused to do or did inadequately.

The depression hit Birmingham early and hard. Tens of thousands of black miners and steel workers were thrown out of work as the big steel companies virtually ceased operations. Getting food and fuel became a major problem for most black families in the city's industrial neighborhoods. The hard times brought a radical political response from some of Birmingham's African Americans, who joined the American Communist party. Unions, however, attracted far more blacks unhappy with their economic situation than the Communist party did. In the 1890s, they had responded enthusiastically to the United Mine Workers' (UMW) organizing efforts among African-American miners. They remained loyal to the UMW despite several efforts on the part of coal companies to break up the union by creating racial tension between black and white workers.

The Civil Rights Era

Civil rights activism began to appear in the 1930s, especially in the area of voting discrimination. It was not, however, until the end of **World War II** (1939–45) that a confrontation between the races became pointed. Tension between blacks and whites increased sharply after World War II, as whites sensed that blacks intended to challenge segregation and other forms of discrimination. In addition to voting, housing patterns became a point of conflict. The need for more and better housing led blacks to build in sections of neighborhoods that had previously been all white.

In 1947 a local black man successfully challenged Birmingham's residential segregation law when the city attempted to prevent him from occupying his new home in North Smithfield, a neighborhood the city had designated as white. Two weeks later his home was blown apart by a dynamite bomb. Other blacks followed him to North Smithfield, but so did more trouble. Several new black homes were bombed in the late 1940s and early 1950s, apparently the work of local Klansmen angry at blacks moving into white neighborhoods. The violence happened with such regularity that this section of town became known as "Dynamite Hill."

In the late 1950s blacks began to challenge the segregation of public schools, but it was not until 1963 when, under federal court order, several all-white schools were desegregated despite bitter opposition from local whites. In the 1960s the national **Civil Rights movement** quickened change in Birmingham. The **sit-in** movement in 1960 and the **freedom-riders** in 1961 challenged "Jim Crow" restaurants and waiting rooms and heightened the fears of segregationist whites. In the spring of 1963 the Rev. Dr. **Martin Luther King, Jr.,** Birmingham minister Fred Shuttlesworth, and the **Southern Christian Leadership Conference** initiated a series of protests against all forms of discrimination in Birmingham.

Daily marches in downtown Birmingham exposed the protesters to the violent tactics of Birmingham Police Commissioner Eugene "Bull" Connor. When thousands of black school children joined the protest, Connor met the challenge with police dogs and firehoses. After King was arrested during the demonstrations, he wrote his "Letter from Birmingham Jail," one of the central statements of his political and spiritual convictions. After several weeks of conflict, business and civil rights leaders arranged a truce, and a settlement that broke down some of the segregation barriers soon followed.

The worst moment of racial turmoil in Birmingham, however, came a few months later, on Sunday morning, September 15, when a bomb exploded in the Sixteenth Street Baptist Church. It killed four young girls—Cynthia Wesley, Addie Mae Collins, Carole Robertson, and Denise McNair.

After the spring demonstrations and the Sixteenth Street bombing, race relations in Birmingham improved. Many new doors were opened, literally and figuratively, to blacks. No achievement was more important than the gaining of the right to vote. Arthur Shores, a local black attorney, was elected to the Birmingham City Council in 1969, and blacks after that won other public offices. The election of Richard Arrington, Jr., a black educator and city council member, to the mayor's office in 1979 was the best evidence of black progress in politics.

Birmingham Today

The years since World War II have brought many changes in the black community not directly related to civil rights. Fewer African Americans work in the steel industry, but more have white-collar occupations. Fewer African Americans live on the Southside, but many more live in the western section of the city in what were all-white neighborhoods. Older neighborhoods like Ensley, Woodlawn, West End, and North Birmingham have gained black population and lost whites at a rapid rate since the mid-1960s.

SPORTS AND ENTERTAINMENT IN BIRMINGHAM

Certain recreational activities have been particularly popular among Birmingham's African Americans. Through the first half of this century, baseball attracted many talented athletes and thousands of avid fans. Many blacks played in industrial leagues, and a few made it to professional teams. The Birmingham Black Barons, whose roster from 1948 to 1950 included baseball Hall of Famer Willie Mays, drew large crowds of both African Americans and whites to Rickwood Field, though white attendance fell when the city commission enforced segregated seating in the 1940s.

Birmingham was also a center for jazz in the 1920s and 1930s. The growth of jazz in Birmingham must be traced to John T. "Fess" Whatley, band director at Industrial High School. A stern taskmaster, Whatley schooled his many students on the basics of reading and performing music. One of Whatley's most famous students, Erskine Hawkins, brought fame to Birmingham jazz and its black neighborhoods in 1939 when he wrote a song entitled "Tuxedo Junction," which became a national hit.

In 1963 Birmingham was accurately characterized as the "most segregated city" in the United States. By the early 1990s, however, schools, playgrounds, parks, and other public facilities had been desegregated. All of the segregation ordinances have been repealed. Although traces of racial segregation remain, communication and cooperation between blacks and whites have greatly improved in an effort to make Birmingham "the Magic City."

(SEE ALSO DISEASES AND EPIDEMICS; KU KLUX KLAN.)

Black Arts Movement

The Black Arts movement (BAM), which occurred roughly between 1965 and 1976, has often been called "the Second Black Renaissance," and the movement is often compared with the **Harlem Renaissance** of the 1920s and early 1930s. In both movements African-American writers and artists produced critically acclaimed works in literature, music, the visual arts, and theater. They also emphasized racial pride and an appreciation of African heritage. BAM reached a wider audience and lasted longer than the Harlem Renaissance, however; it was also dominated by a spirit of aggressive politics that echoed the times.

Black Cultural Nationalism

People involved with BAM wanted to establish a "black" identity, as opposed to an American "Negro" identity. Afro haircuts, daishikis (a traditional African robe), African jewelry, and a militant attitude were among the ways this "blackness" was expressed. In many cases BAM activists dropped their given "slave names" and adopted instead Arab or African names.

BAM was not all about politics, however. It drew inspiration from many different sources, and of course not all BAM artists agreed with one another on every social and artistic issue. Most did agree, however, on one shared philosophy, which was expressed in a 1968 essay by Ron Karenga (later **Maulana Karenga**). The essay, "Black Cultural Nationalism," stated that black art should perform two key functions: expose the enemy, and raise black consciousness. Karenga's theories were embraced by BAM artists, including influential poet LeRoi Jones, who later changed his name to **Imamu Amiri Baraka.**

BAM's most important legacy was probably its search for new ways of expression based on African-American traditions. Part of this tradition was to establish a sense of community, a feeling of black togetherness. This led to the formation of several artists' organizations, schools, and publishing ventures. Although much of the Black Arts activity occurred on the East Coast (and especially in New York), Chicago, Illinois, created two of the movement's most influential institutions: the Organization of Black American Culture (OBAC), founded in 1967, and the Association for the Advancement of Creative Musicians (AACM), founded in 1965.

The most dramatic public statement created by the OBAC was *The Wall of Respect*, a mural painted on a building in Chicago's South Side by members of the visual arts workshop in 1967. The wall depicted black heroes such as **W. E. B. Du Bois, Malcolm X, Nina Simone, Amiri Baraka,** and **Gwendolyn Brooks.** The wall sparked a local and national movement as numerous cities soon produced their own murals. Interestingly, government agencies saw these murals as both fine public art and a way to control urban youth, who could be organized into painting teams during the politically charged summers of the 1960s. The political impact of these projects dwindled as they became more common, and in the 1970s the mural movement withered away. Several OBAC artists formed their own group in 1968, which eventually adopted the acronym **AfriCobra (African Commune of Bad Relevant Artists).**

Music, Dance, and Art

Unlike that of the OBAC, the AACM's inspiration was more economic than political. By the mid-1960s most of Chicago's important jazz clubs had closed, and AACM founders saw a cooperative organization as the best way for musicians to take control of their destinies. The AACM soon attracted many of the best young musicians in Chicago. The group established an educational program and an AACM orchestra that met (and continues to meet) weekly to perform new compositions by AACM members. Most important, the AACM provided a setting in which young musicians could meet, perform together, and exchange ideas.

Chicago also developed notable black theater groups, but New York was the more important city for theater and dance, and most of the famous Black Arts plays premiered there. Although Amiri Baraka was the best known of the BAM playwrights, he had many talented peers. These authors worked in a variety of styles but shared a vision of American society in crisis. Black Arts theater was the theater of a people rebelling against their own oppression, but it was also a theater that looked for solutions and new understandings. Nearly all of the Black Arts theaters held discussions immediately following their productions, involving the director, cast, audience, and sometimes the author.

Black dance also flourished during this period, and several major companies were formed. Although all of these groups specialized in African-American dance, the dancers who made up the companies came from a wide variety of ethnic backgrounds.

BAM had no specific end point; artists continued to grow and evolve along with shifts in American culture. Some say that when the BAM publication *Black World* ceased publication in 1976, the most important voice of the movement ended. Other works published in 1976 by African-American writers such as **Ntozake Shange, Ishmael Reed** (once a noteworthy BAM figure), and **Alice Walker** spoke critically—and in memory of—the movement. Major figures of the movement became less prominent in the late 1970s as new, different African-American voices began to emerge.

BAM's Mixed Legacy

The Black Arts movement is often attacked or dismissed by later artists and critics as having been too hostile and political. For example, many poems of the movement contain attacks on white people and blacks who were accused of being "too white" and not embracing African culture. Musical compositions often included rambling political messages, and images of Malcolm X and the American flag appear repeatedly in the visual arts. These elements, however, do not represent all or even most of the movement's works. Other critics point out that to truly understand the works that BAM produced, it is necessary to understand the period in American history during which they were created. (*See also* **Muralists.**)

Black Entertainment Television (BET)

Black Entertainment **Television** (BET) is a Washington, D.C.–based television station and entertainment company that targets African-American consumers by offering original programming and a wide array of black musical video programming. BET was founded in 1979 by Robert Johnson and aired its first movie, *A Visit to the Chief's Son*, on January 25, 1980. The twenty-four-hour station is part of BET Holdings and boasts a subscriber membership of over forty-five million worldwide.

A graduate of Princeton University (New Jersey), Johnson served as vice president of government relations for the National Cable and Television Association (NCTA) from 1976 to 1979. He started BET by getting loans from the National Bank of Washington and securing the backing of several investors, including John C. Malone, head of Tele-Communications (TCI). By 1989 Johnson was able to repay his investors, and on October 30, 1991, BET became the first black-controlled company to be listed on the New York Stock Exchange. In the first day of its listing, the stock value grew from $9 million to $475 million dollars.

The Black Arts movement is often attacked or dismissed by later artists and critics as having been too hostile and political

In 1995 the company relocated to a new $15 million facility. In 1996 BET added a BET/Starz! Channel 3—a premium movie channel—to its company. That same year, Johnson pledged $100,000 to **Howard University**'s (Washington, D.C.) School of Communication and was awarded the Messenger Award for Excellence in Communication by the university.

BET Holdings also publishes several magazines—*Emerge, Heart and Soul,* and *BET Weekend,*—and also owns three other cable channels. The company formed a **radio** network in 1994 to provide news to radio stations in the urban market. In 1996 the company formed a partnership with Microsoft to form MSBET, an on-line service that offers up-to-date entertainment news and information.

Black Nationalism

The black nationalist movement began in the United States during the eighteenth century as a protest against **slavery.** Rather than become a part of American society, black nationalists believed that African Americans should create their own country. They believed this was the only way that black people would be able to live in freedom and dignity.

Before the 1850s most **free blacks** supported integration (becoming part of white society). But the passage of laws such as the Fugitive Slave Act of 1850 and the Kansas-Nebraska Act of 1854 (both of which were setbacks in the fight against slavery); court rulings such as the Dred Scott decision of 1857 (which expanded the power of slave owners and expanded slavery in the territories); and the spread of "scientific" racist theories all worked together to change the attitudes of many blacks. **Frederick Douglass,** a former slave who had supported nonviolent change, began to believe that freedom could be won only through violence. The changing beliefs of many free blacks, along with previous examples of violent rebellion by slaves, helped inspire John Brown's bloody assault on Harper's Ferry in 1859. Many nationalists saw Brown's rebellion as proof that America was beginning to divide itself over the question of slavery.

In the early twentieth century, **Marcus Garvey** created the **Universal Negro Improvement Association (UNIA).** The UNIA's mission was to return American blacks to Africa. Its members wanted to establish a colony in Liberia, and the organization functioned as a provisional (or temporary) government for that colony. By 1920 the UNIA had hundreds of chapters operating worldwide. It was the largest organized mass movement in black history, with its own official publication (*The Negro World*), flag, constitution, laws, national anthem, and uniformed army. The organization also drafted the "Declaration of the Rights of the Negro Peoples of the World" at its first convention.

Garvey's message helped fuel a new period of political action among blacks, and this period became known as the **New Negro** era. Garvey argued that race was the most important issue for African Americans. Other members of the New Negro Movement also argued that racial inequality was based on social inequality; as a result, many black nationalists became communists (advocates of a classless society, with collective ownership of all property) in order to fight social inequalities. During the **World War I** period (1914–18), Garvey and the New Negro movement led many protests and revolts. In 1923, however, Garvey was convicted of the crime of mail fraud. As a result, membership in the UNIA declined rapidly, and the organization eventually lost much of its power.

In the 1930s Italy's invasion of the African nation of Ethiopia reignited the political activity of black nationalists across the country. During this time black leader **W. E. B. Du Bois** wrote his masterpiece, *Black Reconstruction in America*, which examined national and international problems from the perspectives of both race and class conflicts.

Also during this time, the **Nation of Islam (NOI)** began to gain power in many black communities. One of the most influential black nationalist leaders of the century began his career as a member of the NOI. **Malcolm X** (1925–65), born Malcolm Little, called upon blacks to fight for racial equality and to use "any means necessary" to gain it. Later in his career, Malcolm X called for unity among black nationalists and civil rights leaders, including Dr. **Martin Luther King Jr.,** who supported peaceful political resistance. In fact, just before Malcolm X was killed, he had agreed to enter into a political partnership with King. In addition to emphasizing problems of race, the men agreed to address issues related to social class. After Malcolm X was killed, King called upon the United States to distribute money to all of the people (and nations) it had victimized in the past. After King was assassinated, many other groups continued to work against both racial and social injustice, including the **Black Arts movement,** the **Black Panther Party,** and the Congress of African People.

In the 1970s black nationalist organizations struggled to move forward after the assassinations of both King and Malcolm X. In the 1980s, as communist governments around the world began to collapse, the black nationalist movement stopped emphasizing communism as a part of its philosophy. But black nationalism still remained strong. Organizations such as the Black Workers for Justice, the New Afrikan Peoples Organization, the December 12th Movement, and the Nation of Islam continued into the 1990s. The Nation of Islam is by far the strongest of these organizations, as demonstrated by the Million Man March in October 1995. (*See also* **John Brown's Raid at Harper's Ferry**.)

Black Panther Party for Self-Defense

The Black Panther Party for Self-Defense was a militant (combative) political party formed at the height of the **Civil Rights movement.** It was founded by **Huey P. Newton** and **Bobby Seale** in October 1966, and its members supported extreme actions, even violence, to advance civil rights and opportunities for African Americans. Newton and Seale remained leaders as the party expanded from its Oakland, California, base to become a national organization.

One of the first acts of Newton and Seale as Black Panther leaders was to create a statement of purpose, with these demands: "We want land, bread, housing, education, clothing, justice and peace." The party's appeal among young African Americans had little to do with these goals, however; young people were drawn to its bold combativeness, often expressed in confrontations with police.

After joining the party in 1967, **Eldridge Cleaver,** a former convict and author of a book of essays called *Soul on Ice*, became one of the party's main spokespersons. Cleaver's verbal attacks on white authorities, combined with media images of armed Panthers wearing black leather jackets, attracted publicity and many recruits. Cleaver's prominence in the party increased after October 28, 1967, when Newton was arrested after a dispute that resulted in the death of an Oakland police officer.

The Student Nonviolent Coordinating Committee

Cleaver and Seale joined forces with the **Student Nonviolent Coordinating Committee (SNCC),** a group nationally known as a champion of black power, and the resulting "Free Huey" rallies during February 1968 helped transform the Panthers into a national organization. By the end of 1968, the Black Panther Party ("for Self-Defense" was dropped from its name) had formed chapters in dozens of cities throughout the United States and abroad.

The party's beliefs were never clearly defined, and as it grew it experienced serious internal disputes over its political direction. Cleaver and Seale were unsuccessful in their effort to form a permanent alliance with the SNCC, and when relations between the two groups soured during the summer of 1968, SNCC leader **Stokely Carmichael** decided to remain with the Panthers. His support of black unity and Pan-Africanism (the political and cultural unity of the African continent and the people of African ancestry), however, put him at odds with other Panther leaders, who promoted class unity and close ties with white radicals. Carmichael severed ties with the party after he moved to **Africa** in 1969.

Although the Black Panther Party gradually shifted its emphasis from revolutionary language and armed confrontations with police to community outreach programs, such as free breakfasts for children and educational projects, clashes with police and legal prosecutions nearly wiped out the party's leadership. Soon after finishing his 1968 presidential campaign, Cleaver left for Algeria to avoid returning to prison for parole violation. In March 1969 Seale was arrested for conspiracy to incite rioting at the 1968 Democratic National Convention in Chicago; and in May, Connecticut officials charged Seale and seven other Panthers with murder in the slaying of a party member who was believed to be a police informant. In New York twenty-one Panthers were charged with plotting to assassinate policemen and blow up buildings. Although nearly all of the charges brought against Panther members either did not result in convictions or were overturned on appeal, the prosecutions absorbed much of the party's resources.

In 1970, when Newton's manslaughter conviction was reversed on appeal, he returned to find the party in disarray. Some chapters, particularly those in the eastern United States, resisted direction from the Oakland

headquarters. In 1971 Newton split with Cleaver, charging that Cleaver's influence had created too much emphasis on armed rebellion. The following year, however, Newton fled to Cuba, facing new criminal charges and allegations of drug use. After Newton's departure, Elaine Brown took over leadership of the party, which continued to decline, even after Newton returned in 1977 to resume control. In 1989 Newton was shot to death in a dispute with an Oakland drug dealer.

Several books have been written about the Black Panthers, including works by former members of the organization. Huey Newton's account, *Revolutionary Suicide*, was published in 1995. His cofounder, Bobby Seale, followed two years later with *Seize the Time: The Story of the Black Panther Party and Huey P. Newton*. In 2001, Kathleen Cleaver published *Liberation, Imagination, and the Black Panther Party: A New Look at the Black Panthers and Their Legacy*.

Black Towns

About two hundred black towns were established throughout the United States during the late nineteenth and early twentieth centuries. Largely supported by farming families, the towns had their own black city governments, churches, schools, and businesses. Black towns offered African Americans the chance to control their economic future, to prove that they could govern themselves, and to escape racial oppression.

The First Black Communities

The first attempts at establishing all-black communities were in Upper Canada (later Ontario) during the abolitionist movement, when escaped slaves sought freedom in the northern United States or continued on to Canada, where white charities established settlements to teach them job

MOUND BAYOU, MISSISSIPPI

Founded by the Louisville, New Orleans & Texas Railroad in 1887, Mound Bayou, Mississippi, was the most successful black town. It was surrounded by some of the state's richest cotton-producing lands and was developed by two prominent African-American politicians, James Hill and Isaiah Montgomery. The town's land included two bayous (a marshy body of water that flows into a river or lake) and several Indian burial mounds, which caused Montgomery to name it Mound Bayou. Montgomery knew African-American educator Booker T. Washington, who believed the town was an example of how blacks could help themselves economically. Because of Washington's interest, several articles were written about Mound Bayou, and Washington discussed it in books he published. By 1911 the town had a population of eleven hundred, with nearly eight thousand people living in the surrounding rural area. It had more businesses owned by African Americans, including the only black-owned cottonseed mill in the United States, than any other black town. The town began to decline after Washington's death in 1915, and by the early 1920s it had disappeared like other small Mississippi communities.

skills and give them land to homestead. The first black town in the United States was created in 1835, when Free Frank McWhorter, a former slave from Kentucky, founded the town of New Philadelphia, Illinois. In the first years after the American **Civil War** (1861–65), more black towns were founded so that freed slaves could own and farm their own land. Many of these early towns, such as Shankleville and Kendleton, were in Texas.

Most black towns, however, were established after the end of **Reconstruction**, the period of rebuilding that followed the Civil War. During this time, blacks and whites alike were lured by the promise of cheap or free land, available through the Homestead Act (1862), in the American West. Black towns established in the West included Nicodemus, Kansas; Langston City and Boley, in the Twin Territories, which would later become the state of Oklahoma; Allensworth, California; and Dearfield, Colorado. The most successful black town was Mound Bayou, Mississippi, which had the support of African-American educator and leader **Booker T. Washington** (1856–1915).

A New Generation Moves to the Cities

Many black towns, like Nicodemus, Allensworth, and Dearfield, died out long ago, and none of the surviving towns flourished the way their promoters once hoped. In the late twentieth century they were like thousands of other small towns throughout the United States that depended on highways and railroads, agricultural productivity, favorable county and state political decisions, and increasing settlement patterns to thrive. Black towns with few farms on the surrounding lands were the first to fail.

African Americans of the late 1800s and early 1900s were glad to establish their own towns and make their own government and business decisions, but the next generation was attracted to opportunities in the larger

U.S. cities. When the Great Migration of hundreds of thousands of southern blacks to northern and cities began in 1915, most black communities began to decline. Younger blacks could make some political gains and find jobs by moving to northern cities instead of staying in southern or western black towns. But for one brief period in history, a handful of all-black towns symbolized the hopes of African Americans for political freedom and economic opportunity.

Black Women's Club Movement

The Black Womens Club Movement emerged in the late nineteenth century. It involved local organizations dedicated to improving the lives of African Americans. These social organizations were formed primarily by middle-class women to provide services, financial assistance, and moral guidance for the poor.

Women involved in the club movement gained knowledge about education, health care, and poverty while developing organizing skills. They used these skills to help poor mothers learn how to keep a household, manage a budget, and raise their children. The clubs also supported homes for the aged, schools, and orphanages.

In 1895 women organizing at the local level made attempts to develop national ties. The New Era Club in Boston, Massachusetts, began a publication, the *Woman's Era*, that covered local and national news of concern to club women. Two national federations of local clubs were formed in 1895. The next year, the two merged and became the National Association of Colored Women. Throughout the 1930s the national organization held conventions and conferences for local groups and helped to provide them with training and information. As the reform efforts of African-American women became more political in the late 1930s, both the local and national club movements declined in importance.

Blake, James Hubert "Eubie"

JAZZ PIANIST, COMPOSER
February 7, 1883–February 12, 1983

The son of former slaves, **jazz** pianist and composer Eubie Blake was born in Baltimore, Maryland. He began organ lessons at age six and was soon imitating the tunes he heard in his mother's Baptist church. Blake would go on to have a major impact on jazz. His more than three hundred compositions gave a refined sense of harmony to **ragtime**-style music.

In his teens Blake landed a job as a dancer in a minstrel show (a program of black American songs, jokes, and impersonations), *In Old Kentucky*. During this time he also began to compose music, with his first, "Charleston Rag," appearing in 1899. During his twenties Blake began performing each summer in Atlantic City, New Jersey, where he composed songs and met the piano greats of his day. In 1910 Blake married Avis Lee, a classical pianist.

Blake and **Noble Sissle** teamed up as "The Dixie Duo," a piano-vocal duet in 1916. They traveled around performing on stage and also wrote songs together. In 1921 Sissle and Blake joined with the well-known comedy team of Flournoy Miller and Aubrey Lyles to write *Shuffle Along*. It became so popular that at one point three separate companies were crisscrossing the country performing it.

During the economic hard times of the **Great Depression** in the 1930s, Blake continued to write music for shows. One of them, Lew Leslie's *Blackbirds of 1930*, included "Memories of You," a song that Blake became well known for. During World War II (1939-45) Blake performed in shows for military service personnel. When "I'm Just Wild About Harry," from *Shuffle Along*, became popular during the 1948 presidential campaign of Harry Truman (1884–1972), Sissle and Blake reunited to update the show. The new version failed to gain popularity, however, and Blake retired from public life.

In the 1960s there was renewed public interest in ragtime, and Blake recorded *The Eighty-Six Years of Eubie Blake* (1969), an album that led to a resurgence in his career. After that, Blake performed regularly in concert and on television, and he continued to compose. In 1978 the musical revue *Eubie!* enjoyed a long run on Broadway.

Blake also established a music publishing and recording company and received numerous honorary degrees and awards, including the 1981 Presidential Medal of Freedom, the nation's highest civilian award, given in recognition of exceptional meritorious service. He was active until shortly before his death in 1983, five days after his hundredth birthday. In 1995 Blake was honored for his contribution to music by being featured on a U.S. postage stamp.

Blakey, Art

DRUMMER, BANDLEADER
October 11, 1919–October 16, 1990

Born in Pittsburgh, Pennsylvania, and orphaned as an infant, Art Blakey learned enough piano in his foster home and school to organize a group and play a steady engagement at a local nightclub while in his early teens. He later taught himself to play drums, mimicking the great drummers of the day. He would become famous for his distinctive drumming style and technique.

Blakey left Pittsburgh for New York City with **Mary Lou Williams**'s band in the fall of 1942, leaving her band in 1943 to tour with the **Fletcher Henderson** Orchestra. Shortly after his stint with Henderson, he headed west to St. Louis, Missouri, to join **Billy Eckstine**'s new big-bebop (a peppy form of **jazz**) band. He remained with the band for its three-year duration, working with such modern jazz musicians as **Dizzy Gillespie, Charlie Parker,** and **Sarah Vaughan.**

In 1948 Blakey went to Africa to learn more about Islamic culture and subsequently adopted the Arabic name "Abdullah Ibn Buhaina." During the early 1950s he continued to perform and record with the leading innovators of his generation. With music partner Horace Silver, Blakey in 1955 formed a quintet (five-member band) called the Jazz Messengers. When Silver left in 1956, Blakey assumed leadership of the group, renowned for combining solid, swinging jazz with **blues**, **rhythm and blues**, and **gospel**.

Blakey's commitment to preserving the bebop tradition lasted for over thirty-five years. His group toured widely, serving both as a school for young musicians and as the leading messenger for what has become known as "straight-ahead" jazz. Blakey's Jazz Messengers graduated from its ranks many of the most influential figures in jazz, including **Wayne Shorter** and **Wynton Marsalis**.

Blakey's playing style was influenced by West African and Cuban drumming. His versatility as a drummer received global recognition during his 1971-72 tour with the Giants of Jazz, which included **Dizzy Gillespie**, Sonny Stitt, and **Thelonious Monk**. Blakey died in New York City in 1990.

The Blues

The blues is a type of popular music that developed from southern African-American work songs around the end of the nineteenth century. It blends characteristics of **gospel music** and **jazz**. Most blues lyrics (words) are about life's frustrations and misfortunes; blues artists sing about unfair treatment by lovers or bosses, unemployment, racism, or other troubles. That is why such a song is referred to as "singing the blues" (when someone is down or sad, they are often described as having "the blues").

Although the first recordings of African Americans singing the blues were not made until the 1920s, the blues developed into a recognizable musical style between 1890 and 1920. The blues has had a tremendous effect on jazz, gospel music, theater music, rock, and most popular music of the twentieth century.

Early Blues Artists and Recordings

The earliest written music considered to be the blues was **W. C. Handy**'s (1873–1958) *Memphis Blues* (1912) and *St. Louis Blues* (1914). Handy and another early blues artist, **"Jelly Roll" Morton** (1885–1941), said they first heard the blues along the lower Mississippi River in the 1890s, where it was accompanied by guitars or piano in juke joints and barrelhouses (cheap places to eat, drink, and dance) and at roadside picnics.

Even though many whites and some middle-class blacks disapproved of the blues because it was usually played in bars and at parties where there was drinking, gambling, and fighting, by the 1920s the blues was the most popular African-American music style.

Early classic blues singers were **"Ma" Rainey** (1886–1939), called "the mother of the blues," and **Bessie Smith** (c. 1898–1937). Appearing in vaudeville shows (stage shows with a variety of acts), they appealed to both black and white audiences and sang songs about strong women who overcome mistreatment such as physical abuse and unfaithful husbands. Rainey is considered an early spokeswoman for women's rights.

"Down-home" (simple, unpretentious) blues was recorded beginning in 1926. Record companies took portable recording equipment to the South and recorded singers in juke joints and at country dance parties. Among the earliest blues singers to be recorded were Charley Patton (1887–1934) and **"Blind Lemon" Jefferson** (1897–1929). Down-home blues became so popular in the late 1920s that talent scouts arranged for singers to travel north to make studio recordings.

Development of Blues Styles

Before **World War II** (1914–18), two different blues-guitar styles developed. In Florida, Georgia, and the Carolinas, blues artists played with a fast finger-picking style, similar to **ragtime** piano music. In Mississippi, guitarists did not play a melody that accompanied the singer; instead, they created a single rhythmic pattern of music that was repeated over and over and punctuated the singer's lyrics. These repeated patterns are known as "riffs." Some of the best-known blues artists used this Mississippi Delta style. Among them were "Son" House (1902–1988), **Robert Johnson** (1911–1938), and **Muddy Waters** (1915–1983).

Some of the best down-home blues artists to emerge after World War II were "Lightnin'" Hopkins (1912–1982) and **John Lee Hooker** (1917–). **Muddy Waters** and **Howlin' Wolf** (1910–1976) led bands that helped create the Chicago blues style, which was a version of the Delta blues played with electric and amplified instruments. "Little" Walter Jacobs (1930–1968) invented a completely new sound with his amplified blues harmonica.

Influence of the Blues on Other Musicians

During the late 1930s and 1940s, big-band and jazz musicians like **Count Basie** (1904–1984), **Louis Armstrong** (1900–1971), **Duke Ellington** (1899–1974), **Billie Holiday** (1915–1959), **Charlie Parker** (1920–1955), and **John Coltrane** (1926–1967) used the blues form in jazz music. **Charles Mingus** (1922–1979), one of the most important jazz artists of the 1950s and 1960s, called blues and church music the African-American cornerstones of jazz and the later "soul" music.

Another type of music to evolve from the blues was **rhythm-and-blues (R&B),** led by guitarist-singers like "T-Bone" Walker (1910–1975) and **B. B. King** (1925–). Their use of electric guitars influenced the development of modern blues and rock music. King's album *B. B. King Live at the Regal* (1965) is considered one of the finest blues recording ever made.

Blues Revivals

The first "blues revival" occurred in the 1960s when young white musicians began playing the older down-home blues tunes in coffeehouses and clubs. Blues declined in popularity among African Americans, who preferred the newer sounds of **Motown**, soul music, disco, funk, **rap**, and hip-hop.

A second blues revival began in the 1990s, with older blues recordings being reissued on CDs and blues radio shows and nightclubs boosting the music's popularity. Older blues artists such as Robert Junior Lockwood (1915–), Buddy Guy (1936–), **Etta James** (1938–), R. L. Burnside (1926–),

SELECTED GRAMMY AWARDS GIVEN TO BLUES ARTISTS

The Grammy Award is the recording industry's most prestigious honor and is presented by the Recording Academy. Grammy Awards are given each year in various categories to honor excellence in the recording arts and sciences. Among other awards given by the Recording Academy are the Lifetime Achievement Award and the Grammy Hall of Fame Award.

Blues artists to receive the Grammy Lifetime Achievement Award in recent years are B. B. King, in 1987; Bessie Smith, in 1989; Muddy Waters, in 1992; and John Lee Hooker, in 2000.

The Grammy Hall of Fame Award is given to honor recordings released more than twenty-five years ago that have had a lasting impact or are historically significant. Some blues recordings that have recently been inducted into the Grammy Hall of Fame are the following:

- Inducted in 2000: "Rollin' Stone" (1950), by Muddy Waters

- Inducted in 1999: "Boogie Chillun" (1948), by John Lee Hooker; "Born Under a Bad Sign" (Album, 1967), by Albert King; "Got My Mojo Working" (1957), by Muddy Waters; "Match Box Blues" (1927), by Blind Lemon Jefferson; "Pony Blues" (1929), by Charley Patton; and "Smokestack Lightnin'" (1956), by Howlin' Wolf

- Inducted in 1998: "Cross Road Blues" (1936), by Robert Johnson; "Hoochie Koochie Man" (1954), by Muddy Waters; "The Thrill Is Gone" (1969), by B. B. King

and **B. B. King** have enjoyed new careers and made new recordings. King won a Grammy Award in 2000 for Best Traditional Blues Album with his *Blues on the Bayou*.

When guitarist Jimmy Rogers, the last surviving member of Muddy Waters's first band, died in 1997, he was working on an all-star blues CD featuring rock legends such as Eric Clapton, Jimmy Page, and Mick Jagger and contemporary blues artist Taj Mahal (1942–). After Rogers's death, these artists completed the project, and the CD, *Blues, Blues, Blues*, was issued in 1999. New blues artists emerged during the 1990s, among them The Robert Cray Band, which won a Grammy in 2000 for the album *Take Your Shoes Off* (1999).

Bluford, Guion Stewart Jr. "Guy"

ASTRONAUT
November 22, 1942–

An Eagle Scout who knew he wanted to be an **aerospace** engineer by the time he reached junior high school, Guy Bluford was the first African

Guy Bluford, in the spaceshuttle
Challenger, was the first African American
in space (AP/Wide World Photos.
Reproduced by permission)

American in space. He served as a mission specialist on the eighth *Challenger* shuttle flight in August 1983.

Bluford was born and raised in Philadelphia, Pennsylvania. He received a bachelor of science degree in aerospace **engineering** in 1964 from Pennsylvania State University, where he was enrolled in the U.S. Air Force's Reserve Officers' Training Corps (ROTC). After graduation he joined the air force as a lieutenant colonel. Bluford received his pilot wings in January 1965 and went to Vietnam, where he flew 144 combat missions as a member of the F-4 Fighter Squadron.

From 1967 to 1972 Bluford taught acrobatic flying at Sheppard Air Force Base in Texas. He then served as chief of the aerodynamics and airframe branch of the Flight Dynamics Laboratory at Wright-Patterson Air Force Base in Ohio, while also studying at the Air Force Institute of Technology. He earned a Ph.D. degree in aerospace engineering in 1978.

Bluford was also accepted into the National Aeronautics and Space Administration's (NASA) astronaut program in 1978. After his history-making first flight in 1983, his next mission was again aboard the *Challenger*, in a joint venture with West Germany on October 30, 1985. He flew twice more, in April 1991 and December 1992, aboard the orbiter *Discovery*.

Bluford earned a master's degree in business administration in 1987 from the University of Houston (Texas). In 1993 he resigned from NASA and the air force to become vice president and general manager of an engineering and computer software firm in Greenbelt, Maryland. Bluford has received numerous awards, including the Vietnam Cross of Gallantry with Palm (1967), the **National Association for the Advancement of Colored People's (NAACP)** Image Award (1983), and the **Ebony** Black Achievement Award (1983).

An African-American F I R S T

When he boarded the spaceshuttle *Challenger* in August of 1983, Guy Bluford broke more than twenty years of white-only space exploration, becoming the first African American to travel in outer space.

Bond, Horace Mann

TEACHER, ADMINISTRATOR
November 8, 1904–December 21, 1972

College administrator and scholar Horace Mann Bond was born in Nashville, Tennessee, but lived throughout the South as a boy. His family moved to be near the schools with which his father, a Methodist minister, was affiliated. An unusually advanced student, Bond entered high school when he was nine years old.

At fourteen, Bond enrolled at **Lincoln University** in Pennsylvania. In 1923 he began attending the University of Chicago to pursue his doctorate degree in **education.** At the same time, he worked as a teacher and administrator at several African-American universities.

Bond's first scholarly work, *The Education of the Negro in the American Social Order*, was published in 1934. It linked inadequate education to African Americans' lack of political and economic power. His many publications addressed other issues involving unfair treatment of blacks in the U.S. education system.

In the 1950s and 1960s—while a college administrator—Bond also organized tours, lectures, and articles in support of independence movements in African countries. He was a leader of the American Society for African Culture, which encouraged interest in African culture and warned against the dangers of communism in the African independence movements.

Bond's administrative career included serving as president of Fort Valley State Teachers College in Georgia (1939–45) and as the first black president of Lincoln University (1945–57). He was very successful in attracting financial support for his institutions, turning them into well-respected research and teaching universities. Bond's longest affiliation was with Atlanta University (now Clark-Atlanta University, part of the **Atlanta University Center** in Georgia, where he worked from 1957 to 1971. He was dean of the School of Education and later the director of the Bureau of Educational and Social Research.

Horace Mann Bond, who died in Atlanta in 1972, was the father of **Julian Bond,** the civil rights activist and politician.

Bond, Julian

POLITICAN, POLITICAL WRITER
January 14, 1940–

Julian Bond literally fought his way into the Georgia House of Representatives at the peak of the **Civil Rights movement.** On January 10, 1966, fellow legislators voted to prevent him from taking his seat in the house when he refused to retract his outspoken support of draft evasion and anti–**Vietnam War** (1959–75) activism. With the help of Rev. **Martin Luther King Jr.** (1929–1968) and Vice President Hubert Humphrey (1911–1978), Bond fought them and ultimately won his seat in a Supreme Court decision.

Bond was born in Nashville, Tennessee, and grew up in **Lincoln University**, Pennsylvania, surrounded by **education** (his father was president of Lincoln University). In the early 1960s he attended **Morehouse College** (Atlanta, Georgia), where he helped create the Committee on Appeal for Human Rights. In 1968, after serving in the Georgia legislature (1966–75), Bond was considered for the Democratic vice presidential nomination. He was too young, however, to serve, not having reached the mandatory age of thirty-five set by the U.S. Constitution. Bond then served in the Georgia Senate (1975–87).

In 1972 Bond wrote a book called *A Time to Speak, a Time to Act* and narrated a Public Broadcast System (PBS) television feature on the **Civil Rights movement** called *Eyes on the Prize*. In 1986 he ran for U.S. Congress but lost to John Lewis. In the 1990s Bond served as a visiting professor at Drexel University (Philadelphia, Pennsylvania) and Harvard University (Cambridge, Massachusetts), among others, and hosted a television program called *TV's Black Forum*. In 1998 he was elected chairman of the board of the **National Association for the Advancement of Colored People (NAACP).**

Politician and activist Julian Bond
(Courtesy of Library of Congress)

Bonner, Marita

WRITER
June 16, 1899–December 6, 1971

Writer Marita Bonner was born and raised near Boston, Massachusetts. She was admitted to Radcliffe College (Cambridge, Massachusetts) in 1918 and also began a career as a high school teacher. After graduating in 1922, she taught high school in Bluefield, West Virgina, and then in Washington, D.C. In 1930 she married William Almy Occomy and moved with him to Chicago, Illinois, where she taught in the public schools and spent the rest of her life.

Bonner published her first story, "The Hands," in 1925. This was followed by an autobiographical essay, "On Being Young—a Woman—and

Colored" (1925), and several short stories, including "Nothing New" (1926), her first story about Chicago's "black belt," where most African Americans lived. During this period she also wrote three plays: *The Pot Maker* (1927), *The Purple Flower* (1928), and *Exit—An Illusion* (1929).

After leaving Washington, D.C., in 1930, Bonner turned her attention exclusively to fiction, publishing under her married name. Many of the stories she wrote while living in Chicago consist of what she called a "black map" of the city's African-American communities: class distinctions between the communities, the ways in which blacks interacted with other ethnic groups, and the social and economic hardships they endured. Bonner's Chicago stories—many set in fictional Frye Street—frequently worked together to build single, elaborate tales but were narrated from different perspectives and printed independently of one another.

After 1941 Bonner wrote infrequently and published nothing. She continued to teach, raised her three children, and became involved with the Christian Science movement. She died in 1971 of injuries she received when her apartment caught fire.

Bontemps, Arna

WRITER
October 13, 1902–June 4, 1973

Arna Bontemps—poet, playwright, novelist, critic, and editor—was a leading figure in the surge of black artistic development of the 1920s known as the **Harlem Renaissance.** He was born in Alexandria, Louisiana, in 1902 to members of the Seventh-Day Adventist Church and grew up in Los Angeles, California. After graduating from San Fernando Academy in 1920, he enrolled in Pacific Union College, from which he graduated in 1923.

In 1924 Bontemps went to New York City, where he met other young writers, including **Langston Hughes, Countee Cullen,** and **Claude McKay.** In New York he taught in Adventist schools and began his writing career. His first novel, *God Sends Sunday* (1931), was transformed by Bontemps and Countee Cullen into a musical that played on Broadway in 1946. One of the first African-American historical novels published, Bontemps's *Black Thunder* (1936) was based on a Virginia slave revolt in 1800.

Bontemps also produced numerous nonfictional historical works, including *They Seek a City* (1945), written with Jack Conroy. The book, about black migration, was updated in 1966 as *Any Place but Here*. Bontemps and Conroy also created a series of original tales for children, including *Sam Patch, the High, Wide and Handsome Jumper* (1951). In 1956 Bontemps received the Jane Addams Children's Book Award for *Story of the Negro* (1948). Throughout his career Bontemps also wrote poetry. *Personals*, a collection of his poems, was published in 1963.

In 1943 Bontemps became head librarian at **Fisk University** in Nashville, Tennessee, and from 1966 to 1969 he was a professor at the

Chicago Circle campus of the University of Illinois. In 1970 Bontemps returned to Fisk as writer-in-residence. He died there in 1973.

Borican, John

MIDDLE-DISTANCE RUNNER
1913–December 22, 1942

John Borican was a record-setting runner from Bridgeton, New Jersey. In 1941 he became the first person to win the U.S. pentathlon (which consists of five **track-and-field** events) and the decathlon (which has ten events) in the same year. He also set world records in middle-distance track races, such as the 600-yard and 1,000-yard events. Not only fast on his feet, Borican was also a fast learner. He attended Temple University (Philadelphia, Pennsylvania) and Virginia State College and pursued a master's degree at Columbia University (New York City). Borican died at the young age of twenty-nine from unknown causes.

Bouchet, Edward Alexander

SCIENTIST, EDUCATOR
September 15, 1852–October 28, 1918

The first African American to earn a Ph.D. degree from an American university, Edward Bouchet was born in New Haven, Connecticut. He received his early schooling at Sally Wilson's Artisan Street Colored School, New Haven High School (1866–68), and Hopkins Grammar School, where he graduated at the head of his class in 1870. That same year, Bouchet enrolled at Yale University in New Haven.

Bouchet was a very motivated student, received high grades, and was elected into the academic fraternity Phi Beta Kappa, a very high honor. He received his Ph.D. in physics from Yale in 1876.

From 1876 to 1902 Bouchet designed and taught laboratory courses in chemistry and physics at Philadelphia, Pennsylvania's Institute for Colored Youth (later Cheney State College), a Quaker institution with a highly regarded academic department. From 1902 to 1905 he held various positions in St. Louis, Missouri. He was director of academics at St. Paul's Normal and Industrial School in Gallipolis, Ohio, from 1906 to 1908 and taught at Bishop College in Marshall, Texas, from 1913 to 1916. Bouchet, who never married, remained active in the Episcopal Church, the Yale Alumni Association, and the **National Association for the Advancement of Colored People (NAACP)** before his retirement in 1916. He died in 1918 in New Haven.

An African-American FIRST

Edward Bouchet was the first African American to earn a Ph.D. from an American university—a physics degree from Yale University in 1876

Bowman, Sister Thea

EVANGELIST, TEACHER
December 29, 1937–March 30, 1990

Educator and champion of peace Sister Thea Bowman was born in Yazoo City, Mississippi, the daughter of a physician. Named Bertha by her parents, she became a Catholic at age nine and was christened Sister Thea when she became the first black novitiate (a girl in training to be a nun) of the Franciscan Sisters in 1956.

Sister Bowman obtained her undergraduate degree in English from Viterbo College (LaCrosse, Wisconsin) and master's and doctorate degrees in linguistics and English literature from Catholic University of America (Washington, D.C.). She taught in Mississippi public schools during the 1960s and at Viterbo from 1971 to 1978. While teaching at Viterbo she founded the Hallelujah Singers, a touring group that performed traditional black spirituals. She was even lead singer on an album of spirituals.

In 1978 Sister Bowman, whose teaching always included emphasis on customs and values of different races and cultures, became the consultant on interracial awareness for the Franciscans of Jackson, Mississippi, while also teaching at Xavier University in New Orleans, Louisiana. For her dedication to promoting awareness between cultures, she was awarded the LaCrosse

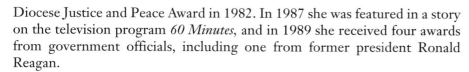

Diocese Justice and Peace Award in 1982. In 1987 she was featured in a story on the television program *60 Minutes*, and in 1989 she received four awards from government officials, including one from former president Ronald Reagan.

A cancer sufferer since 1984, Sister Bowman was given the American Cancer Society's Courage Award in 1988 in a ceremony in the White House Rose Garden. Shortly before she died in 1990, she was the first recipient of the Sister Thea Bowman Justice Award. The award is presented each year to a minister whose leadership exemplifies the energy and determination necessary to make a difference in the church and society.

Boxing

Prior to the 1900s few blacks, foreign or native American, gained prominence, let alone dominance, in prizefighting. Until professional boxing was divided into weight divisions in the late nineteenth century, and continuing well after that, white promoters conspired to deny African-American fighters opportunities to obtain title fights. For decades, black fighters typically fought more often and for less money than their white counterparts; many black pugilists died young and penniless for their efforts. Among the few American-born boxers to rise to the top of the sport in the nineteenth century was George Dixon, who reigned as champion of the bantamweight and, later, featherweight divisions in the late 1800s. A handful of foreign-born black fighters also made names for themselves in that era, including Virgin Islands–born heavyweight Peter Jackson and Barbados-born lightweight-welterweight Joe Walcott.

Early-Twentieth-Century Black Boxers

For all practical purposes, African-American boxers entered the sport successfully only during the twentieth century, with most of that success occurring in the century's latter half. Black boxers of note in the century's first half were regarded as trailblazers by the African-American community and earned a celebrity status far beyond the realm of the sport. One such fighter, Joe Gans, a lightweight who reigned as champion for six years just after the turn of the century, is regarded by boxing historians as one of the greatest ever to fight in that division. Others to gain prominence in the first decades of the century were middleweight-heavyweight Sam Langford, light heavyweight–heavyweight Joe Jeannette, and heavyweight Harry Wills. Their fame, however, paled considerably to that of **Jack Johnson,** the first black heavyweight titleholder.

Johnson, who held the crown from 1908–15, took advantage of a rare title shot for a black heavyweight to obtain the title in a bout staged in Sydney, Australia. Johnson was arrogant and outspoken at a time when **Jim Crow** laws and racist attitudes, generally, were at their highest in the United States. That public persona (also hurt considerably by his preference for white women) soon infuriated whites, regardless of their interest in boxing. Trouble with American authorities was a constant for Johnson, and he only managed to hold his title for as long as he did by fighting in Europe during much of his reign. Due to Johnson's notoriety, it again became more difficult for black boxers to gain title shots.

The 1930s to 1960s

African-American fighters continued to have greater luck rising through the ranks of the lower weight divisions. Among those who managed to make that journey was **Henry Armstrong,** who many consider to be among the best boxers of all time. Armstrong held the featherweight, lightweight, and welterweight titles simultaneously in the late 1930s. A considerable cultural shift in the glamour division of heavyweight came with the success of **Joe Louis,** who won the title in 1937 and held it until 1949. Louis was everything that Johnson had not been: humble, soft-spoken, gracious. The key moment in his career was one for which he even had white America solidly in his corner. Louis's 1938 rematch with former champion Max Schmeling, set up by Schmeling's second-round knockout of Louis in 1936, pitted an American against a German (and possible Nazi) in the early days of Hitler's conquest of Europe. His first round knockout of Schmeling made Louis a national hero across race lines. Louis increased his standing among whites by serving in the U.S. Army during **World War II**.

In the decade after the Second World War, black boxers went from being exceptions to becoming regulars among the ranks of contenders. In the late 1940s boxing proved a natural sport for coverage by the still-limited technology used in the production of live television. An immensely popular fighter of the time was **Sugar Ray Robinson,** a flashy and fluid welterweight-middleweight who enjoyed a long career in the spotlight. Robinson won a combined six titles covering three weight classifications. Other champion boxers who were seen routinely on weekly, nationally televised fights were welterweight Kid Gavilan, light heavyweight **Archie Moore,** and heavyweight **Floyd Patterson.**

The 1960s to 1980s

In the early 1960s welterweight–junior middleweight Emile Griffith was conspicuous as a combined six-time titleholder in that range of three divisions. Television, however, was increasingly devoting its decreasing boxing coverage to the heavyweight division. Boosted by his earlier gold medal–winning light heavyweight performance in the 1960 Olympic Games, Cassius Clay Jr. really burst on the national scene with his 1964 upset of feared heavyweight champ **Sonny Liston.** Combining poetry and boastfulness, Clay knew how to use the television medium to his advantage—and television was only too happy to provide him the forum. Later, when he fought induction into the army during the Vietnam War (1959–75) on religious grounds as a Black Muslim, he became an outcast for a time, especially after he publicly changed his name to **Muhammad Ali.** Within a few years, after sentiment turned against the war, Ali was forgiven, even embraced, by the American public. Ali held the heavyweight title an unprecedented three times. At the height of his fame, he may well have been the most recognizable person on the planet. Ali was just one of several gifted black heavy-

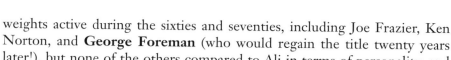

weights active during the sixties and seventies, including Joe Frazier, Ken Norton, and **George Foreman** (who would regain the title twenty years later!), but none of the others compared to Ali in terms of personality, and hence, popularity.

The 1980s to the Early Twenty-First Century

The biggest names in boxing during the 1980s may have been those fighting in the middle divisions. The most successful of these was **Sugar Ray Leonard,** who won titles in five weight classifications. Leonard combined uncommon grace and speed to outbox his opponents, often ending a fight, however, with a flurry of punches resulting in a knockout. Leonard, however, was joined by **Thomas Hearns,** who also piled up titles in five divisions. Like Leonard, Hearns started as a welterweight and moved up through several divisions as he matured and added weight. Unlike Leonard, however, Hearns's strength was unquestioned put-away power that he used to end many a fight with an early knockout.

Both Leonard and Hearns were joined in those divisions by such other notables as Marvelous Marvin Hagler and Dwight (Braxton) Qawi. The heavyweight division was dominated in the early to mid-eighties by Larry Holmes, but later fell into disarray as a number of fighters claimed the title for short periods. Among those was **Mike Tyson,** a ferocious fighter who seemed invincible in the late eighties before personal problems outside the ring began to disastrously affect his performances inside the ring.

In the 1990s the most notable heavyweight champion was Evander Holyfield, a former cruiserweight champ who stepped up in weight to face many of the top contenders. He twice won the championship and recorded a pair of decisive victories over Tyson, who continued to be a top challenger for much of the decade. One of the best fighters in the world at the beginning of the twenty-first century was Roy Jones Jr., who has fought in the middleweight to light heavyweight divisions.

Bradley, David Henry Jr.

WRITER
September 7, 1950–

Writer David Bradley was born and raised in rural Bedford, Pennsylvania, and attended the University of Pennsylvania, where he studied English and wrote his first novel, *South Street,* graduating in 1972. Afterward, he moved on to King's College in London, England, where he earned a degree in 1974. After working for two years in publishing, Bradley became a member of the English department at Temple University in Philadelphia, Pennsylvania.

South Street, a tale of alienation from the lifestyles and politics of the university environment, was published in 1975. Bradley's second novel, *The Chaneysville Incident* (1981), won several awards: the PEN/Faulkner Award, the largest juried award for fiction in the United States; the American

David Bradley (AP/Wide World Photos. Reproduced by permission)

Academy and Institute of Arts and Letters award for literature; and a *New York Times Book Review* "Editor's Choice" citation. The core of this novel is an incident from Bedford's own family history. In doing research for the area's two hundredth anniversary celebration) in 1969, Bradley's mother discovers thirteen unmarked graves on the property of a Bedford County landowner. In doing so, she confirms a local myth concerning thirteen runaway slaves on the **Underground Railroad** who, on the point of recapture, preferred death to slavery and asked to be killed.

In addition to two novels, Bradley has written articles and essays for many publications, including *Esquire*, the *New York Times Book Review*,

Redbook, and the *Southern Review*. He was awarded a Guggenheim Fellowship in 1989 and a National Endowment for the Arts Fellowship in 1991.

Bradley, Thomas "Tom"

POLITICIAN
December 27, 1917–September 29, 1998

Tom Bradley was born in Calvert, Texas. Although his father and mother were both sharecroppers (they rented the land they farmed, paying with a share of the crops), he would one day become mayor of one of the largest cities in the United States, Los Angeles, California.

When Bradley was four, his family moved to Dallas, Texas, and when he was six, to Somerton, Arizona, where they lived with relatives and he first attended school. In 1924 the family moved to Los Angeles. Bradley attended Polytechnic High School, where he was one of 113 blacks out of a student population of 1,300. He excelled as a scholar and athlete and won a scholarship to the University of California at Los Angeles (UCLA).

In 1941 Bradley left UCLA to enter the police academy. He remained in the Los Angeles Police Department (LAPD) until 1961, rising to the rank of lieutenant, the highest position achieved up to then by an African American. During his years on the police force, Bradley also attended Loyola University Law School and Southwestern University Law School at night and became a lawyer in 1956.

Bradley left the police force in 1961, and in 1963 he ran successfully for the city council seat for Los Angeles's predominantly white Tenth District. He was one of the first blacks in the western part of the United States to be elected in an area that was mostly white. He would remain in that office until 1973.

In August 1965, when riots erupted in the Watts area of Los Angeles, Councilman Bradley's criticism of police brutality created conflicts between him and his former colleagues in the LAPD and Mayor Sam Yorty. Bradley, however, because of his law enforcement background and his dignified, unthreatening public image, remained popular with the people of Los Angeles. In 1969 Bradley challenged Yorty for the office of mayor but was narrowly defeated.

In 1973 Bradley ran for mayor again and defeated Yorty to become Los Angeles's first black mayor, as well as the first African-American mayor of a predominantly white city. He would be reelected four times. A major highlight of Bradley's period as mayor was the 1984 Summer Olympics. The Bradley administration also spurred downtown development. Bradley, however, was accused of neglecting working-class and inner-city neighborhoods, particularly black areas. Nevertheless, he won the 1982 Democratic Party nomination for governor of the nation's largest state. He narrowly lost to Republican George Deukmejian. In 1986 he again ran for governor but lost again.

Bradley was reelected mayor for the fourth time in 1989, completing his last term in 1993. He died of a heart attack in Los Angeles on September 29, 1998.

Braithwaite, William Stanley Beaumont

AUTHOR, EDUCATOR
December 6, 1878–June 8, 1962

The son of an emigrant from British Guiana (in northern South America) and the daughter of a former slave, author William Stanley Braithwaite was born and raised in Boston, Massachusetts. His father's death in 1884 left the family destitute, and Braithwaite left school when he was twelve to work full time. He worked several other jobs before finding employment as an errand boy at the publishing firm of Ginn & Co., where he eventually worked as a typesetter.

Braithwaite later claimed that he had been setting type for the first lines of English poet John Keats's "Ode on a Grecian Urn" when he realized his passion for poetry and became determined to write his own. His first book of verse, *Lyrics of Life and Love*, was published in 1904; his first anthology (collection), the *Book of Elizabethan Verse*, appeared in 1906; and a second volume of poetry, *House of Falling Leaves*, appeared in 1908.

Braithwaite continued to support himself and his family through writing and editing before accepting a professorship at Atlanta University (now Clark-Atlanta University, part of the **Atlanta University Center**) in Georgia, where he taught for ten years. During this time he started to work on his autobiography, *The House Under Arcturus*, which was published in three parts in 1941. Braithwaite retired from teaching and moved to the Harlem district of New York City in 1945. He published a volume of his selected poems in 1948.

Breakdancing

Breakdancing is a form of dance that was developed by teenage African-American males on the streets of the South Bronx in New York City. During the 1970s breakdancers (nicknamed "B-Boys") often performed to rap music, then an emerging style of music. The dance form became part of a young inner-city culture that included a certain look (unlaced sneakers, hooded sweatshirts, loose-fitting jeans, baseball caps, and windbreakers), graffiti art, and a distinct dialect (language).

Breakdancing is believed to have developed from *capoeira*, a Brazilian martial arts form disguised as dance. Originally a form of competition between gangs, breakdancing shows off the physical strength and style of the dancer. Dancers perform acrobatics such as multiple spins and flips. Some moves are even dangerous: in the "windmill," for example, the dancer spins quickly on his shoulders; the "suicide" has the performer throwing himself forward to land flat on his back on a hard (usually cement) surface. Other

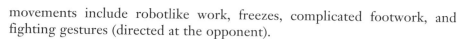

movements include robotlike work, freezes, complicated footwork, and fighting gestures (directed at the opponent).

Dance crews, often gangs, met on street corners, at subway stations, or on dance floors to "battle" other groups. The winning crew was the one to demonstrate the greatest precision, strength, style, and, most important, nerve. The more daring the performance, the better. Breakdancing was made popular in part by pop superstar **Michael Jackson,** who performed the "moonwalk," a complex move in which a person appears to be walking forward but moving backward, on national television. Featured in several movies during the 1980s, breakdancing dropped out of the limelight later that decade. During the 1990s it reemerged as a **social dance** form, performed in nightclubs.

Briggs, Cyril Valentine

ACTIVIST

1888–October 18, 1966

Cyril Briggs was a journalist and political activist who spoke out against the U.S. government's treatment of African Americans and workers. Born in the British West Indies, Briggs got his early start in journalism working on local newspapers. He moved to the United States to work in 1905, and by 1915 he was appointed editor of the *Colored American Review*, located in New York City. *The Review* featured articles about black economic success and racial pride. Briggs eventually went to work as a writer for the *New York Amsterdam News*. At the *News*, Briggs criticized the U.S. government for fighting a war (**World War I**; 1914–18) to defend democracy in Europe while denying African Americans rights at home.

In 1919 Briggs left the *News* to devote all of his time to the *Crusader*, a newspaper he had begun publishing a year earlier. Originally the *Crusader* focused on civil rights for blacks. As Briggs gradually became a supporter of Communism, admiring a political system in which all goods are supposedly owned by all of the people and distributed as needed, the *Crusader* focused more on spreading Communist ideas.

When the *Crusader* shut down in 1922, Briggs continued to work for the rest of his life as a journalist supporting Communist ideas and civil rights, and as a political activist. He organized many black groups within the Communist Party, such as the American Negro Labor Congress and the League of Struggle for Negro Rights.

Brimmer, Andrew Felton

ECONOMIST

September 13, 1926–

Economist Andrew F. Brimmer is an expert in international finance and often writes about employment and business issues concerning African Americans. Born and raised in Louisiana, he served in the U.S. Army

Baseball great Lou Brock (AP/Wide World Photos. Reproduced by permission)

(1945–46) before earning bachelor of arts (1950) and master of arts (1951) degrees from the University of Washington. He earned a Ph.D. degree in **economics** from Harvard University (Cambridge, Massachusetts) in 1957.

Brimmer became deputy assistant secretary of commerce for economic policy in 1963 and then assistant secretary for economic affairs under President John F. Kennedy (1961–63). In 1966 President Lyndon B. Johnson (1963–69) made him the first black member of the board of governors of the Federal Reserve Bank, which controls credit and money flow in the United States.

In 1974 Brimmer began teaching at Harvard's Graduate School of Business. Two years later, he founded Brimmer and Company, a consulting firm in Washington, D.C. He was still professionally active in 1997, when Congress put him in charge of sorting out financial problems for the city of Washington, D.C.

In his writings, including a column for *Black Enterprise* magazine, Brimmer has argued that racial discrimination, rather than education, is keeping African Americans from higher-paying jobs. He also believes that teen pregnancy and unemployment among young black people cannot be blamed on the economy. He has encouraged African Americans to look for economic opportunities in the corporate arena and other areas, not just in small business.

Brock, Louis Clark "Lou"

BASEBALL PLAYER
June 18, 1939–

Baseball player Louis "Lou" Brock played outfield for the Chicago Cubs from 1961 to 1964 before being traded to the St. Louis Cardinals, where he played for the next fifteen years. Despite his batting record—he retired in 1979 with more than three thousand career hits to his credit—Brock is best remembered for his speed and superior base-stealing ability. Brock was such a clever base stealer that he set a record for the most bases stolen in a season (118) in 1974.

Brock was born in El Dorado, Arkansas. He won a scholarship to Southern University in Baton Rouge, Louisiana. While with the Cardinals, he led the team in hits from 1967 to 1969, appeared in three World Series, and played in three All-Star Games. In 1985 he was voted into the Baseball Hall of Fame.

Brooke, Edward W. I. III

POLITICIAN, LAWYER
October 26, 1919–

Edward W. I. Brooke was the first African American elected to the U.S. Senate. Throughout his political career he fought hard to ensure that blacks were given the same civil rights as whites.

Born in Washington, D.C., Brooke earned a degree from D.C.'s **Howard University**. In 1941 he was called to serve in **World War II** (1939–45). While serving in the war, Brooke defended soldiers in court cases. This experience encouraged him to enter Boston (Massachusetts) University Law School in 1945. In 1962 Brooke became the attorney general, or chief law officer, of Massachusetts. He became known for prosecuting dishonest politicians. In 1966 Brooke was elected to the U.S. Senate as a Republican. He served two terms in the Senate, after which he returned to practicing law in Boston and Washington, D.C.

Brooks, Gwendolyn Elizabeth

POET, NOVELIST, TEACHER
June 7, 1917–

Recognized internationally as a major literary figure, Gwendolyn Brooks succeeded the famous poet Carl Sandburg (1878–1967) as poet laureate (an honorary title bestowed in recognition of excellence in poetry) of Illinois in 1968. She is also the first African American to win a Pulitzer Prize for excellence in poetry, for *Annie Allen* (1950). Winner of two Guggenheim Fellowships, Brooks in 1976 also became the first black woman elected to the National Institute of Arts and Letters.

Born in Topeka, Kansas, Gwendolyn Brooks was raised in **Chicago, Illinois**, where she lives today. In her autobiography, *Report from Part One* (1972), she describes a happy childhood. Her father, the son of a runaway slave, was a janitor who had hoped to become a doctor, and her mother was a fifth-grade teacher who wished to write. They nurtured their daughter's writing talents. Years later, Brooks's mother took her to meet the authors **James Weldon Johnson** and **Langston Hughes** at church. Hughes became an inspiration to the young poet, and also a friend and teacher.

Brooks graduated from Wilson Junior College (now Kennedy-King) in 1936. In 1939 she married the poet and writer Henry Lowington Blakely II, with whom she had a son and a daughter.

As poet laureate, Brooks supports the creativity of other writers. Her annual Poet Laureate Awards distribute considerable sums of her own money, chiefly to the schoolchildren of Illinois. She visits prisons, where her readings have inspired poets such as the late **Ethridge Knight**.

Brooks's work is notable both for its exquisite craft and its social depth; her works span six decades of social and political changes. Although she has always experimented with traditional forms of poetry, her later work became much more free verse and open, a quality that can be seen in her epic *In the Mecca* (1968). In 1971 Brooks began an annual literary magazine, *The Black Position*, and made the first of her two trips to Africa. Her experiences there are the focus of later works, including *Winnie* (1988), a poem honoring Winnie Mandela, president of the African National Congress Women's League.

Brooks continues to be honored for her work and her driving spirit. She was elected to the National Women's Hall of Fame and given the National

An African-American FIRST

In 1966 Edward W. I. Brooke became the first African American elected to the U.S. Senate. As a legislator Brooke helped pass the 1968 Civil Rights Act, which marked a turning point in U.S. social, cultural, and political history. Specifically, Brooke lobbied for "open housing" laws to prevent people from discriminating against home buyers on the basis of race.

An African-American FIRST

Gwendolyn Brooks, who began writing poetry at seven, was the first African American to a win a Pulitzer Prize for poetry, for *Annie Allen* (1950). The Pulitzer Prize is awarded annually to individuals for excellence in several fields, including music, literature, and journalism.

Endowment for the Arts Lifetime Achievement Award in 1989. In 1999 she received a "First Women" Award during the National First Ladies Library Award ceremony in Washington, D.C. In addition, the National Academy of American Poets awarded her the fellowship for distinguished poetic achievement in 2000.

Broonzy, William Lee Conley "Big Bill"

SINGER, GUITARIST, FIDDLER, SONGWRITER
June 26, 1893–August 14, 1958

A singer, guitarist, fiddler, and songwriter, William Broonzy became one of the most recorded **blues** singers in the United States during the 1930s to 1950s. He reached the height of his popularity in the 1950s, appearing with such musical artists as Pete Seeger and **Sonny Terry.** He appeared on radio and television and toured in Africa, South America, and the Pacific.

Born in Scott, Mississippi, Broonzy was one of seventeen children. Music was part of his life from an early age, and he learned spirituals in church and work songs in the field. At age ten he learned to play the guitar and violin on homemade instruments. By 1907 he was good enough to play at picnic dances for blacks and whites.

After brief stints as a preacher and a sharecropper (a person who rents land to farm, paying the rent with a share of the crops produced), Broonzy joined the army during **World War I** (1914-18). By 1920 he was in Chicago, Illinois, working at odd jobs and performing at parties and clubs with musicians such as Papa Charlie Jackson. In the 1930s he also began recording widely with several record labels. His singing style linked country and urban blues music, and his guitar playing was light and lilting. His songs could be wistful and mournful, as in "Friendless Blues" (1934), or humorous, as in "Keep Your Hands Off Her" (1935).

Performing and recording with numerous groups throughout the 1930s, Broonzy was invited to play in promoter John Hammond's 1938 "From Spirituals to Swing" concert at New York City's Carnegie Hall. He then began touring extensively in the United States and Europe, greatly benefiting from a post–**World War II** (1939-45) folk music revival. One of his most famous songs from the postwar period was "Black, Brown, and White Blues," in which he addressed the struggle for civil rights, singing, "Now if you's white, you's right, but if you's brown, stick around, and if you's black, oh brother, git back, git back, git back."

Despite his popularity and success, it was not until 1953 that Broonzy earned his income as a full-time musician, giving up his jobs as cook, janitor, and porter. He died of cancer in 1958.

Brotherhood of Sleeping Car Porters

Organized in secret on August 25, 1925, the Brotherhood of Sleeping Car Porters (BSCP) became the first successful African-American labor

union (an organization of workers formed to promote better wages, benefits, and working conditions for its members). Not only did the BSCP successfully negotiate wage agreements between the Pullman Company and its porters (baggage handlers) through the years, it also supported civil rights activities by providing labor and money to various movements. The BSCP also stimulated black participation in unions and fought to end discrimination in organized labor and in the U.S. defense industries and the military.

African-American sleeping car porters were employed by the Pullman Company from its beginning in 1867 because they were dependable and would work for low wages. Porters worked in the sleeping cars of passenger trains, helping with luggage, making beds, polishing shoes, and waiting on passengers twenty-four hours a day. They earned little pay and only small tips, but because they had steady jobs and could travel, they were considered well off among black workers.

Asa Randolph listened to the porters' complaints and taught them about trade unions and collective bargaining (negotiations between a labor union and an employer for better wages, hours, and working conditions). He began organizing them in 1925 and served as president of the BSCP from 1925 to 1968. Because the porters feared losing their jobs, they at first hesitated to join a trade union like the BSCP. As the union grew, the Pullman Company was said to frame (contrive false evidence against), beat, and fire employees to discourage others from joining.

Randolph made several attempts to bring the Pullman Company to the bargaining table with the sleeping car porters but was unsuccessful. He even tried to organized a strike (a work stoppage to protest working conditions, such as low pay or excessive hours) in 1928. The strike never happened, however, because the porters were afraid that other blacks would be only too happy to step in and take their jobs. After the strike failed, the BSCP lost many members.

By the mid-1930s, with the passage of more favorable national labor laws, membership increased. A particular high point was when the American Federation of Labor (AFL) gave the BSCP an international charter in 1935. (Prior to this time, the AFL had refused to officially recognize the BSCP, probably because it was considered a black union.) And, after twelve years of negotiations, the Pullman Company finally signed a contract with the BSCP on August 25, 1937, agreeing to improved working conditions and some $2 million in pay for the porters.

After this success, Randolph and the BSCP fought for fair rights in other areas. When black workers found themselves locked out of new jobs in the defense industry during **World War II** (1939–45) because of racial discrimination, Randolph and the BSCP threatened to march on Washington with one hundred thousand blacks to demand defense jobs for blacks and integration (including members of all races as equals) of the armed forces. President Franklin D. Roosevelt's (1882–1945) administration created the Fair Employment Practices Committee (FEPC) in 1941 in exchange for cancellation of the march. The FEPC helped provide job training for many African Americans.

When the AFL merged with the Congress of Industrial Organizations (CIO) in 1955, Randolph became a vice president of the new union, and the

BSCP worked to get the AFL-CIO to give financial backing to civil rights activities in the 1950s and 1960s. The BSCP supported Randolph's marches on Washington for integrated schools in 1958 and 1959 and the March on Washington for Jobs and Freedom in 1963, the largest civil rights demonstration in U.S. history. Many organizers for the BSCP later had important roles in the **Civil Rights movement,** such as E. D. Nixon, who was a key figure in the **Montgomery bus boycott** of 1955–56 in Montgomery, Alabama.

As rail transportation declined and commercial airlines began carrying more passengers, the BSCP merged with the Brotherhood of Railway and Airline Clerks in 1978, leaving behind a legacy to organized labor and to future workers in the struggle for civil rights.

Brown, Claude

WRITER
February 23, 1937–

Claude Brown was born in the Harlem district of New York City. He had behavioral problems, and by the time he was ten he had a long history of skipping school and being expelled. Eventually, he was sent to the Warwick reform school. After his release he worked a series of odd jobs and enrolled in night courses. Brown earned his high school degree in 1957 and returned to Harlem, where he sold cosmetics and played piano for a living.

In 1959 Brown won a grant to study government at **Howard University,** which awarded him a bachelor of arts degree in 1965. While in his last year of college he published an article about growing up in Harlem that attracted the attention of an editor at Macmillan Publishing Company. The editor offered Brown an advance payment to write what would become his celebrated 1965 **autobiography,** *Manchild in the Promised Land.* The book was a piercing account of coming-of-age in stormy Harlem and was praised for its honesty in depicting a difficult childhood. The best-seller made Brown a celebrity, but his second book, *Children of Ham* (1976), about a group of Harlem youths struggling to succeed, failed to have the same impact.

Since the 1970s, Brown has worked as a freelance writer, commenting on the status of urban America. His articles have been published in such leading periodicals as the *New York Times,* the *Los Angeles Times,* and *Esquire.*

Brown, Hallie Quinn

EDUCATOR, ACTIVIST, WRITER
1850–1949

Educator and social activist Hallie Quinn Brown, a child of former slaves, was born in Pittsburgh, Pennsylvania. Her family later moved to

Ohio, where she received a bachelor of science degree from **Wilberforce University** in 1873. Her long teaching career included jobs at plantation schools during **Reconstruction** (the reestablishment of the Southern states after the American **Civil War**, 1861–65) and at the Tuskegee Institute (now **Tuskegee University**) in Tuskegee, Alabama.

During the 1890s Brown traveled extensively to do fund-raising for Wilberforce University. Her dramatic presentations on African-American **folklore** and black life made her a popular public speaker. She also addressed the 1895 world conference of the Women's Christian Temperance Union in London, England. On another trip to England, she met twice with Queen Victoria (1819–1901).

Brown founded the National Association of Colored Women, the first national club for black women. Supporting the successful presidential campaign of Warren G. Harding campaign in 1920, she served as national director of Colored Women's Activities and spoke at the Republican National Convention in Cleveland, Ohio.

Brown's books include *Bits and Odds: A Choice Selection of Recitations* (1920) and *Homespun Heroines and Other Women of Distinction* (1926).

Brown, Hubert G. "H. Rap"

WRITER, POLITICAL ACTIVIST
October 4, 1943–

Hubert "H. Rap" Brown is a civil rights leader who is fully committed to ensuring equal treatment for blacks. Known for his combative approach to fighting for racial justice, Brown is also the author of the harshly titled book *Die Nigger Die!* (1969), which deals with Brown's experiences with racism.

Born in Baton Rouge, Louisana, in 1943, Brown joined the **Civil Rights movement** in high school and continued as an activist at Southern University in Baton Rouge. In 1962 he joined the Nonviolent Action Group (NAG) and was soon elected chairman. Brown was also active in the **Black Panther Party for Self-Defense**. Wearing black leather jackets and influenced by **Malcolm X**, the Panthers were known for their violent stance against racism. According to Brown, violence is "as American as cherry pie."

In 1967 Brown was arrested for carrying a gun and was sentenced to five years in prison. Just before being sent to prison, however, Brown fled for his life when two of his friends were killed in a car explosion. He was caught by the Federal Bureau of Investigation (FBI) in 1972 and served four years in prison.

Brown later converted to **Islam** and changed his name to "Jamil Abdullah Al-Amin." He lives in Atlanta, Georgia, and has served as the *imam*, or leader, of the community mosque, which is the place of worship for Muslims, the followers of Islam. In May 2000 Brown was charged with murdering a police officer. Brown claims he is innocent and awaits trial.

Brown, James Joe Jr.

SINGER, SONGWRITER
May 3, 1933(?)–

James Brown: Selected Recordings

"Try Me"
(1958)

"Out of Sight"
(1964)

"I Feel Good (I Got You)"
(1965)

"Papa's Got a Brand New Bag"
(1965)

"Cold Sweat"
(1967)

"Say It Loud—I'm Black and I'm Proud"
(1968)

"Living in America"
(1986)

James Brown was born near Barnwell, South Carolina. His early life was marked by difficulty: his mother left the family when James was four, and Brown spent his early, impressionable years in a bordello run by his aunt in Augusta, Georgia. As a boy he received musical tutoring from neighbors, and he entered and won local talent contests while not yet in his teens. At thirteen, he formed his first musical group.

These early musical endeavors were cut short in 1949 when Brown landed in juvenile prison on theft charges. Paroled three years later, he formed a group that would soon become known as the Famous Flames. Their first single, "Please, Please, Please," was released in 1956 and climbed to number six on the **rhythm-and-blues** (R&B) charts.

In 1958, with the ballad "Try Me," Brown achieved the top position on the R&B charts and began to realize his own distinctive style. He became a tireless performer, playing as many as three hundred dates a year. He developed into one of pop music's most exciting live performers, capping his shows with a trademark "collapse-and-resurrection" routine. With the album *Live at the Apollo* (1963), Brown brought the excitement of his stage show to a worldwide audience and was propelled to international stardom.

Plagued by personal problems throughout much of the 1970s, Brown went into semi-retirement, although he never entirely stopped performing. In the early 1980s he staged a successful comeback, making brief appearances in motion pictures such as *The Blues Brothers* (1980) and returning to extensive recording and performing. In 1986 he became one of the first performers inducted into the Rock and Roll Hall of Fame.

In 1988 Brown was sentenced to six years in prison for failing to stop for a police officer and aggravated assault; he served two years. His legal troubles continued into the 1990s: in 1995 he was arrested for domestic violence (charges were later dropped), and in 1998 he was arrested on marijuana and gun possession charges.

Despite his personal troubles, Brown is one of the world's towering figures of popular music. He has influenced musicians performing in styles ranging from rock and **jazz** to dance pop, **reggae,** and hip-hop (music with elements of **rap** and **breakdancing**). Critics now generally recognize him as one of the most influential American musicians of the last half of the twentieth century. He continued to receive awards throughout the 1990s, including a 1993 star on Hollywood's Walk of Fame and a lifetime achievement award from the national Rhythm and Blues Foundation.

Brown, James Nathaniel "Jim"

FOOTBALL PLAYER, ACTOR
February 17, 1936–

According to some, Jim Brown was the greatest National Football League (NFL) fullback of all time. Brown was not just a tremendous **football** player, however; he was a tremendous all-around athlete.

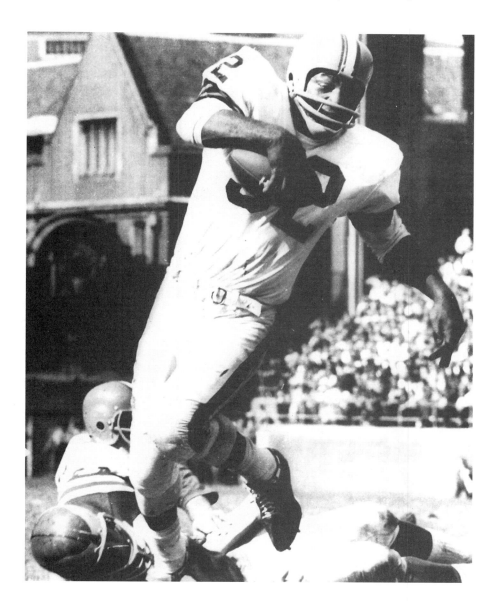

Football legend and actor Jim Brown when he played fullback for Cleveland (AP/Wide World Photos. Reproduced by permission)

Born in St. Simon's Island, Georgia, Brown moved to Long Island, New York. He excelled in every sport he played in high school and college, including football, basketball, baseball, boxing, track, and lacrosse. From 1954 to 1957 he attended Syracuse University (Syracuse, New York), where he scored a record 43 points in one football game. In 1957 Brown had offers to become a professional boxer, baseball player, basketball player, and football player. To the delight of football fans across the United States, he chose to play football for the Cleveland Browns.

Included among his career highlights are 12,312 career rushing yards, 126 touchdowns, and an average of 5.2 yards per carry (a record that still stands today). Every year he played, he was elected to the Pro Bowl, and he was voted to the Football Hall of Fame in 1971.

Brown was just as energetic after he retired from football. He began an acting career, starring in **film**s such as *The Dirty Dozen* (1967), *He Got Game* (1997), and *Any Given Sunday* (2000) and in the **television** shows *Chips* (1983) and *The A-Team* (1986).

Brown has also actively promoted the welfare of African Americans. He founded the Black Economic Union, which helps black business owners, and in the 1990s he established the Amer-I-Can program, which helps young blacks in Los Angeles, California, develop self-pride. Additional Amer-I-Can programs have been set up in other areas of California and in Chicago, Illinois. Perhaps his most stern statement against racism came in 1990 when he threatened to withdraw his name from the Football Hall of Fame because he believed that black players were not being recognized equally.

Brown's personal life, however, has been less inspiring than his life in football. He has appeared in court on several charges of domestic violence, and in early 2000 he faced prison time for failing to attend domestic violence counseling.

Brown, Joe "Old Bones"

BOXER
May 18, 1926–

Joe "Old Bones" Brown was a lightweight (127-135 pounds) boxer who, instead of punching hard, outsmarted his opponents with graceful footwork. He served in the U.S. Navy during **World War II** (1939–45), winning the all-service (all branches of the military service) title. Brown called himself "Old Bones" because he felt he was older and weaker than his opponents.

Brown worked his way into professional **boxing** and became the lightweight champion in 1955 when he beat Wallace "Bud" Smith, even though his hand was broken. Brown defended his title ten times, until he lost to Carlos Ortiz in 1962. He retired with an impressive 104 wins (47 knockouts) and 57 losses.

Brown, Sterling Allen

POET, SCHOLAR
May 1, 1901–January 13, 1989

Sterling A. Brown's poetry, teaching style, and personality captured the humor and resilience of the black folk tradition. He was born on the **Howard University** (Washington, D.C.) campus, where his father taught religion. Brown remained there most of his life and retired from his own teaching career there in 1969.

Brown graduated from Williams College (Massachusetts) in 1922 and went on to earn a master's degree in English from Harvard University (Cambridge, Massachusetts) the following year. Before returning to Howard in 1929, he taught for several years at a seminary and a number of universities in the United States.

Brown achieved a lasting reputation as a poet, scholar, and teacher. His most celebrated volume of poems was *Southern Road* (1932). Brown was different from such contemporary (living at the same time) poets as **Claude**

McKay (1889–1948) and **Countee Cullen** (1903–1946), who wrote sonnets imitating the English poets John Keats (1795–1821) and William Shakespeare (1564–1616). Brown preferred the folk-ballad form and used common black people as his subjects. Brown was influenced by the poet as A. E. Housman (1859–1936) as well as by African-American **folklore, blues,** and work songs. The characters of Brown's poems, such as Slim Greer, Scrappy, and Old Lem, are tough, worldly, and courageous. At once unsentimental and unapologetic, these characters embody the strength and forthrightness that were typical of all of Brown's work.

As a scholar, Brown is best remembered for two books: *The Negro in American Fiction* (1937) and *Negro Poetry and Drama* (1937). These works document the African-American influence in American literature from its beginnings to the 1930s. *The Negro in American Fiction* has been a foundation for all following studies of blacks in American fiction.

From 1936 through 1940 Brown served as national editor of Negro affairs for the Federal Writers' Project. He reviewed how African Americans were portrayed in the publications sponsored by the project. Although the task was frustrating, the appointment reflected how highly regarded Brown was. The 1930s were the most productive years of Brown's life.

Brown was a pioneer in the teaching of African-American literature, and many black writers, scholars, and political figures have studied with him. Outside the classroom, Brown held informal listening sessions, using his own massive record collection to introduce students to **jazz, the blues,** and other black musical forms. His power as a teacher came from his rare ability to combine the traditions of the United States with progressive political values and a blunt, down-to-earth personal style.

Brown's literary productivity decreased after the 1940s, partly due to repeated illnesses. He remained active as a guest lecturer and poetry reader and taught at several universities during his forty-year tenure at Howard. Brown died in Takoma Park, Maryland, on January 13, 1989.

Brown v. Board of Education of Topeka, Kansas

The most important legal case affecting African Americans in the twentieth century, and one of the most important Supreme Court decisions in U.S. constitutional history, was *Brown v. Board of Education of Topeka, Kansas*. Although the case addressed the issue of segregated public schools, it also became the legal basis for other controversies in the **Civil Rights movement** of the 1950s and 1960s.

In 1954 laws in eighteen states plus the District of Columbia required segregated school systems in which only whites attended white schools and only blacks attended black schools. Although supposedly guaranteeing blacks "separate but equal" education, black schools were never equal to those for whites. They were often in run-down buildings, and classrooms were overcrowded. Many black schools had no indoor plumbing or heating, and there was very little money for books and supplies. Bus service was rarely provided to black students who lived in the country.

THE COURT'S DECISION

Speaking on behalf of the Supreme Court, Chief Justice Earl Warren made public the Court's decision in the case *Brown v. Board of Education of Topeka, Kansas*. Warren found that "in the field of public education the doctrine of 'separate but equal' has no place. Separate education facilities are inherently unequal."

Linda Brown, whose father, Rev. Oliver Brown, sued the Topeka, Kansas, school system on her behalf, had to travel on the bus an hour and twenty minutes to school and an hour and twenty minutes back home. If her bus was on time, she was dropped off at school half an hour before it opened. Her bus stop was six blocks from her home, past a hazardous railroad yard; her school was twenty-one blocks from her home. The neighborhood school her white playmates attended was only seven blocks from her home and required neither bus nor hazardous crossings to reach.

Attorney **Thurgood Marshall** of the **National Association for the Advancement of Colored People (NAACP)** decided to challenge segregation in schools and took the *Brown* case to the highest court in the country, the Supreme Court. After reviewing the histories of the Fourteenth Amendment (which guarantees citizens equal protection under the law), public education, and segregation, the Supreme Court ruled that segregated schools were illegal.

Brown signaled the end to the legality of segregation. Within a dozen years the Supreme Court would strike down all forms of legalized segregation.

Brown, William Wells

NOVELIST, HISTORIAN
1814–1884

William Wells Brown was a writer of fiction and history whose writing reflected his experiences as a slave and as a free man. Brown escaped from **slavery** in 1834 and adopted the name of an Ohio farmer who helped him. Settling in Cleveland, Ohio, Brown helped numerous slaves escape to Canada. After moving to Buffalo, New York, he continued his participation in the **Underground Railroad** and spoke publicly on behalf of women's rights, peace, and antislavery activities.

In 1847 Brown moved to Boston, Massachusetts, where he published a successful book, *Narration of William W. Brown, a Fugitive Slave*. In 1949 he traveled to Europe to attend the Paris Peace Congress and to create support for American antislavery activities. There, he wrote the first African-American travel book and what is considered to be the first African-American novel, *Clotel: or The President's Daughter: A Narrative Slave Life in the United States*. Brown also published the first play by an African American, *The Escape; or, A Leap for Freedom*.

An African-American FIRST

William Wells Brown is considered the first black novelist. His novel *Clotel: or The President's Daughter: A Narrative Slave Life in the United States,* was published in England in 1853. He was also the first African American to write a travel book, called *Three Years in Europe* (1852), and the first to write a dramatic work, *Experience; or How to Give a Northern Man a Backbone* (1856).

Brown continued to write fictional and historical works for the rest of his life. He also worked as a physician in Boston, where he died in 1884.

Browne, Marjorie Lee

MATHEMATICIAN
September 9, 1914–October 19, 1979

Marjorie Lee Browne ((c)Patricia Kenschaft. Reproduced by permission)

One of the first African-American women to receive a Ph.D. degree in mathematics, Majorie Lee Browne grew up in Memphis, Tennessee. Her father, Lawrence J. Lee, a postal worker, was an avid reader and instilled in his daughter his excitement for learning and travel. She became obsessed with reading—especially the classics and mysteries—which helped her develop the analytic skills she would use as a mathematician and educator. Browne was also an excellent tennis player and won many women's singles championships in Memphis.

Browne graduated with honors from **Howard University** (Washington, D.C.) in 1935 and received master's (1939) and Ph.D. (1949) degrees in mathematics from the University of Michigan (Ann Arbor). She was appointed to the mathematics faculty at North Carolina Central University in Durham in 1949; her career there would span the next thirty years. Under her leadership as chairman of the mathematics department, the university achieved many firsts. In 1961 she received a $60,000 IBM (International Business Machines) educational grant to establish the first academic computer center at the university. In 1969 she received the first of seven Shell Foundation scholarship grants to be awarded to outstanding mathematics students. Browne was also a lecturer in thirteen National Science Foundation Institutes for science and math teachers from 1951 to 1971.

Browne specialized in topology (a branch of mathematics that deals with certain geometric aspects of spaces and shapes). She did research and studies in that field in several postdoctoral fellowship programs during the 1950s and 1960s, including stints at Cambridge University in England and Stanford University in California.

During the 1950s Browne fought for the integration of professional teaching and mathematics organizations, eventually joining the North Carolina Teachers Association, the Mathematical Association of America, and the American Mathematical Society.

Browne died in 1979. That year, four of her former students established a fund in her name to award an annual scholarship in mathematics. In 1981 she was one of six African-American women included in the Smithsonian Institution's traveling exhibition "Black Women: Achievements Against the Odds."

Brownsville, Texas, Incident

On the night of August 13, 1906, a shooting spree occurred in Brownsville, Texas, leaving one man dead and two others wounded. Sixteen days earlier, three African-American companies of the First Battalion of the U.S. 25th Infantry, Colored, had arrived and were stationed at Fort Brown, just outside town. The white citizens of Brownsville believed the black soldiers were guilty of the crime, even though the soldiers and their white officers denied any involvement in the shooting. The investigation that followed sparked controversy throughout the United States.

Because the shooting might have involved members of the U.S. Army, President Theodore Roosevelt (1858–1919) called for an investigation. The inspector assigned to the case reported that some of the soldiers were guilty but their white officers were not responsible. He recommended that all of the black soldiers be discharged from the army because he believed some of the soldiers knew who did the shooting but would not tell.

After a second investigation, during which the soldiers continued to say they were innocent, all were given "dishonorable discharges" from the U.S. Army, because none would point a finger at the supposedly guilty parties. The soldiers who could prove they were innocent were allowed to reenlist in the army; fourteen of them did.

When an interracial civil rights organization, the Constitution League, reported to the U.S. Congress that evidence showed the soldiers were innocent, Senate hearings were held and the Brownsville incident became a national concern.

In March 1910 three Senate committees issued reports. The first found that some of the soldiers did the shooting but it was uncertain which ones. The second found there was no evidence to press charges against any particular soldier and no reason for discharging them all. The third committee found that most of the testimony proved that none of the soldiers participated in the shooting.

After these findings, Senator Joseph Benson Foraker of Ohio made a political issue of the Brownsville incident in his campaign against Theodore Roosevelt for the 1908 presidential nomination. Foraker charged that Roosevelt had allowed a decision based on flimsy evidence to stand. Although Foraker lost the nomination, the Brownsville incident had become an important racial issue.

The incident widened a split that had first occurred in 1905 among two African-American groups. One group followed black educator **Booker T. Washington**'s (1856–1915) philosophy that blacks should accept segregation and work to improve their conditions through education and job training. The other group, members of the new **Niagara movement** (established 1905; the forerunner of the **National Association for the Advancement of Colored People**) believed blacks should press for civil rights on the basis that segregation and racism were unacceptable. Although Washington had privately tried to stop Roosevelt from discharging the soldiers of the 25th Infantry, he was unwilling to criticize Roosevelt publicly. Because of this, many of Washington's supporters deserted him and joined the Niagara movement.

The soldiers charged in the Brownsville incident were never proved guilty, although they remained dishonorably discharged until 1973, when they were granted honorary discharges. By that time, however, only one of the soldiers was still alive.

Bryant, Hazel

SINGER, ACTRESS, PRODUCER
September 8, 1939–November 7, 1983

Hazel Bryant was a classically trained singer who became a multitalented theater producer. Bryant received her early musical training in church choirs and went on to study music at the Oberlin Conservatory of Music (Oberlin, Ohio), where she earned her bachelor of arts degree in 1962.

Bryant moved to New York City, where in 1968 she began the Afro-American Total Theater. The theater was dedicated to supporting blacks in every aspect of the arts, from theater to film to music. During her career Bryant acted, wrote, directed, and produced for her own company as well as other organizations. In 1971 she was the subject of a short film entitled *Hazel, Hazel, Hazel, Hazel, Hazel*. Bryant died in 1983 of heart failure.

Bubbles, John

TAP DANCER
February 19, 1902–May 18, 1986

Known as "the father of rhythm tap," John Bubbles was born John William Sublett in Louisville, Kentucky. At the age of ten he and Ford Lee Washington (1906–1955) teamed up as "Buck and Bubbles." Bubbles sang and danced while Buck played piano accompaniment. After winning a series of amateur-night shows, they began performing in Louisville, Detroit, Michigan, and New York City.

Bubbles developed his own style of tapping, featuring a difficult technique called "double over-the-tops" that looks like self-tripping. Bubbles complicated it further by traveling backward and forward and from side to side. His other innovations were slowing the tempo, adding complex rhythms, and tapping with his heels and toes, rather than dancing on his toes.

By 1922 the team was playing the biggest vaudeville (traveling stage shows popular from the late 1800s to 1920s and featuring a variety of songs, dances, acrobatics, magic acts, and skits) theaters. Bypassing black-owned theaters, they headlined shows for white audiences across the country. During the 1930s Buck and Bubbles became the first black performers to appear in many theaters, including Radio City Music Hall in New York.

Some of the team's most notable appearances were in the Broadway Frolics of 1922, Lew Leslie's Blackbirds of 1930, and the Ziegfeld Follies of 1931. In 1935 Bubbles created the acting, singing, and dancing role of Sportin' Life in composer George Gershwin's (1898–1937) **opera** *Porgy and Bess*.

After Buck's death in 1955, Bubbles appeared with comedian Bob Hope (1903–), entertaining military personnel in Vietnam during the Vietnam War (1959–75). He also recorded albums, including *From Rags to Riches* (1980). Bubbles was partly paralyzed by a stroke in 1967. He made one of his last public appearances as a singer in *Black Broadway*.

Bullins, Ed

PLAYWRIGHT
July 2, 1935–

Born in Philadelphia, Pennsylvania, Ed Bullins is one of the most influential and productive of African-American dramatists, with more than fifty plays to his credit. His plays focus on ordinary African-American life, the sorrows and frustrations of black ghetto life, and race relations.

From 1952 to 1955 Bullins served in the U.S. Navy. He received a bachelor of arts degree from Antioch University in San Francisco, California, in 1989 and did graduate work at San Francisco State University.

During the 1960s Bullins was one of the leaders of the **Black Arts movement.** In the mid-1960s he was a founder and producer of Black Arts/West, an African-American theater group in San Francisco. He also cofounded the Black Arts Alliance and Black House, a militant (combative) cultural-political organization.

Working at the New Lafayette Theatre in Harlem, New York, from 1968 to 1973, Bullins was playwright-in-residence and, later, associate director. He also edited *Black Theatre* magazine. He worked for the New York Shakespeare Festival from 1975 until the early 1980s and then relocated to San Francisco to teach and write.

Audiences, critics, and publishers have praised Bullins's plays, for which he earned Obie Awards for distinguished playwriting in 1971 and 1975. *The Taking of Miss Janie* (1975), one of his best-known plays, received the Drama Critics Circle Award as the best American play of 1974-75.

Bullins has also written two children's plays, *I Am Lucy Terry* and *The Mystery of Phillis Wheatley*, both produced in 1976. In 1997 a new play by Bullins, *Boy × Man* ("boy times man"), was presented by the Negro Ensemble Company in New York. Bullins has taught at several colleges and universities, including New York University and the University of California at Berkeley.

Playwright Ed Bullins (AP/Wide World Photos. Reproduced by permission)

Bumbry, Grace Ann

OPERA SINGER
January 4, 1937–

Born in St. Louis, Missouri, Grace Bumbry has performed at all of the major **opera** houses of the world. She displayed her musical talents at an early age and at seventeen won first prize in a radio-sponsored contest, a $1,000 scholarship to the St. Louis Institute. She could not attend, however, because the institute did not admit blacks. Soon after, she won a talent contest and an appearance on the *Arthur Godfrey* television show.

Bumbry attended Boston University in Massachusetts and Northwestern University in Illinois in the mid-1950s. From 1956 to 1959 she studied at the Music Academy of the West in Santa Barbara, California.

In 1961 Bumbry became the first African American to sing at the Bayreuth (Germany) Festival, devoted to the operas of German composer Richard Wagner. In 1965 she made her debut at the New York Metropolitan Opera (the Met) as Princess Eboli in *Don Carlos* (1867), by Italian composer Giuseppe Verdi.

Possessing a rich and highly expressive voice, Bumbry has sung many leading roles. At the Met in 1985, she sang the role of Bess in American composer George Gershwin's famous folk opera *Porgy and Bess* (1935). She has appeared on numerous recordings, including a 1996 tribute to the legendary James Levine celebrating his twenty-fifth year as conductor of the Met.

Bunche, Ralph Johnson

SCHOLAR, DIPLOMAT, INTERNATIONAL CIVIL SERVANT
1904–1971

Ralph Johnson Bunche was a scholar, diplomat, and international civil servant whose negotiating abilities earned him the Nobel Peace Prize in

Ralph Bunche (AP/Wide World Photos. Reproduced by permission)

1950. He was the first African American and the first United Nations (UN) figure to win the prestigious prize. Bunche was also the author of one of the most widely respected books ever written on race relations in the United States, *An American Dilemma: The Negro Problem and Modern Democracy* (1944).

Born in Detroit, Michigan, Bunche moved to New Mexico after his mother's death in 1917. He graduated first in his class in both high school and at the University of California at Los Angeles (UCLA; 1927). His hard work earned him a scholarship to Harvard University (Cambridge, Massachusetts), where he earned a master's degree in 1928. After teaching at **Howard University** (Washington, D.C.), Bunche returned to Harvard to become the first black to earn a Ph.D. degree in political science.

Bunche believed that the major problems facing blacks in the United States were economic, with race playing a secondary role. He believed that encouraging working-class economic improvement would be the best way for blacks to achieve progress. In an effort to bring together black leaders and white–collar workers with black laborers, Bunche and others formed the National Negro Congress. It was soon taken over by Communists, however, and Bunche resigned.

In 1945 Bunche became the first black to head a State Department "desk" (a division specializing in a particular activity), the Division of Dependent Area Affairs (dealing with the affairs of colonial territories and determining their future following the end of **World War II** in 1945).

Bunche went to work for the UN in 1946. In 1947 he was assigned to the UN Special Commission on Palestine shortly before the First Arab–Israeli War in 1948. For his efforts in resolving the war, Bunche received the 1950 Nobel Peace Prize.

Although U.S. President Harry Truman (1884–1972) offered to make him assistant secretary of state in 1950, Bunche decided to remain at the United Nations in New York, citing as his reason racism and segregation in Washington, D.C. He worked at the UN and was actively involved in the **Civil Rights movement** until his death in 1971.

Burnett, Charles

FILMMAKER
April 13, 1944–

In his **film**s Charles Burnett depicts African-American culture and experience. Many of his films focus on the tensions and frustrations of urban black families, especially relationships between fathers and sons and between brothers. A major concern of storytelling, says Burnett, should be restoring values.

Born in Vicksburg, Mississippi, Burnett moved with his family to Los Angeles, California, during **World War II** (1939-45). He received a bachelor's degree in theater arts from the University of California at Los Angeles (UCLA), where he made his first **film,** *Several Friends* (1969), about a group of young African-American men who are unable to see or understand that

something has gone wrong in their lives. Burnett also completed a master's degree at UCLA. As a graduate student in 1977, he made a fourteen-minute film, *The Horse*, about a boy who has to witness the death of an old horse. It won first prize at a film competition in West Germany.

Killer of Sheep (1977), Burnett's first feature film, received critical acclaim and appeared in many independent film festivals (programs showing movies by persons not working for major Hollywood studios). In 1990 it was selected for the National Film Registry at the U.S. Library of Congress as one of twenty-five "culturally and historically significant American films."

In 1980 Burnett received a Guggenheim Fellowship (a grant of money from the Guggenheim Foundation for a period of six months to one year that allows recipients to concentrate on their creative work without having to worry about a steady source of income) to work on *My Brother's Wedding*. In 1988 he received a John D. and Catherine T. MacArthur Foundation Award, given to highly talented and exceptionally creative individuals in a wide range of endeavors. The award funded a production company and professional actors (including Danny Glover) for *To Sleep with Anger*, Burnett's most critically acclaimed work. The film earned a special jury prize at the 1990 Sundance Film Festival, a leading film festival founded by actor Robert Redford in Utah, which premieres new and independent American films.

Burnett's film *The Glass Shield*, which depicts the troubles of the first black cop in an all-white police squad, opened to enthusiastic reviews in 1995. In 1998 Burnett directed *The Wedding*, adapted from a novel, and in 1999 directed the romantic comedy-drama *The Annihilation of Fish*.

Butler, Octavia Estelle

NOVELIST, SHORT STORY WRITER
June 22, 1947–

Octavia Butler is one of only a few African-American **science fiction** writers. The only surviving child of Laurice and Octavia M. Guy Butler, she was raised in a racially and culturally diverse neighborhood of Pasadena, California. Dyslexic (a learning disorder that involves reading and language), extremely shy, and therefore solitary, Butler began writing as a child, convinced she could write better science fiction stories than those she saw on television.

Butler has been respected by the science fiction community of writers, critics, and fans as an important author ever since her first books earned excellent reviews. Her first published novel, *Patternmaster* (1976), is one of five books in her *Patternist* saga (a long, detailed story). The books present interrelated stories reaching from the time shortly before **Africa** was colonized by European countries to a distant future after Earth has undergone major destruction.

In each of these novels, Butler introduces issues of race and gender to science fiction. Her female characters are African, African-American, or mixed-race women who are powerful and capable. Butler's *Xenogenesis* series (beginning with *Dawn* in 1987 and ending with *Imago* in 1989) continues an examination of women in differing roles as it explores issues of human survival in another grim future after major devastation of Earth. In 2000 the *Xenogenesis* series was published in a single volume titled *Lilith's Brood.* Her most recent series, *The Parable of the Sower,* is a frighteningly believable tale set in a ruined civilization.

Although she is primarily a novelist, Butler's short stories have won two coveted science fiction awards. "Speech Sounds" (1983) received a Hugo Award; "Bloodchild" (1984) earned both a Hugo and a Nebula Award. Her most prestigious award, however, came in 1995, when her body of work earned Butler a $250,000 MacArthur Fellowship.

Butts, Calvin O. I. III

MINISTER
July 22, 1949–

Calvin Butts, the son of a restaurant chef and a welfare services administrator, was born in New York City. He was class president in high school in 1967 and graduated from **Morehouse College** in Atlanta, Georgia, in 1971. While studying at Union Theological Seminary in New York in 1972, he became assistant pastor of the four-thousand-member Abyssinian Baptist Church, the largest and most prestigious church in the city's Harlem district.

During the 1970s and 1980s Butts earned a reputation as a community leader and activist. He was head of Harlem's Young Men's Christian Association (YMCA) branch, toured neighborhood schools to report on education, condemned police brutality, and, in 1988, joined a march to protest the shooting of an African-American teenager. He also created controversy with his attacks on liquor and tobacco billboard advertisements in black communities and his attacks on New York's political leaders, both white and black.

In 1989 Butts became the chief pastor of Abyssinian. During the following years he devoted more time to managing the church's finances, assisting with employment and welfare programs, and attracting economic investment in the community. Butts remained an activist, however, continuing his campaigns against alcohol and cigarette advertising and gambling. In 1993 he began a well-publicized crusade against **rap** music, which he denounced as violent and indecent. (*See also* **Baptists.**)

Caesar, Adolph

ACTOR
1934–March 6, 1986

Adolph Caesar was a twentieth-century actor well known for playing strong characters in both plays and movies. In 1970 Caesar got his start in theater when he joined the Negro Ensemble Company in New York City. He also performed with many other theater groups, including the New York

Shakespeare Festival and the Lincoln Center Repertory Company. Caesar worked as an announcer for television and radio commercials, as well as a narrator for the Public Broadcasting Service (PBS) series *Men of Bronze* (1977) and *I Remember Harlem* (1981).

Caesar came to public attention in 1981 with his strong performance in the Pulitzer Prize-winning drama *A Soldier's Play*. His portrayal of Sergeant Vernon C. Waters, an abusive officer in the U.S. Army's segregated forces during **World War II** (1939–45), earned him several awards. He also played Sergeant Waters in *A Soldier's Story*, the 1984 film version of the play, and was nominated for an Oscar as best supporting actor that year. In 1986 Caesar suffered a fatal heart attack while filming the movie *Tough Guys*.

Caesar, Shirley

GOSPEL SINGER
October 13, 1938–

The winner of ten Grammy Awards (the record industry' most prestigious prize), Shirley Caesar was born in Durham, North Carolina. Inspired by her father, "Big Jim" Caesar of the Just Come Four **gospel music** quartet (a group of four), "Baby Shirley" made her first recording, "I'd Rather Have Jesus," in 1951.

In 1958 Caesar became nationally known as a soloist with the Caravan Singers. She was using the "sanctified" style of gospel singing that uses fast tempos and extensive improvisation (making up the music as one performs it, rather than following a "script"). In 1966 Caesar formed the Caesar Singers and adopted a less energetic and flashy approach, called the "song and sermonette" style.

In addition to performing and recording, Caesar has had several other careers. She received a bachelor of science degree in business education from Shaw University (Raleigh, North Carolina) and served on the Durham City Council (1987–91). She then became pastor of the Mt. Calvary Word of Faith Church in Raleigh, as well as president of Shirley Caesar Outreach Ministries, an emergency social services organization. In 1998 Caesar published her **autobiography**, *The Lady, the Melody & the Word*.

Shirley Caesar: Selected Recordings

"I've Been Running for Jesus a Long Time, and I'm Not Tired Yet"
(1958)

"Hallelujah, It's Done"
(1961)

"I Won't Be Back"
(1962)

"Don't Drive Your Mama Away"
(1969)

"No Charge"
(1978)

"Faded Roses"
(1980)

"Martin"
(1985)
Stand Still (1993)

Shirley Caesar Live ... He Will Come
(1995)

Christmas With Shirley Caesar
(1999)

California

First African-American Settlers: Some blacks arrived in California when it was under Spanish and, later, Mexican control (mid-1500s to mid-1800s), and most were integrated into Spanish-speaking society. Significant numbers of African Americans migrated there during the California gold rush, which began in 1849.

Free Black Population: California became a state in 1850. By 1860, 4,000 African Americans resided in the state. Some of those who had arrived during the gold rush were slaves, but the majority of California's blacks were free. When, in the mid-1800s, the state refused to allow African Americans the right to vote or testify in court, black leaders formed the Franchise League, California's first black civil rights organization.

The Great Depression: The Great Migration, during which tens of thousands of African Americans looking for jobs migrated to California in the 1910s and 1920s, continued into the 1930s despite the depression. By 1940 nearly 125,000 African Americans called California home. Most found low-paying jobs in the service sector as cooks, janitors, or unskilled laborers. During and after **World War II** (1939–45), defense-related industry lured nearly 250,000 African Americans to the state.

Civil Rights Movement: Although their increasing population gained them greater political representation, black Californians continued to experience discrimination and often complained of police brutality. In 1965 a riot was sparked in Los Angeles that led to increased attempts at integration. The **Black Panther Party for Self-Defense,** which had its roots in Oakland, California, argued that integration was futile. The Panthers provided important social services such as child care for residents of the ghettos in Oakland and San Francisco.

Current African-American Population: According to U.S. Census Bureau estimates, the total black population in California was 2,455,570 (7.5 percent of the state population) as of July 1, 1998.

Key Figures: Tom Bradley (1917–1998), five-term mayor of Los Angeles; **Wilson Riles** (1917–1999), former state superintendent of public instruction; **Willie Brown** (1934–), speaker of the state assembly.

(SEE ALSO **WEST, BLACKS IN THE.**)

Calloway, Cabell "Cab"

JAZZ SINGER, BANDLEADER
December 25, 1907–November 18, 1994

With a show business career spanning more than sixty years, **jazz** singer and bandleader Cab Calloway was one of the twentieth century's most popular performers. Born in Rochester, New York, Calloway grew up in Baltimore, Maryland. In high school he sang with a vocal group called the Baltimore Melody Boys.

The Calloway family later moved to Chicago, Illinois, where young Calloway attended Crane College. He began his career as a singer, drummer, and master of ceremonies at nightclubs in Chicago and other midwestern cities. In the late 1920s Calloway became bandleader of the Alabamians, and in 1929 the band played at Harlem, New York's famed **Savoy Ballroom.**

During the 1930s Calloway became a household name, renowned for his infectious vocal dramatics, his frenzied dashing up and down the stage in a white satin suit, and his inspirational leading of audience sing-a-longs. His biggest hit, "Minnie the Moocher" (1931), with its "Hi-de-ho" chorus, was a million-copy seller and earned him the nickname "Hi-de-ho Man."

Calloway's band was one of the most popular in the country, with such hits as "At the Clambake Carnival" (1938), "Jumpin' Jive" (1939), and "Pickin' the Cabbage" (1940). Calloway also nurtured some of the best instrumentalists of the day, including saxophonist **Chuck Berry**, trumpeter **Dizzy Gillespie**, bassist **Milt Hinton**, and drummer **Cozy Cole**. In addition to its success in nightclubs and on the concert stage, the Calloway orchestra also appeared in movies, including *The Big Broadcast* (1932), *St. Louis Blues* (1939), and *Stormy Weather* (1943).

Throughout the 1950s and 1960s Calloway continued to perform both as the leader of big bands and as a solo act. In the mid-1960s he toured with the **Harlem Globetrotters** comic basketball team as the halftime performer. In 1974 Calloway appeared in an all-black version of *Hello, Dolly!* and two years later he published his **autobiography**, *Of "Minnie the Moocher" and Me*. Calloway appeared on Broadway in *Bubbling Brown Sugar* in 1975, and his role in the 1980 film *The Blues Brothers* brought him many new fans.

In 1980 Calloway received the **Ebony** Lifetime Achievement Award for his outstanding career, and President Bill Clinton presented him with the National Medal of Arts in 1992.

Cambridge, Godfrey MacArthur

ACTOR
February 26, 1933–November 29, 1976

Godfrey Cambridge was an actor and **comedian** who refused to be limited to the usual black roles. Cambridge grew up in New York City and became such an excellent student he won a scholarship to Hofstra University (Long Island, New York). After racial threats forced him to leave Hofstra, Cambridge transferred to City College in New York in his junior year. Upon graduating, he worked a variety of jobs, including airplane wing cleaner, judo instructor, and cab driver.

In 1956 Cambridge landed his first professional role, as a bartender in the play *Take a Giant Step.* The play ran for nine months and led to many television appearances. In 1961 Cambridge appeared in French writer Jean Genet's play *The Blacks*, a savage **drama** about racial hatred. For his performance the *Village Voice* newspaper in New York's Greenwich Village gave him its OBIE Award for best performer of 1961. Cambridge went on to perform in *A Funny Thing Happened on the Way to the Forum* (1962), *The Living Promise* (1963), and *How to Be a Jewish Mother* (1967), in which he played every part but the title role.

Cambridge was able to choose his roles carefully, and he turned down **film** parts that he thought would typecast him, or have him play the same type of character over and over. Instead he played a wide variety of movie characters, including an Irishman in *Troublemaker* (1964), a Jewish cab driver in *Bye, Bye Braverman* (1968), and a concert violinist in *The Biggest Bundle of Them All* (1968). Cambridge is probably best known for his leading roles in the popular films *Watermelon Man* (1970) and *Cotton Comes to Harlem* (1970).

In addition to his film appearances, Cambridge was a successful stand-up comedian. His sense of humor, while not offensive to white audiences, did not lack bite. His comedy often dealt with ordinary people, black and white, struggling with the problems of everyday life. During the **Civil Rights movement,** Cambridge performed at rallies and organized support for the employment of more African Americans in the entertainment industry. In 1976 Cambridge collapsed and died on the set of the television movie *Victory at Entebbe*, in which he played the Ugandan dictator Idi Amin.

Campanella, Roy

BASEBALL PLAYER
November 19, 1921–June 26, 1993

In 1948 Roy Campanella became the first African American to play catcher in major league **baseball.** Campanella, who had an Italian father and a black mother, was born in Philadelphia, Pennsylvania. At the age of sixteen he was already showing signs of greatness. He played in the Negro National League for a while before signing a contract with the Los Angeles Dodgers. Campanella broke into the big leagues with style, winning three Most Valuable Player awards and setting batting records. In 1957 a car crash

Roy Campanella when he was catcher for
the Brooklyn Dodgers (AP/Wide World
Photos. Reproduced by permission)

brought Campanella's career to an end. Being the fighter that he was, however, he came back from the injury to help out with his community and teach for the Dodgers. In 1969 he was voted to the Baseball Hall of Fame.

Canada

Canada, like the northern United States, became a refuge for African Americans seeking freedom from **slavery** in the American South during the 1700s and 1800s. Hoping for a chance to prosper and enjoy equal rights with whites, many blacks immigrated (moved) to Canada, only to find much of the same segregation and discrimination there that they faced in northern U.S. cities. As in the United States, all-black settlements were established in Canada, but most eventually failed. Although many black Canadians gained a good education and enjoyed successful careers and even international fame during the twentieth century, racism and interracial violence persisted in Canadian cities into the late 1990s.

Slavery and Abolition in Canada

The territories of British North America, which were united into Canada in 1867, had a long history of slavery before the British Parliament abolished slavery everywhere in the British Empire in 1833. Early French settlers had African household slaves as early as 1629. The number of slaves increased after 1763, when the British took over French possessions on mainland North America and made the slave system legal.

In 1793, however, about the same time that the United States passed the first Fugitive Slave Law, making it legal to capture runaway slaves in northern states, the Upper Canada (later Ontario) Abolition Act freed young slaves at age twenty-five and banned further enslavement. This ban on slavery soon spread to Lower Canada (later Quebec), and Britain's **abolition** decree of 1833 included all of Canada.

Early Migrations from the United States

Blacks in the United States began to migrate to British North America (Canada) in 1783. The first immigrants were a group of African Americans who fought for the British in the American Revolution (1775–83). When the Americans won the war, these black Loyalists were granted land and freedom in Nova Scotia and New Brunswick. Although free, they were considered just a step above slaves by local whites. They earned low wages and had difficulty supporting themselves.

The second wave of blacks to settle in Canada was made up of refugees who had served with the British forces during the War of 1812 (1812–15) between Great Britain and the United States. Many were forced to live in poor, segregated sections, where they farmed small plots of land. Because they were so poor, some sold themselves back into slavery. In 1820 many families left Nova Scotia for the Caribbean island of Trinidad, where they were welcomed. The rest remained, and some, like William Hall, who won the Victoria Cross for service in the British military, became British patriots.

Canada Bound on the Underground Railroad

After 1840 Canada became the main destination of black slaves fleeing the United States via the **Underground Railroad**, a secret network that helped **fugitive slaves** reach sanctuary in the free states or in Canada). Canada refused to send fugitive slaves back to their U.S. owners, and about thirty thousand slaves escaped from 1830 to 1860. About ten thousand free-born African Americans also immigrated to Canada during this period. Most settled in Upper Canada, known as Canada West, near Toronto, Niagara, and St. Catherine's, close to the American border.

Before the American **Civil War** (1861–65), blacks chose to immigrate to Canada, which was close to home and to relatives in the United States, rather than to the African colony of Liberia, established by American abolitionists. The passage of the U.S. **Fugitive Slave** Act of 1850, which made it easier to have runaway slaves returned, spurred new interest in mass settlement in Canada. Former slave **Henry Bibb** (1815–1854) and other abolitionists organized efforts for immigration to Canada. Bibb's newspaper, *The Voice of the Fugitive*, first published in 1851, became the first black Canadian newspaper. Black abolitionist **Harriet Tubman** (c. 1820–1913) settled in St. Catherine's and set up the interracial Refugee Slaves' Friends Society. Other black leaders, such as **Frederick Douglass** (1817–1895), opposed emigration, saying African Americans should stay and work to improve conditions at home.

Hard Times for Blacks in Canada

Loyal Canadian blacks called Canada "the North Star." Many blacks enjoyed legal equality and voting rights in Canada, but most faced harsh difficulties. Canadian whites opposed slavery but many also opposed large-scale black settlement, and segregation was widespread, often leading to racial violence. In 1850 Canada West passed the Common School Act, which permitted separate schools or classrooms for blacks and whites. Most white Canadians never accepted blacks as true Canadians, and many black refugees moved back to the United States after the passage, in 1865, of the Thirteenth Amendment to the Constitution, banning slavery in the United States.

When a new wave of black immigration began in the early 1900s, Canadian whites pressed the government to ban further migration. Canadian railway agents and border officials were told to use various methods to slow immigration, and black migration to Canada soon stopped, without official action by the Canadian government.

During the twentieth century, blacks were treated about the same in Canada as they were in the northern United States. Segregation and housing discrimination were widespread, especially in cities, often forcing blacks to live in ghetto areas like those in American cities. Both private and government employers practiced job discrimination against blacks.

Improvements in the Twentieth Century

Life improved for Canadian blacks during the second half of the twentieth century. After protests by civil rights groups, court decisions and legis-

BLACK SETTLEMENTS IN CANADA

From 1830 to 1860 blacks and whites who wanted to help fugitive slaves become established in free society set up several black settlements in Canada. The most famous was Wilberforce, established for a group of free blacks who left Cincinnati, Ohio, in 1829 after the city decided to enforce Ohio's racial restrictions. City officials ordered black residents to pay a $500 tax within thirty days or leave the city. Members of the Quakers, a religious group, gave two black leaders, Israel Lewis and Thomas Cresap, money to purchase land on Lake Huron in Canada, but Canadian whites did not want blacks to settle there. When Cincinnati blacks learned this, Lewis and Cresap could persuade only two hundred to join the Canadian settlement. It was unsuccessful and disbanded in 1836.

Another settlement was Dawn, which was part of a project to teach fugitive slaves skills for surviving in Canada's cold, harsh environment. White abolitionists and missionaries provided funds to establish the British-American Institute, a training school and sawmill, in Chatham, Canada, in 1843. The surrounding black settlement was named Dawn for the settlers' hopes for the future. In the years that followed, more than five hundrfed blacks came to the settlement, but by 1849 Dawn's funding was running out. The settlement closed during the 1850s, and the institute closed in 1868.

lation slowed discrimination in housing and employment. In 1960 a federal bill of rights was passed that outlawed racial discrimination.

By 1980 people of African descent—about 3 percent of Canada's population in 1990—averaged a higher education level than whites in most provinces. But as blacks gained more rights during the 1970s through the 1990s, white supremacist groups like the **Ku Klux Klan** became more active. Police shootings of blacks in Canadian cities resulted in mass protests and racial violence.

Cardozo, Francis Louis

MINISTER, EDUCATOR, POLITICIAN
February 1, 1837–July 22, 1903

Francis L. Cardozo was born in Charleston, South Carolina, in 1837. His father was a prominent Jewish businessman; his mother was a **free black** woman. Cardozo attended a free Negro school until he was twelve, when he was apprenticed to a carpenter. He worked as a carpenter until he was twenty-one, when he went to Great Britain to study for the ministry.

Cardozo became a Congregational minister in 1864. After the **Civil War** (1861–65), he returned to Charleston with the American Missionary Association. The South now offered a large missionary field for black ministers who wanted to work with freedmen.

In 1866 Cardozo helped establish the Avery Normal Institute in Charleston, becoming its first superintendent. Avery trained black teachers, and in the post–Civil War South the school played an important role in the education of blacks.

Reconstruction, the political reorganization of the Southern states after the Civil War, drew Cardozo into politics. He served as South Carolina's secretary of state from 1868 to 1872 and was the first black in South Carolina's history to hold government office. He was state treasurer from 1872 to 1877. Among the black preacher-politicians of Reconstruction, Cardozo was fairly moderate. For example, he did not urge freedmen to seize their former masters' land, as Tunis G. Campbell did in Georgia. When the Reconstruction government of South Carolina was overthrown in 1877, Cardozo moved to Washington, D.C., where he became a member of the city's black elite. He died there in 1903.

Cary, Mary Ann Shadd

ABOLITIONIST EDITOR, EDUCATOR, ATTORNEY
1823–1893

Mary Ann Shadd Cary was born in Wilmington, Delaware, to free parents who were active in the abolitionist movement. She became the first African-American woman in North America to edit a newspaper and the first to practice law in the United States. Throughout her career she advocated that through education, thrift, and hard work black people could successfully achieve integration.

Quaker educated, Cary began a school for African Americans in Delaware and taught in neighboring states. She wrote for **Frederick Douglass**'s *North Star* and published *Hints to Colored People of the North*, a pamphlet on black self-reliance. In 1851, while attending a lecture in Canada on the recently implemented Fugitive Slave Act, Cary met **Henry Bibb,** publisher of the abolitionist paper *Voice of the Fugitive*. Bibb convinced her to teach **fugitive slaves** in Canada West (Ontario) yet opposed her strong stance in favor of integration.

Cary taught in Canada in the 1850s while editing her newspaper, *The Provincial Freeman*, but struggled financially to keep the paper in publication. With the outbreak of the **Civil War** (1861–65), she returned to the United States and served as a recruitment officer for black volunteers in the Union army. After the war she settled in Washington, D.C., where she worked as a teacher and principal. At the age of forty-one she became the first woman to attend **Howard University** Law School. She completed her studies in 1871, but the university refused to grant her law degree until 1881, believing that a woman's graduation would attract negative publicity.

After addressing the National Women's Suffrage Association in 1878, Cary spent the remaining years of her life concentrating her efforts on advancing the struggle for women's right to vote. She maintained an active schedule until her seventieth year, when she was stricken with rheumatism followed by terminal cancer in the summer of 1893.

Activist Stokely Carmichael speaking at a rally (AP/Wide World Photos. Reproduced by permission)

Carmichael, Stokely

ACTIVIST
July 29, 1941–November 15, 1998

Stokely Carmichael was an outspoken activist for black rights. Born in Port of Spain, Trinidad, in the West Indies off the northeastern coast of Venezuela, Stokely Carmichael graduated from **Howard University** (Washington, D.C.) in 1964. During his college years he participated in a variety of civil rights demonstrations sponsored by the **Congress of Racial Equality (CORE)**, the Nonviolent Action Group (NAG), and the **Student Nonviolent Coordinating Committee (SNCC)**. As a participant in **freedom rides,** he was arrested in 1961 for violating Mississippi segregation laws and spent seven weeks in jail. After college he directed SNCC voter registration efforts and helped organize black voters.

Elected SNCC chairman in 1966, Carmichael supported radical ideas that distanced the SNCC from the moderate leadership of other civil rights organizations. A chief spokesperson for Black Power, which was a movement for blacks to take pride in their culture, Carmichael coauthored *Black Power* (1967) and published a collection of his essays and addresses, *Stokely Speaks* (1971). In 1968 he was made prime minister of the **Black Panther Party**; in 1969 he quit the Panthers and became an organizer for the All-African People's Revolutionary Party. In 1978 he changed his name to Kwame Toure. For the last thirty years of his life, he made the West African port town of Conakry, Guinea, his home, and he continued working in political education and promoting the goal of a unified socialist **Africa**. He died of prostate cancer in 1998.

Carpetbaggers

The period following the American **Civil War** (1861–65) was known as **Reconstruction** because Northern and Southern states struggled to "reconstruct" or reunite the Union (the United States), which had been torn apart by war. During this period of rebuilding, a number of individuals from the North moved to the South. These individuals were known as "carpetbaggers."

"Carpetbagger" was a derogatory, or negative, term. It was used by Southerners to describe Northerners who were perceived as sweeping into the South to reap economic and political benefits in a region that had been ravaged by war. It was assumed that carpetbaggers were from the lower classes. While some carpetbaggers may have been, the large majority were well-educated, middle-class lawyers, businessmen, newspaper editors, and teachers. Some were members of the Freedmen's Bureau and hoped to assist former slaves. (The Freedmen's Bureau was an agency created in 1865 to help former slaves find jobs and to protect them against discrimination.)

The majority of carpetbaggers were veterans of the Union (Northern) army who decided to remain in the South when the war ended. They were eager for economic opportunities that came from purchasing land from or going into business with Southern planters, whose fortunes had been destroyed by the war.

Some carpetbaggers moved to the South for political opportunity. Among the most well known white carpetbaggers were Republican governor Robert K. Scott, who moved south from Ohio with the Union army and directed the Freedmen's Bureau in South Carolina; Henry C. Warmoth and William P. Kellogg of Louisiana, army veterans from Illinois; and Mississippi governor Adelbert Ames, who was originally from Maine.

Although the term "carpetbagger" generally applies to whites, a number of black Northerners also migrated south during Reconstruction. Black carpetbaggers were veterans of the Union army, ministers and teachers who had moved south to work for the Freedmen's Bureau, and the children of Southern **free blacks** who had been sent north years before for an education.

After the Civil War, more than one hundred African Americans from the North moved to the South and held public office. Among the most well known were Mifflin Gibbs and Jonathan Gibbs, who were born in Philadelphia, Pennsylvania, and who held major positions in Arkansas and Florida, respectively; and Stephen A. Swails, a veteran of the **Fifty-fourth Regiment of Massachusetts Voluntary Infantry,** who became the most prominent political leader in Williamsburg County, South Carolina.

It is uncertain how many Northerners moved to the South during Reconstruction, but estimates say that Northerners made up approximately 2 percent of the total Southern population. They particularly influenced politics in Florida, Louisiana, and South Carolina. After Reconstruction, most carpetbaggers returned to the North. Today, the term "carpetbagger" refers to an individual who runs for office in a district to which he or she has only recently moved. (*See also* **Scalawags.**)

Carroll, Diahann

SINGER, ACTRESS
July 17, 1935–

Entertainer Diahann Carroll was born Carol Diahann Johnson in **New York City.** She took voice and piano lessons from an early age and attended

New York City's High School of Music and Performing Art. In 1954 Carroll was chosen for a role in the play *House of Flowers.* The same year, she made her screen debut in the **film** *Carmen Jones.* She went on to perform in such films as *Porgy and Bess* (1959) and *Paris Blues* (1961). She returned to the theater in 1962 as the lead in the musical *No Strings,* for which she won a Tony Award.

In 1968 Carroll became the first African-American woman to have her own **television** series, *Julia.* She played a widowed mother who worked as a nurse. The role bothered some blacks, who felt that the character was too "white," representing white images of African Americans rather than being authentically black. Nevertheless, the program was a success. Carroll next played a single ghetto mother in the film *Claudine* (1974), for which she was nominated for an Academy Award. In 1976 she was inducted into the Black Filmmakers' Hall of Fame.

In the 1970s Carroll revived her singing career and returned to television in guest roles. In 1984 she took the role of Dominique Devereaux on the television series *Dynasty,* thus becoming the first African American to star in a nighttime soap opera. Carroll felt that her portrayal of a character as mean-spirited as her white peers was both her best work and an important step forward for black actors.

Carter, Betty

JAZZ SINGER
May 16, 1930–September 26, 1998

Jazz singer Betty Carter began her career in Detroit, Michigan. As a teenager, she sang with jazz greats **Dizzy Gillespie** and **Charlie Parker.** From 1948 to 1951 she sang and adapted music for the **Lionel Hampton** band. In 1951 Carter settled in New York City and sang in clubs and theaters, including Harlem's famed **Apollo Theater.** She toured with singer **Ray Charles** and traveled to Europe and Japan in the 1960. Carter organized her own trio in 1969 and formed her own recording company in 1971.

Carter's jazz roots can be traced to singing legends **Billie Holiday** and **Sarah Vaughan,** but her her particular way of singing and her ability to improvise, or make up music as she performs, is uniquely her own. She is best known for her adaptations of popular tunes and jazz originals. Carter died of cancer in Brooklyn, New York, on September 26, 1998.

Carter, Ronald Levin "Ron"

JAZZ BASSIST
May 4, 1937–

One of the most in-demand musicians in the **jazz** world, Ron Carter began playing the cello at age ten. He switched from studying classical music to studying bass instruments in 1954. Carter won a scholarship to the prestigious Eastman School of Music in Rochester, New York, where he received a bachelor's degree in 1959. He went on to receive a master's degree in bass performance from the Manhattan School of Music, New York City, in 1961. During this period Carter performed regularly with several classical orchestras, becoming one of the first African-American bassists to do so. He also performed with various jazz groups. From 1963 to 1968 he worked with **Miles Davis**'s quintet (a five-member band).

Carter, known for his solid, "straight-ahead" jazz, left the quintet in 1968. He worked on his own and made several recordings. He continues to perform, mostly as the leader of his own group. Carter has written three books on jazz bass technique, including *Building a Jazz Bass Line*. He has taught at Washington University in St. Louis, the Manhattan School of Music, and the University of Buffalo (New York).

Carver, George Washington

SCIENTIST, EDUCATOR
c. 1864–January 5, 1943

Born in Diamond, Missouri, George Washington Carver did not remember his parents. His father is believed to have been accidentally killed before Carver was born, and his mother was apparently kidnapped by slave raiders when he was very young. He and his brother were raised by his mother's former owners.

Carter was refused admission to his local school because of his race, so he was privately tutored before moving to a nearby town in the mid-1870s to attend school there. He soon realized that he knew more than his teacher and left school. He roamed around the Midwest for almost fifteen years, supporting himself by cooking, doing laundry, and homesteading (settling and farming a piece of land) while trying to educate himself.

In 1890 Carver enrolled at Simpson College in Iowa. Originally, he wanted to be an artist, but he was talked into giving up his plans by his teacher, who convinced him that a black man could not make a living as an artist. He then went to Iowa State College, where, as the only black student, he earned a master's degree in agriculture.

At the invitation of **Booker T. Washington,** Carver became the head of the agriculture department at Tuskegee Institute (now **Tuskegee University** in Alabama). He spent the next forty-six years at Tuskegee, building a family of friends, both black and white, with his outgoing and giving personality. At Tuskegee, Carver became known for advocating the growing of peanuts as an inexpensive source of protein, and he published many peanut recipes. He soon developed a national reputation as "the peanut wizard."

Often overlooked is the contribution Carver made toward bridging the gap between blacks and whites. When he earned a lecturing sponsorship to speak on white campuses in the 1920s and 1930s, he won the hearts of the American public. He did just as much for the fight against racism by simply being a good person as those who actively campaigned against hatred. He

George Washington Carver working on an experiment in his lab (Courtesy of the Library of Congress)

became the trusted friend of many influential whites, such as automobile giant Henry Ford, as well as friends with poor sharecroppers, black and white. His work and his warm personality greatly enriched the lives of thousands of others.

Catlett, Elizabeth

PRINTMAKER, SCULPTOR
April 15, 1919–

Pioneering artist Elizabeth Catlett graduated *cum laude* (with praise or distinction) from **Howard University** (Washington, D.C.) in 1937. She then earned a master's degree from the University of Iowa (1940), where she studied with painter Grant Wood (1892–1942) and shifted from **painting** to sculpture. The sculpture Catlett created as part of the requirements for obtaining her master's degree, titled *Mother and Child*, took first prize in the 1941 American Negro Exposition in Chicago, Illinois.

While studying ceramics at the Art Institute of Chicago in 1941, Catlett met and married Charles White. In 1945 she received an award to do a series on African-American women and went to Mexico with White to work. Catlett briefly returned to New York to divorce White before marrying Mexican artist Francisco Mora in 1947.

In 1958 Catlett became the first woman to teach at the National University of Mexico's School of Fine Arts. From 1959 until 1976 she served as the head of the sculpture department.

Catlett's artwork has appeared in numerous solo and group exhibitions. It often deals with African-American women, sometimes with the theme of mother and child. Both Mexican and African-American cultures have influenced her sculptures and prints, both of which can be realistic in style or abstract (a painting that represents the qualities of something by using shapes, lines, and color, rather than showing its outer appearance as a photograph would). Her best-known abstract works are *Sharecropper* (1968) and *Malcolm X Speaks for Us* (1969).

Catlett was still active—and living in Mexico—at the time of a fifty-year retrospective of her work (1946–96; a "look back" at her work over that period) in New York in 1998.

Chamberlain, Wilton Norman "Wilt"

BASKETBALL PLAYER
August 21, 1936–October 12, 1999

Wilton Norman Chamberlain, known to the world as Wilt Chamberlain, was one of the best **basketball** players of all time. His athletic ability, combined with his imposing height, seven feet two inches, transformed him into an offensive wonder.

Born in Philadelphia, Pennsylvania, Chamberlain had such a natural presence on the court that he was drafted by the Philadelphia Warriors to play in the National Basketball Association (NBA) before he graduated from high school. Chamberlain declined, however, deciding to attend college at the University of Kansas. During college Chamberlain was so unstoppable on the court that they changed the rules to make it easier for teams to guard him. He began playing in the NBA in 1959 for Philadelphia, where he continued to defy opponents, earning Rookie of the Year and Most Valuable Player awards.

Chamberlain's career was filled with spectacular highlights, including two NBA championships (1967 and 1972), a single-season scoring record of 4,029 points (averaging over 50 points per game), thirteen trips to the All-Star Game, and scoring an incredible 100 points in a single game (1962). He was voted to the Naismith Memorial Basketball Hall of Fame in 1978.

Despite his achievements on the court, Chamberlain was haunted by a reputation for poor performance in big games. He also disliked the nickname he was given ("Wilt the Stilt") because he felt it implied that his only advantage was his height. Chamberlain published an **autobiography,** *A View*

Wilt Chamberlain going up against Bill
Russell in a basketball game (Corbis
Corporation. Reproduced by permission)

From Above, in 1991). In 1999 Chamberlain died suddenly of an apparent heart attack, leaving behind a legacy of basketball triumphs.

Chaney, James Earl

CIVIL RIGHTS ACTIVIST
May 30, 1943–June 21, 1964

Civil rights activist James Chaney came from a Mississippi family who instilled in him a sense of racial pride from an early age. In 1963 he became directly involved in civil rights activities and joined the **Congress of Racial Equality (CORE),** which was part of the Council of Federated Organizations (COFO). In 1964 COFO planned a massive voter registration and desegregation campaign in Mississippi called the **Freedom Summer.** Events of that summer eventually led to Chaney's death.

Chaney, along with two white men who also worked for CORE, Michael Schwerner and Andrew Goodman, were assigned to investigate a church burning in Neshoba County, Mississippi. The church had been a potential site for a Freedom School that would teach literacy and voter education. The **Ku Klux Klan,** an organization that opposed equal rights for blacks, was suspected of burning the church down.

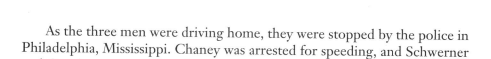
As the three men were driving home, they were stopped by the police in Philadelphia, Mississippi. Chaney was arrested for speeding, and Schwerner and Goodman were arrested as suspects in the church burning.

When Deputy Sheriff Cecil Ray Price discovered that the car Chaney had been driving was registered to CORE, he alerted local Klan leader Edgar Ray Killen. Killen, along with twenty other Klansmen, plotted against the CORE members. Later that same night, Price released the three activists from jail after Chaney paid a fine. They were followed out of town by a Klan posse, forced from their cars, driven to an isolated wooded area a few miles away, and killed. Their bodies were buried in an earthen dam near Philadelphia.

When the trio did not call to check in, other CORE members began to worry. Agents from the Federal Bureau of Investigation (FBI) were called in to investigate. When the burned shell of Chaney's car was found a few days after the incident, Neshoba County was flooded with journalists who reported to the shocked nation the hostility of some Mississippi whites toward blacks and civil rights workers.

The FBI recovered the bodies of the three men from the earthen dam on August 4, 1964, and four months later nineteen men were charged with the conspiracy. Despite a number of confessions and eyewitness accounts, only seven defendants were convicted. The conspirators were all paroled before serving full jail terms, and most returned to the Mississippi area by the mid-1970s.

Charles, Ray

MUSICIAN
September 23, 1930–

Singer and pianist Ray Charles is often called "the father of soul" for his creative blending of **gospel, blues,** and **jazz.** His best-known recording is "Georgia on My Mind," chosen as the state of Georgia's official song in 1977.

Born in Albany, Georgia, and raised in Greenville, Florida, Charles was five when he developed glaucoma, the disease that blinded him. He spent eight years at the School for the Deaf and Blind in St. Augustine, Florida, learning composition, writing musical scores in braille, and playing several instruments.

Charles left school in 1945 and later moved to Seattle, Washington, where he played in **jazz** trios and developed a piano and vocal style influenced by **Nat "King" Cole.** In 1955 Charles made a musical breakthrough with the recording "I've Got a Woman." The song combines a bluesy physical energy with the emotional sound of gospel, a mix that was shocking to many critics. This style is heard in some of Charles's most successful songs, including "Hallelujah, I Love Her So" (1956) and "What'd I Say" (1959).

As his popularity grew, Charles also developed an addiction to heroin. He was arrested three times for drug possession but never served a long

A true legend of rhythm and blues, Ray Charles (AP/Wide World Photos. Reproduced by permission)

prison term. In 1965 he stopped performing for a year while breaking his addiction.

Since then, Charles has enjoyed a long series of successes and honors. In the late 1960s he started his own record label and music-publishing firm. His accomplishments have included winning a **National Association for the Advancedment of Colored People (NAACP)** Hall of Fame Award (1983), being among the first ten artists named to the Rock and Roll Hall of Fame (1986), and even earning the French title Master of Arts and Letters. Charles has also won twelve Grammy Awards, the record industry's most prestigious prize.

Charles has said that he will never stop performing. In the 1990s he formed a seventeen-piece band and a five-member backup group known as the Rayletts. He continues to make television commercials, following an enormously popular 1991 Diet Pepsi ad campaign. Charles has used his high profile to help support social causes, including civil rights issues, African famine relief, and aid to the disabled.

Chase-Riboud, Barbara Dewayne

SCULPTOR, POET, NOVELIST
June 26, 1939–

Author Barbara Chase-Riboud (© Jerry Bauer. Reproduced by permission)

Sculptor, poet, and novelist Barbara Chase-Riboud was born and raised in Philadelphia, Pennsylvania. She earned art degrees from Philadelphia's Temple University (1957) and from Yale University in New Haven, Connecticut (1960). Early in her career she learned how to sculpt in bronze in Italy and studied Egyptian art.

Chase-Riboud married the French photographer Marc Riboud in 1961. Soon after, the couple traveled to China, Nepal, and Inner Mongolia. Her notes from the trip were transformed into a collection of poems titled *From Memphis to Peking* in 1974.

African and Asian influences can be seen in Chase-Riboud's sculptures from the late 1960s. She became known for using unusual combinations of materials, such as bronze and wool, or steel and synthetics. She also used hemp, wood, leathers, metals, and feathers in works resembling African masks.

By the early 1970s Chase-Riboud was world famous. Her work has been exhibited at the Smithsonian Institution in Washington, D.C., New York's Whitney Museum, and the Museum of Modern Art in Paris, France, among others.

Chase-Riboud published her first novel, *Sally Hemings*, in 1979. The book suggests that Thomas Jefferson's (U.S. president, 1801–1809) relationship with his slave mistress, **Sally Hemings,** produced seven children. Chase-Riboud was both complimented and criticized for her novel. In 1998 DNA testing (gene comparison) confirmed that Jefferson had in fact fathered at least one of Hemings's children.

Chase-Riboud made headlines in 1997 when she sued the makers of the film *Amistad* and director Steven Spielberg for plagiarizing (illegally using) her novel *Echo of Lions*. Chase-Riboud later withdrew her lawsuit and strongly praised the **film.**

With homes in Paris and Rome, Chase-Riboud has continued to travel widely, write, and produce visual art. During the late 1990s she worked on plans to create a massive bronze memorial honoring the eleven million individuals who died on slave ships crossing the Atlantic Ocean.

Chavis, Benjamin Franklin Jr. "Muhammad"

CIVIL RIGHTS ACTIVIST
January 22, 1948–

Benjamin Chavis Jr., who went on to become a leading civil rights activist, first became involved in the struggle for civil rights at age twelve. He was determined to use a whites-only library in Oxford, North Carolina, and his desire led to its integration (use by both blacks and whites). Chavis remained active in civil rights organizing in college. He then spent a year as a labor organizer. Chavis later joined the Washington field office of the United Church of Christ's Commission for Racial Justice (UCCCRJ).

In 1971 Chavis was sent to Wilmington, North Carolina, to assist local ministers. The racial climate in Wilmington had become explosive when court-ordered desegregation (ending the practice of separating blacks and whites) began in 1969. Chavis was to help organize a black students' boycott of a local school. (A boycott is an intentional refusal to use a facility or to buy or use a product.) Within two weeks of his arrival, Wilmington erupted in a week-long riot.

In March 1972 Chavis and fifteen former students were arrested for setting fire to a white-owned grocery store and shooting at firemen and policemen who answered the call. Chavis and nine others, who became known as the Wilmington Ten, were convicted of arson and assault, and in 1975 Chavis entered prison. The case received national and international support, and in 1980 a federal appeals court overturned the convictions. While in prison, Chavis taught himself Greek, translated the New Testament, wrote two books (*An American Political Prisoner Appeals for Human Rights*, 1979, and *Psalms from Prison*, 1983), and earned a master's degree. After his release he earned a doctor of ministry degree.

In 1986 Chavis became the executive director of the UCCCRJ. He focused on combating both what he called "environmental racism"—the government and industry's practice of burdening poor and predominantly black neighborhoods with toxic waste dumps—and gang violence. In 1993 Chavis became the executive director of the **National Association for the Advancement of Colored People (NAACP).** He pledged to revitalize the organization and to sharpen its focus, but he was later removed for using NAACP funds to make an out-of-court settlement in a sexual harassment case brought against him.

Following his resignation from the NAACP, Chavis joined the **Nation of Islam (NOI).** In 1997 he announced his conversion to Islam, and he took the name Benjamin Chavis Muhammad. He was defrocked by the United Church of Christ. He was named by NOI leader **Louis Farrakhan** to lead Black Muslim activist **Malcolm X's** (1925–1965) old mosque in Harlem, New York.

Checker, Chubby

ROCK-AND-ROLL SINGER
October 3, 1941–

Chubby Checker's recording of "The Twist" launched an international dance craze in the early 1960s. During high school in Philadelphia, Pennsylvania, Checker, born Ernest Evans, worked at a poultry market, singing as he plucked chickens. Impressed by his voice, Evans's boss took him to a record company, where he signed a recording contract in 1959. His imitation of popular singer Fats Domino caught the attention of Dick Clark, the host of *American Bandstand*, a nationally televised dance show. It was Clark's wife who gave Evans the name Chubby Checker, a play on Fats Domino's name.

At Clark's urging, Checker recorded "The Twist," and he appeared on *Bandstand* to perform the mildly suggestive dance that accompanied it. "You

Chubby Checker dancing the twist, the dance craze he made popular (Archive Photos. Reproduced by permission)

move your hips like you're drying yourself with a towel," Checker explained. Boosted by television, Checker's record shot to the top of the pop charts in September 1960. In January 1962 Checker's record returned to the top of the charts, the only time a song has reached number one on two separate occasions. Checker recorded other songs and dance numbers, but none had the Twist's impact or success.

Chesnutt, Charles Wadell

WRITER
June 20, 1858–November 15, 1932

Born in Cleveland, Ohio, to freeborn mulattoes (persons of mixed black and white ancestry), Charles Wadell Chesnutt lived for most of his childhood in Fayetteville, North Carolina. As an adult, he served for a time as a school principal and a Sunday school superintendent in North Carolina, but he became determined to escape the racism of the South. Eventually, he returned to Cleveland, which became his permanent place of residence. By the 1890s he had launched a successful business in legal stenography (taking notes of law proceedings).

Chesnutt, a fiction writer, was dissatisfied with the way the black experience was portrayed by southern white writers, and he vowed to create stories that were more accurate and faithful. In 1899 he published two well-received collections of stories, *The Wife of His Youth and Other Stories of the Color Line* and *The Conjure Woman*. The stories in *The Conjure Woman* depict magical events and the horrors of **slavery** while exploring the complex attachments that linked former slaves to their ancestors and to their masters. The book was a great success and was closely followed by his first novel, *The House Behind the Cedars* (1900).

Chesnutt's next books proved too bitter for his audience, however, and his popularity faded. His second novel, *The Marrow of Tradition* (1901), for example, was filled with the political arguments that followed the **Civil War**.

As one of the wealthiest black men in Cleveland, Chesnutt had a powerful political voice. Until his death, he was so outspoken in defense of blacks against discrimination that in 1928 he was awarded the Spingarn Medal, the highest award bestowed by the **National Association for the Advancement of Colored People (NAACP)**, given each year for the most distinguished service of any black person in advancing the cause of blacks in the United States. Chesnutt continued to write and publish until 1930, despite poor critical reception and sales.

Chess

Traditionally, chess has not been a popular activity in African-American culture. Blacks did not begin to appear on the chess scene until the latter half of the twentieth century. The game has been gaining popularity among blacks in recent years, however.

Theophilus Thompson was the earliest recognized African-American chess player, in the second half of the nineteenth century. Blacks then seem to have disappeared from the chess scene until the 1940s. It was not until 1960 that Walter Harris became the first black to be crowned a chess "master" by the United States Chess Federation (USCF). In the 1960s and 1970s chess began to grow in popularity among blacks; however, there were still very few black chess masters.

There has been some debate among experts as to why so few blacks have become masters. Some argue that blacks have not developed an interest in the game, while others suggest that racism has prevented them from participating in major tournaments. In the 1980s several African Americans won the Armed Forces chess championship, which helped the game gain in popularity among blacks. Perhaps the best-known African-American chess player in modern times is Maurice Ashley, who in 1999 became the first black to earn the title "grandmaster."

MAURICE ASHLEY: CHESS CHAMPION

In March 1999 Maurice Ashley became the first African American to be named a chess grandmaster. Ashley was born to a poor family in the Caribbean island of Jamaica; the family moved to the United States when he was twelve. He became interested in chess after a schoolmate challenged him to a game and badly beat him. After reading up on the game, Ashley's interest quickly turned into obsession. He would play for hours with a group of chess players called "the Black Bear School of Chess" in Brooklyn, New York.

Ashley used to boast to his friends that one day he would become a grandmaster—an elite class of chess players. There are only 470 grandmasters in the world, 48 of whom are from the United States. Having realized his ambition in 1999, Ashley continues to enter competitions and funds his passion by announcing chess matches for television and coaching for the Harlem Educational Activities Fund. He spends his spare time practicing his moves on the computer or training with Gregory Kaidanov, who is ranked fifth in the United States.

There have been efforts among African Americans to establish chess organizations designed to promote interest in the game. Groups with such colorful names as the Kingsmen Chess Club, the Bad Bishops, and the Raging Rooks (all takeoffs on chess playing pieces) were founded in eastern U.S. cities in the 1980s and have managed to recruit blacks and organize competitions.

Chicago, Illinois

Chicago Beginnings

Chicago's African-American community emerged in the 1840s, sixty-one years after the arrival of Jean Baptiste Pointe du Sable, an Afro-French immigrant and Chicago's first non-Native American settler. Kept out of most jobs and lacking money to establish businesses of their own, black Chicagoans filled less rewarding roles in the city's growing economy. Resisting discrimination, these African Americans agitated against slavery, formed vigilance committees to defend fugitive slaves, and worked for the repeal of the Illinois Black Laws.

The Civil War Years

Laws passed during the **Reconstruction** period following the **Civil War** (1861–65) forced state legislators to reconsider legal restrictions on black citizens. Black men won the right to vote in 1870, while legislation overturned school segregation in 1874 and prohibited discrimination in public facilities in 1885. Integrationist in outlook, business and professional leaders had strong ties to white Chicagoans and laid the groundwork for black participation in civic life. They published Chicago's first black newspaper, built churches, and organized the election of the city's first black public official in 1871.

The Early Twentieth Century

Between 1890 and 1915, migration—largely from the upper South—tripled Chicago's black population to fifty thousand. Employers' beliefs regarding particular abilities of the various races excluded African Americans—supposedly incapable of regular, disciplined industrial work—from nearly all but the least skilled jobs. Black women, more likely than other women to enter the paid labor force, were even more concentrated than men in these dead-end occupations. African Americans earned less than their white counterparts, but paid higher housing prices. Limited to residences in certain areas, black Chicagoans concentrated in two emerging ghettos—a long thin sliver on the South Side and a smaller area on the West Side.

In response to exclusion coupled with population growth, Chicago's black male leadership turned inward. Between 1890 and 1915 a new generation of leaders focused its energies on developing black community life. Women were more likely than men to be active in interracial reform movements, but men occupied positions of power within the community. Oscar DePriest, the first black alderman in a city where power resided in the city council, won election in 1915. By then black Chicago had its own YMCA, settlement houses, hospital, military regiment, and bank, and a vital business and entertainment district along the State Street "Stroll."

The manufacturing boom brought about by **World War I** (1914–18) transformed Chicago and other centers of industry. The need for workers to fill the newly created jobs forced factory owners to lay aside their beliefs about black workers. Approximately sixty thousand black Southerners—largely from the deep South—relocated in Chicago. Men worked in steel mills, packinghouses, other heavy industries, and traditional service jobs. Women worked in light industry and domestic service. Postal workers and Pullman porters anchored a middle class defined more by lifestyle than by income. Chicago had more black-owned stores by the end of the 1920s than any other city in the United States. A small professional and business elite began to be formed. Black politicians sat in the city council, the state legislature, and, by 1929, the U.S. House of Representatives.

The weight of the **Great Depression** hit the black community hard. Last admitted through the factory gates, black workers were the first to be laid off. Eviction often followed unemployment. Black Chicagoans responded to the depression with renewed activism. Reviving "Don't Buy Where You Can't Work" campaigns started during the 1920s, ghetto residents successfully picketed stores and office buildings.

During **World War II** (1939–45), the New Deal, industrial recovery, and the emergence of the Congress of Industrial Organization (CIO) opened new economic and political opportunities. By the end of the war, thousands of black Chicagoans held union jobs, and a new generation of black activists emerged from the CIO and, later, the Negro American Labor Council.

THE CHICAGO RENAISSANCE

The growth and prosperity of the period after World War II produced a cultural flowering often referred to as the "Chicago Renaissance." Extending beyond the jazz and blues innovations usually associated with Chicago musicians like Muddy Waters and Dizzy Gillespie, this creative blossoming included literature (Richard Wright, Arna Bontemps, Willard Motley, Margaret Walker, and Gwendolyn Brooks), dance (Katherine Dunham), and art (Archibald Motley, George Neal, Richmond Barthé, and Margaret Taylor Goss).

The Civil Rights Era

Migration from the South surged during the 1940s and 1950s, with the ghetto expanding along its edges. Attempts to leapfrog across boundaries, whether by individuals or by means of government programs, attracted violent resistance by whites. By the early 1950s the housing authority had shifted from being a force for integration to becoming a developer of high-rise ghettos constructed in black neighborhoods. In 1959 the U.S. Commission on Civil Rights labeled Chicago "the most residentially segregated city in the nation."

Housing segregation combined with unfairly divided public-school districts to dominate the attention of Chicago's postwar civil rights movement. The formation of the Coordinating Council of Community Organizations in 1962 focused mainly on school desegregation. The entrance of the **Southern Christian Leadership Conference** and the Rev. Dr. **Martin Luther King, Jr.**, in 1965 and 1966 shifted the focus toward open housing. Marches through white neighborhoods encountered violent opposition, bringing Mayor Richard Daley to the bargaining table, but black leaders lacked the resources to secure more than just empty words and promises. By 1967 only **Jesse Jackson**'s employment-oriented Operation Breadbasket was achieving real gains. Riots in 1966 and 1968 gave voice to people's rage and provoked temporary civic concern about racial injustice and poverty, but left mainly devastation in their wake.

Continued organizing efforts paid off, however, in 1983, with the election of Chicago's first African-American mayor, Harold Washington. Frequently blocked in his efforts by city council, Washington had begun to wield effective power only two years before his death in 1988. Washington's group of supporters became divided after his death, but remained a force in city politics and within the black community into the 1990s.

Chicago Today

In the 1990s Chicago's African-American population remained largely on the South and West Sides. Block after block of working-class bungalows and apartment buildings housed families struggling to maintain their standard of living amid deteriorating public schools, a declining industrial base, and a weakened public sector. The effects of unemployment or low-wage service jobs were visible nearby, in neighborhoods characterized by run-down housing and dwindling business activity. Public-housing projects held a population often largely made up of children and unemployed or under-employed women. But prosperous middle-class neighborhoods, while losing some residents to increasing opportunities in the suburbs, continued to include a black elite that has maintained its commitment to black institutions while taking its place among the city's power brokers.

(SEE ALSO **RECONSTRUCTION; THE BLUES; MUDDY WATERS; DIZZY GILLESPIE; GWENDOLYN BROOKS.**)

Children's Literature

Children's literature that gives a true picture of the African-American experience did not really develop until about the 1940s, even though some books featuring black characters were written during the 1800s and early 1900s. These early books, such as Helen Bannerman's *Little Black Sambo* (1928), although quite popular, presented a stereotypical (one-sided) picture of African-American life. The characters were drawn with exaggerated features, and the stories were usually about wide-eyed, smiling slaves or servants.

There were few books written for children about African Americans even by 1965, but after the civil rights era, African-American characters were found in about twice as many publications. During the 1990s new authors emerged, and established authors wrote new books that more accurately portrayed the culture and daily life of both historical and contemporary African Americans.

The 1930s to 1960s

By the late 1930s several works appeared that gave a realistic picture of the African-American experience. Among these were two works by the African-American author **Arna Bontemps** (1902–1973), *You Can't Pet a Possum* (1936) and *Sad-Faced Boy* (1937).

By the middle to late 1940s children's books began to address the issue of civil rights. **Carter Woodson** (1875–1950), considered the father of African-American historical writing, wrote several children's books in the 1940s documenting African-American history. Among them were *African Heroes and Heroines* (1944) and *Negro Makers of History* (1948). During the 1950s African-American poet **Langston Hughes** (1902–1967) wrote a series of educational books for children, such as *Famous American Negroes* (1954).

The 1960s

By the 1960s well-written children's books about African Americans were being published, including white author Ezra Jack Keats's (1916–1983) *The Snowy Day* (1962) and **Ann Petry**'s (1908–1997) *Tituba of Salem Village* (1964).

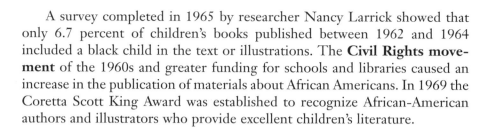
A survey completed in 1965 by researcher Nancy Larrick showed that only 6.7 percent of children's books published between 1962 and 1964 included a black child in the text or illustrations. The **Civil Rights movement** of the 1960s and greater funding for schools and libraries caused an increase in the publication of materials about African Americans. In 1969 the Coretta Scott King Award was established to recognize African-American authors and illustrators who provide excellent children's literature.

The 1970s

During the 1970s outstanding authors and poets began writing children's books. Among them was the poet Lucille Clifton (1936–), whose books of poetry and stories are considered valuable introductions to African-American heritage. Other important children's authors during this period included **June Jordan** (1936–), author of *His Own Where* (1971) and *Kimako's Story* (1981). **Julius Lester** (1939–) combined black southern folklore and contemporary political issues in his children's books, which included *The Long Journey Home: Stories from Black History* (1972), a nonfiction collection of **slave narratives** that was a finalist for a National Book Award.

Other authors to make their mark on children's literature during this period included the Nigerian Chinua Achebe (1930–), known for *How the Leopard Got His Claws* (1973); Virginia Hamilton (1936–), winner of the Coretta Scott King Award; and Walter Dean Myers (1937–) and Eloise Greenfield (1929–).

A study of African-American characters in children's literature done in 1979 showed that 14.4 percent of books published between 1973 and 1975 had black characters in the text or illustrations, more than double the percentage found in Nancy Larrick's 1965 study.

Although the publication of children's books about the African-American experience slowed in the late 1970s and 1980s, new authors emerged, such as **Ossie Davis** (1917–), who wrote books about important African Americans in history, including *Escape to Freedom: A Play About Young Frederick Douglass* (1978). Author Mildred Taylor (1943–) also entered the children's book arena with *Song of Trees* (1975) and *Roll of Thunder, Hear My Cry* (1976), recipient of the American Library Association's Newbery Medal, awarded each year to the author of the most distinguished children's book.

The 1980s and 1990s

As mainstream publishers printed fewer books about African Americans in the 1980s, small presses, such as Black Butterfly Press, began publishing new African-American authors, and the demand for African-American materials continued to increase during the 1990s. Because of the demand, the big publishing houses followed suit and began to publish more books by and about African Americans.

The 1990s saw the publication of some excellent African-American books, including Mildred Taylor's (1943–) *Mississippi Bridge* (1990) and Angela Johnson's (1961–) *When I Am Old with You* (1990) and *Heaven* (1998; winner of the 1999 Coretta Scott King Book Award). Among the award-winning children's authors who portrayed the black experience in the late

Selected Children's Books with African-American Themes for Readers in Grades 5 to 8

The Watsons Go to Birmingham—1963 (1997), by Christopher Paul Curtis

Francie (1999), by Karen English

Childtimes: A Three-Generation Memoir (1987), by Eloise Greenfield and Lessie Jones Little

Sweet Whispers, Brother Rush (1982), by Virginia Hamilton

Breaking Ground, Breaking Silence: The Story of New York's African Burial Ground (1998), by Joyce Hansen and Gary McGowan

The Other Side: Shorter Poems (1998), by Angela Johnson

Toning the Sweep (1993), by Angela Johnson

Dark Thirty: Tales of the Supernatural (1992), by Patricia C. McKissack

Rebels Against Slavery: American Slave Revolts (1996), by Patricia C. McKissack and Frederick L. McKissack

Sojourner Truth: Ain't I a Woman? (1994), by Patricia C. McKissack and Frederick L. McKissack

Aida (1990), by Leontyne Price

The Block: Poems (1995) by Langston Hughes, illustrations by Romare Bearden, introduction by Bill Cosby

Get on Board: The Story of the Underground Railroad (1997) by Jim Haskins

(Source: American Library Association. "Coretta Scott King Discussion Guide." http://www.ala.org/srrt/csking/cskread.html (accessed June 2000).)

CORETTA SCOTT KING AUTHOR AWARDS, 1993–2000

The Coretta Scott King Award is presented to authors and illustrators of African descent whose books promote an understanding and appreciation of the "American Dream" for African Americans. Presented annually by the Coretta Scott King Task Force of the American Library Association's Social Responsibilities Round Table, the award commemorates the life and work of Dr. **Martin Luther King Jr.** and honors his widow, Coretta Scott King, for her courage in continuing King's work for peace and world brotherhood. In the Author category of the award, one book published during the previous year is chosen, and other books are given the "Honor Book" title for the year. The following are Author Award winners.

2000: *Bud, Not Buddy,*
by Christopher Paul Curtis

1999: *Heaven,*
by Angela Johnson

1998: *Forged by Fire,*
by Sharon M. Draper

1997: *Slam,*
by Walter Dean Myers

1996: *Her Stories,*
by Virginia Hamilton

1995: *Christmas in the Big House, Christmas in the Quarters,*
by Patricia C. and Frederick L. McKissack

1994: *Toning the Sweep,*
by Angela Johnson

1993: *Dark Thirty: Southern Tales of the Supernatural,*
by Patricia C. McKissack

(Source: American Library Association. "The Coretta Scott King Award Book List." http://www.ala.org/srrt/csking/csking/cskawin.html (accessed June 2000).)

1990s were Christopher Paul Curtis, Nikki Grimes, Joyce Hansen and Gary McGowan, and Karen English.

Childress, Alice

PLAYWRIGHT
October 12, 1920–August 14, 1994

Born in Charleston, South Carolina, and raised by her grandmother in Harlem, New York, Alice Childress grew up economically poor but culturally rich. Her grandmother exposed her to the arts and taught her to strive for excellence. Her grandmother also encouraged her to write by creating a game that allowed Childress to develop fictional characters. Forced to drop out of high school when her grandmother died, Childress continued her education by reading books from the public library.

Childress began her career in the late 1940s while helping develop and strengthen the American Negro Theatre (ANT), where she studied acting and directing. She wrote and produced more than a dozen plays, including *Wedding Band: A Love Hate Story in Black and White* (1966; televised on ABC in 1974) and *Moms* (1987). Childress was the first black woman to win an Obie Award for the best original Off-Broadway play (a play performed somewhere other than New York's main theater district, known as Broadway), *Trouble in Mind* (1955). Childress's plays concern the poor and the opressed, often transforming underdogs into winners by showing their dignity and will to survive.

Childress also wrote many novels, including hard-hitting stories about teenagers with problems. Her novel *A Hero Ain't Nothin' but a Sandwich* (1973), about a thirteen-year-old addicted to the drug heroin, was banned in parts of the country because of its strong language and blunt character portrayals.

Alice Childress: Works for Young Readers

Rainbow Jordan
(novel, 1981)

Those Other People
(novel, 1989)

When the Rattlesnake Sounds
(play, 1975)

Let's Hear It for the Queen
(play, 1976)

Chisholm, Shirley

POLITICIAN
November 30, 1924–

Shirley Chisholm's career places her among the most significant black politicians of the twentieth century. After earning a master's degree from Columbia University in New York City, Chisholm helped to form the Unity Democratic Club in New York, and in 1965 she ran a successful campaign for a position in the New York State Assembly. There, she pressed her interest in education and helped to establish programs to assist poor students.

In 1969 Chisholm won a seat in the U.S. House of Representatives, becoming the first African-American woman to be elected to Congress. She was an outspoken opponent of the **Vietnam War** (1959–75) and continued to fight for economic justice and women's rights.

In 1972 Chisholm announced her candidacy for the Democratic Party nomination for president. She was the first African American ever to do so. Although her campaign was unable to gain enough support to be successful, her effort was nonetheless groundbreaking. Shirley Chisholm retired from Congress in 1982. She has since taught at several colleges and continues to be active in politics as the founder of the National Political Congress of Black Women.

An African-American **F I R S T**

Shirley Chisholm paved the way for black women politicians by being the first African-American woman elected to Congress, in 1968. During her fourteen years in the House of Representatives, Chisholm sponsored several education bills and bills to help the poor. She also served on the Veterans' Affairs Committee, the Education and Labor Committee, and the influential House Rules Committee.

Chong, Albert

PHOTOGRAPHER
November 20, 1958–

Art photographer Albert Chong is famous for work that explores his Jamaican identity as well as his mixed racial and religious background. He was born in Kingston, Jamaica, West Indies, into a family of African and

Asian heritage. At nineteen he won silver and bronze medals for **photography** at the 1977 Jamaica Festival of Arts.

That same year, Chong immigrated to the United States. He earned a bachelor's degree at New York City's School of Visual Arts in Manhattan (1981) and a master's degree from the University of California at San Diego (1991).

Chong's work from 1980 to 1985 was a series of family and self-portraits or "I-traits," as he calls them. In one, *Natural Mystic* (1982), he sits naked on a chair against a background of tree branches and burlap cloth. Time-lapse photography makes Chong's figure blurred and ghostlike.

Since 1986, Chong has created numerous still-lifes about personal memory and ancestor worship. Images in these photographs include objects used in Jamaican and African rituals and Chong's dreadlocks and Jamaican passport.

Chong has taught photography at the School of Visual Arts, the University of Colorado at Boulder, Mira Costa College in California, and more recently at the Rhode Island School of Design. During the late 1990s he began working with other artists on multimedia and performance art.

Christian Methodist Episcopal Church

Selected Leaders of the Christian Methodist Episcopal (CME) Church

Lucius Henry Holsey (1842–1920),
founder of CME schools

Channing Heggie Tobias (1882–1961),
chair of the board (1953–59) of the NAACP

John Hope Franklin (1915–),
historian

Alex Haley (1921–1992),
acclaimed author (*Roots: The Saga of an American Family*, 1976)

Based on the ideas of the Methodist Church, which was founded by English religious leader John Wesley (1703–1791) and brought to the United States in 1784, the Christian Methodist Episcopal Church also embraces characteristics of African heritage, giving the church its own unique shape. Founded December 16, 1870, in Jackson, Tennessee, as the Colored Methodist Episcopal Church, the Christian Methodist Episcopal (CME) Church was organized by former slaves. After **emancipation**, or freedom, African-American members of the Methodist Episcopal (ME) Church, South realized the importance of establishing their own church for the continuation of their faith and to help build a sense of community. According to cofounder Isaac Lane (1834–1937), who became a bishop (high-ranking minister) of the CME Church in 1873, the church was organized after "our own [African American] ideas and notions."

Work began in 1866, and by the time the church was officially founded in 1870, it included several hundred ordained ministers and congregations (individual churches), seventy-eight thousand members, and an official publication, *The Christian Index*. Properties formerly used by the black congregations of the ME Church were transferred to the CME Church.

As African Americans migrated from the South to the North, Midwest, and Pacific Coast during the late 1800s and early 1900s, the Colored Methodist Episcopal Church grew. New congregations were founded in communities where black people settled around the United States. After **World War II** (1939–45), as the **Civil Rights movement** gained strength, the church decided to change its name: in 1954 the restrictive term "colored" was dropped in favor of "Christian."

The CME Church was active in the Civil Rights movement and has a long history of leadership in education, community outreach, and other charitable works, including antipoverty and drug prevention programs. In the 1990s the church's membership was 812,000, and the church directed twenty-one schools, four colleges, and a school of theology (religion).

Citizenship Schools

During the mid-1950s through the 1960s, citizenship schools played a vital role in promoting literacy, increasing voter registration, and developing community leadership skills among African Americans in the South. Under the direction of Myles Horton, the **Highlander Citizenship School** in Monteagle, Tennessee, had emerged as a champion of racial equality and integration by the early 1950s. In 1953 a grant from the Emil Schwartzhaupt Foundation (a major benefactor of progressive community organizations) gave Horton the resources to create a series of education programs that would help African-American adults become informed voters. These programs became known as "citizenship schools."

Horton and Highlander black community activists attended workshops to discuss strategies for carrying out their voter registration efforts. In attendance at one of the early workshops were two activists who played central roles in creating the citizenship school program: **Septima Clark** and Esau Jenkins.

Through discussions with Jenkins and Clark, Horton became convinced that Johns Island in South Carolina should be the site of the first citizenship school. After many months of community planning, the Johns Island Citizenship School was founded in 1957. The school had an initial enrollment of fourteen students. Because the school was unable to afford a building or a paid staff, classes were held in the back room of a small store. Students were taught practical skills that they could use in their daily lives—such as reading the Bible, signing their names, and making out money orders—as well as how to fill out voter registration forms.

The classroom curriculum also centered on teaching students to address the social conditions in their community. The school served as a site of political discussion, where students were encouraged to speak up and to examine the world more closely. The knowledge students gained at the school allowed them to tackle problems differently and make better use of local resources. As the school began to "graduate" successful new voters and community political awareness grew, enrollment rapidly increased. From 1956 to 1960 voter registration on Johns Island increased 300 percent.

Citizenship schools were created on the other South Carolina sea islands as the success of the Johns Island's school became evident and the **Civil Rights movement** spread throughout the South. Teacher-training workshops at Highlander brought together experienced teachers with new teachers. The workshops were forums for discussions of current events and local **politics** and created a sense of community among participants. By early 1961 eighty-two teachers had been trained by Highlander and were teaching in citizenship schools in Alabama, Georgia, South Carolina, and

Tennessee. By that same year, citizenship schools had registered hundreds to vote.

In February 1961 Horton, anticipating that the citizenship school program would soon outgrow Highlander's funding capabilities, negotiated the transfer of the program to the **Southern Christian Leadership Conference (SCLC)** to ensure the program's survival. Septima Clark joined the staff of the SCLC to direct the citizenship school program, which was renamed the Citizenship Education Project (CEP). By 1966 the project had trained more than ten thousand teachers for the citizenship schools.

Citizenship schools grew to become a key grassroots support for the Civil Rights movement throughout the Deep South. By 1970, thirteen years after the first citizenship school was formed with only fourteen students, eight hundred citizenship schools graduating more than one hundred thousand African Americans had been formed in the South.

As time passed, however, many in the Civil Rights movement felt that involvement in local politics was no longer a central goal of the movement. Also, despite the continued overall success of the CEP in training teachers, many of the schools closed because of inadequate funding. By 1970 the schools had faded out of existence.

Civil Rights Movement

Although the fight for equal rights has been an ongoing struggle in the United States, activities during the 1950s and 1960s reached new heights. During this period, called the Civil Rights Movement, African-American reformers and white supporters helped pass national laws and secure Supreme Court decisions that would protect the constitutional rights of all people, regardless of color.

The U.S. Constitution guarantees certain rights to all people in the nation. These civil rights allow people to choose their religion, gather and speak freely, and publish their ideas; they also say that the laws apply to all people equally and that the justice system should treat all people the same.

In 1865 slavery was outlawed and the Fourteenth and **Fifteenth Amendment**s were added to the Constitution, extending all rights to black people. But some laws and policies kept African Americans separate from, and treated them differently than, white people. Southern states passed laws that discriminated against and segregated (set apart) African-American citizens. Called **Jim Crow** laws, they prevented black people from voting and required blacks to use separate drinking water fountains, bathrooms, bus seats, train cars, and recreational facilities. Since 90 percent of African Americans lived in the South until 1910, these laws affected most of the black community.

The NAACP Is Founded

In the early 1900s reform-minded African Americans began organizing and speaking out to end discrimination and segregation. Among the earliest advocates of full racial equality was educator and writer **W. E. B. Du Bois**

(1868–1963). In 1905 he founded the **Niagara Movement**, a short-lived organization that supported "the total integration of blacks into mainstream society, with all the rights, privileges, and benefits of other Americans." In 1909 Du Bois was among the founders of the NAACP, **National Association for the Advancement of Colored People**. The organization began working through the courts to bring about change.

In 1915 NAACP lawyers argued in the Supreme Court case of *Guinn v. United States* that the "grandfather clauses" passed by some southern states to keep black people from voting were against the constitution. These clauses had required black voters to pass difficult tests before they were allowed to vote or stated that only people whose grandfathers were able to vote as of a certain date (usually a date when no black person in the South was free to vote) could go to the election booths.

Encouraged by this victory, the NAACP pressed for equal school facilities for blacks. In the 1930s the group succeeded in desegregating all-white graduate schools in some states. The NAACP also worked with elected officials to try to pass national laws against lynching but their efforts were frustrated.

During the administration of President Franklin Roosevelt (1882–1945; president 1933–45), a small but important victory was won in 1941 with the establishment of the Fair Employment Practices Committee. The group worked to improve racial integration in factories producing materials for **World War II** (1939–45).

"Separate-but-Equal" Is Overturned

After World War II the way in which Americans viewed racism and discrimination began to shift. After fighting a war to protect democracy, many questioned how it could be right to prevent any individual in the United States from having full equal rights. In December 1946 President Harry Truman (1884–1972; president 1945–53) appointed a committee to investigate violations of black rights. Three months later the committee released its report, titled "To Secure These Rights." The report, a federal attack on state Jim Crow laws, was approved by the president. In 1950 Truman began to desegregate the armed forces.

By this time the NAACP's chief lawyer, **Thurgood Marshall** (1908–1993), had begun fighting segregation in public schools. In several court cases Marshall argued that segregation denied blacks "equal protection of the laws" as guaranteed by the Fourteenth Amendment. In 1954 the Supreme Court ruled in the case of ***Brown v. the Board of Education*** that in public schools the "separate-but-equal" policy has no place. (*See also* **Plessy v. Ferguson**.)

But the Brown ruling angered white supremacist groups, such as the **Ku Klux Klan** (KKK), that had emerged in the South. By the mid-twentieth century, the number of KKK members grew and the acts of violence they carried out grew as well. This "massive resistance," approved by some southern lawmakers and citizens, aimed to keep black people "in their place." Many schools did not desegregate and those that did often met with violence.

President John F. Kennedy urged Congress to pass a strong civil rights law that gave racial intolerance "no place in American life"

Nonviolent Protest Becomes Force for Change

The civil rights movement was sparked by a single act of defiance of a reform-minded seamstress named **Rosa Parks** (1913–). In December, 1955, Parks refused to give her bus seat to a white rider. Her stance set off the **Montgomery, Alabama, Bus Boycott**, led by an Atlanta minister, the Rev. Dr. **Martin Luther King Jr.** He gained national attention, calling on supporters to follow a policy of nonviolent resistance—to keep the struggle peaceful. In November 1956 the boycott triumphed. A Supreme Court decision overturned Montgomery's laws enforcing bus segregation.

In January 1957 King organized the **Southern Christian Leadership Conference** (SCLC), a network of nonviolent civil rights activists. In September the U.S. Congress passed the first Civil Rights Act in nearly 100 years. The act created a commission to monitor civil rights violations and authorized the U.S. Justice Department to protect black voting rights by taking violators to court.

Sit-Ins: African-American activists began using the "sit-in" as an effective form of protest. For example, on February 1, 1960, four students at a Woolworth's lunch counter in Greensboro, North Carolina, refused to leave their seats when they were refused service. The protest was covered in the news and set off similar demonstrations against segregation in public places. Hundreds of young protesters joined forces in April 1960, forming the **Student Nonviolent Coordinating Committee** (SNCC, pronounced "snick") to promote peaceful resistance to segregation.

The Freedom Ride: In May 1961 educator **James Farmer** (1920–), co-founder of the **Congress of Racial Equality** (CORE), led fourteen white and black volunteers on a "freedom ride" through the South. They were testing whether southern states were complying with a Supreme Court order to desegregate interstate bus terminals. Arriving in **Birmingham, Alabama,** on May 14, the freedom riders were met with a violent white mob; on May 20, federal marshals protected the riders from a similar "reception" in Montgomery.

The problem of racism seemed to only grow deeper. A May 3, 1963, event turned the tide of public opinion in favor of the extension of civil rights. That day, as nonviolent followers of Dr. King marched in protest in Birmingham, Alabama, police beat participants and unleashed trained dogs on them. The horrible scene was taped by television news cameras and replayed across the country. In response, President John Kennedy (1917–1963; president 1961–63) urged Congress to pass a strong civil rights law that gave racial intolerance "no place in American life."

March on Washington: In support of the proposed law, Dr. King led a peaceful march on Washington, D.C., on August 28, 1963. He delivered his famous "I Have a Dream" speech on the steps of the Lincoln Memorial. The rally encouraged a diverse group of people to support civil rights and work for interracial harmony.

On July 2, 1964, President Lyndon Johnson (1908–1973; president 1963–69) signed the Civil Rights Act, forbidding segregation in public places, ending federal aid to segregated institutions, outlawing racial dis-

crimination in the work place, strengthening black voting rights, and extending the life of the Civil Rights Commission.

Voting Rights

In the summer of 1964 civil rights groups invited white college students from the North to travel through the South to encourage and aid African Americans to register to vote. The program, called **Freedom Summer**, was countered by violence staged by white supremacists. Bombs and fires claimed black homes, churches, businesses, and lives. The events highlighted the need for laws to protect black voters at the state level.

In support of such laws, African-American marchers set out from Selma, Alabama, toward Montgomery on March 7, 1965. As they did, they suffered assaults by state and local police. Television news cameras caught the incident on tape and the images of unprovoked violence were broadcast around the nation, strengthening public support. On August 6, President Johnson signed the Voting Rights Act, authorizing the U.S. attorney general to send federal examiners tooversee local registrars (officials who register voters).

The Movement Splinters

With many important battles won, the civil rights movement turned its attention to other problems of racism, including poverty, unequal housing opportunities, and old patterns of segregation. But there was not widespread agreement on how to solve these deep problems. Meanwhile, frustration with ongoing discrimination mounted. On August 11, 1965, the Watts area of South-Central Los Angeles (California) erupted in rioting after a confrontation between police and a black motorist turned violent.

The civil rights movement began to split. During a march with Dr. King through Mississippi in June 1966, the SNCC leader **Stokely Carmichael** (1941–1998) mocked the policy of nonviolence. Instead, he called for "black power," or militance on the part of black people. The stance put off many liberal whites and divided the black community. While King continued to lead nonviolent protests, some African Americans responded to Carmichael's cry for disobedience regardless of the cost. The summer of 1967 saw the outbreak of violence in 100 U.S. cities and came to be called "the long, hot summer." The following April (1968), King was assassinated in Memphis, Tennessee. Sadly, news of his death set off more rioting, leaving Washington, D.C., in flames for three days. The following week, Congress passed the Civil Rights Act of 1968, which banned discrimination in the sale and rental of most housing.

The Struggle Continues

While schools had been ordered to desegregate in the 1954 ruling of *Brown v. the Board of Education*, as the 1970s began, integration still had not been achieved. In 1971 the Supreme Court ruled it was acceptable to bus children across districts in order to integrate schools. The policy of busing set off more protests, including in Boston, where white demonstrators turned violent. In 2000, nearly 50 years after Brown, the problem of integrating public schools had still not been wholly solved.

The NAACP and the National Urban League remain at the forefront of the civil rights struggle. While conservative politics of the 1980s set back the initiative, African Americans (and other minorities) were being elected to office in greater numbers. In positions of power they have worked with community groups to get ever closer to the ultimate goal of the civil rights movement—full equality among all groups, regardless of color. (See also **Affirmative Action**.)

Civil War

The American Civil War (1861–65) was the result of years of disagreement between Northern and Southern states. People living in the American South depended on agriculture to make a living, and wealthy individuals who lived on large plantations relied on African slave labor to keep the economy going. The Northern states relied more on industry, so, although slavery did exist in the North, the number of slaves was far less than in the South. There was also disagreement over states' rights. Southern states believed they should have more power to make their own laws, while Northern states believed the federal government should have more power. Although there were many disagreements that contributed to the beginning of the Civil War, the emotional focus of the conflict quickly became the end of **slavery.**

Black leaders suffered many disappointments in the decade before the Civil War. The greatest setback came in 1857 with the Supreme Court's decision in the Dred Scott case. In that decision, the Supreme Court stated that blacks were "beings of an inferior order ... so far inferior, that they had no rights which the white man was bound to respect." As a result, many black leaders lost all hope that African Americans would ever be treated equally in the United States. They supported plans for **free blacks** to leave this country and start life over again in **Africa** or the Caribbean. Despite these disappointments, most free blacks in the North agreed with **Frederick Douglass** (1817–1895), a former slave and political leader who insisted that the best future for African Americans still lay in America.

As the 1850s came to a close, African Americans were encouraged by signs that the country was growing more divided over the question of slavery. In Congress, Northern and Southern states battled fiercely over whether or not to expand slavery into the West, and a new political party was formed. This was the Republican Party, and it was created as an antislavery party. In 1860 Abraham Lincoln became the first Republican to be elected president, and in 1861 the Civil War began. Across the North free black communities sent petitions to state legislatures and wrote to the secretary of war to volunteer for battle. At that time, however, blacks were not allowed to serve in the army, and their requests were denied.

Angered by this policy, some blacks withdrew their support from the war. Frederick Douglass, in his newspaper the *Douglass Monthly*, demanded that black men be allowed to serve. He accused President Lincoln of fighting with his "white hand" while allowing his "black hand to remain tied."

Southern Blacks

In the South, African Americans found themselves living in the Confederate States of America, a newly created nation preparing itself for war and determined to maintain slavery. In a speech comparing the Confederacy to the federal government created in 1787, the vice president of the Confederate States, Alexander Stevens, stated that the Confederacy was founded upon the belief that "the Negro is not equal to the white man; subordination to the superior race is his natural and moral condition."

One of the Confederacy's economic strengths was its huge supply of black slave labor. Tens of thousands of slaves were forced into service by their owners to work at sites of military production, to transport materials to build fortifications, or to work for Confederate troops. Many blacks were separated from their families as men were forced into Confederate labor gangs. For many black men, however, this work allowed them to escape to freedom. Many slaves slipped away from Confederate railroad crews or joined Union forces after major battles.

Black Enlistment and Emancipation

Thousands of blacks were "employed" (they were not always paid) as military laborers on the Union side as well. Wherever Union armies advanced into the South, blacks served as wagon masters, construction workers, and cooks. Former slaves who were familiar with the South also served as spies. **Harriet Tubman,** famous for her earlier career helping slaves escape to freedom along the **Underground Railroad,** was one of the countless blacks who served the Union as a guide and a spy. She was later commended by the secretary of war for her work as a nurse and scout during the war.

As the war continued, the Union's policy of not allowing black men to enlist became impossible to maintain. As the North lost more and more white soldiers in bloody battles, support for black troops began to grow. In 1862 the North changed its policy and allowed blacks to enlist as soldiers. By August of that year, the War Department had authorized the recruitment of five regiments of black infantry.

Following Lincoln's Emancipation Proclamation in January 1863 (which freed the slaves in the states "in rebellion," or the Southern states), the governors of Massachusetts, Connecticut, and Rhode Island were authorized to enlist black troops. The Union needed as many men as it could recruit, and black enlistment became the best way to weaken and destroy slavery. For the rest of the war, the Union army focused its efforts on freeing blacks and enlisting black soldiers.

During the war black soldiers suffered not only the same hardships as their white comrades but also the effects of racism. They did not receive the same level of medical care that white troops received; they faced reenslavement or execution if captured by Southern troops; and they were discriminated against by white Union soldiers and the federal government. In fact, the Union government broke its promise and paid all black soldiers, regardless of rank, less than it paid the lowest-paid white soldier. The unequal pay they received angered black soldiers more than any other form of discrimi-

An African-American sailor from the Civil War. Service records show that over 18,000 African Americans served as seamen in the Civil War (Courtesy of the Library of Congress)

nation, and many black regiments refused to accept any pay until it was equalized. Under pressure from black communities, abolitionists, and governors, Congress finally granted equal pay for black and white soldiers in June 1864.

In spite of unfair treatment, black soldiers participated in 39 major battles and 410 minor engagements during the last two years of the war. Many black units fought heroically and suffered terrible losses. In all, nearly three thousand blacks died in battle during the Civil War, and another thirty-three thousand died of disease.

With the passage of the Thirteenth Amendment in February 1865, slavery was legally abolished in America. For African Americans the end of the Civil War was a time of great hope and fear. Political and social equality were now possible, but racism remained a constant threat. The years ahead would bring great advancement in black politics, civil rights, and institu-

tions, as well as great disappointment and betrayal. But freedom had finally come at last.

Clark Atlanta University

Founded: Clark Atlanta University was formed in 1988 when two historically black colleges, Clark College (founded 1869) and Atlanta University (founded 1865), merged. Clark Atlanta is now the largest of the United Negro College Fund institutions.

Location: Atlanta, Georgia

Known For: Excellence in research; many of the university's research projects are sponsored by U.S. government agencies, including the Department of Defense and the Department of Energy.

Religious Affiliation: United Methodist Church

Number of Students (1999–2000): 5,410

Grade Average of Incoming Freshman: 3.0

Admission Requirements: Recommended high school courses include at least four years of English, three years of mathematics, two years of science, two years of foreign language, three years of social studies; SAT or ACT scores; one letter of recommendation from a teacher and one from a counselor.

Mailing Address:
Clark Atlanta University
Office of Admission
223 James P. Brawley Dr., SW
Atlanta, GA 30314

Telephone: (800) 688-3228

E-mail: admin@cau.edu

URL: http://www.cau.edu

Campus: The 113-acre campus is located one mile from downtown Atlanta. The Building for Science Research and Technology houses many research facilities under one roof, including the Center for Excellence in Teaching and Learning and the Environmental Justice Research Center. The academic heart of the campus is the Center for Academic Achievement, which includes a language laboratory and a writing laboratory. Other buildings include a computer lab and several art galleries. Because Clark Atlanta is part of the **Atlanta University Center,** students are able to use many of the facilities located throughout Atlanta, including the Robert Woodruff Library, which contains over 500,000 volumes.

Special Programs: African and African-American studies; honors program; independent study.

Extracurricular Activities: Student government; school newspaper, *The Panther*; radio station; television station; athletics (men's basketball, football, tennis, track; women's basketball, tennis, track, volleyball); CAU band; four sororities and four fraternities; over sixty organizations, including theater groups and jazz ensembles.

Clark Atlanta Alumni: Louis Tompkins Wright (1891–1952), Clark University alumni and first African-American physician to head Harlem Hospital's surgery department; songwriter **James Weldon Johnson** (1871–1938), Atlanta University alumni and author of "Lift Ev'ry Voice and Sing," considered the Negro national anthem; Kenny Leon, the first African-American artistic directory of a national theater company (the Atlanta Alliance Theater).

Clark, Kenneth Bancroft

PSYCHOLOGIST, WRITER, ACTIVIST
July 24, 1914–

Kenneth Clark: Selected Publications

Prejudice and Your Child
(1955)

Dark Ghetto: Dilemmas of Social Power
(1965)

A Relevant War Against Poverty
(1969)

The Pathos of Power
(1974)

Psychologist Kenneth Clark was instrumental in the U.S. Supreme Court decision in the case of *Brown v. Board of Education of Topeka, Kansas,* in 1954. The historic case put an end to segregation (the separation of blacks and whites in public facilities) and played a vital role in the **Civil Rights movement** of the 1950s and 1960s. The Court used Clark's psychological research on race relations in its ruling outlawing segregation. Clark attended **Howard University** (Washington, D.C.) and earned a Ph.D. degree from Columbia University (New York). He taught at the City College of New York from 1942 until 1975. He is the author of several books and articles. He has been recognized for his scholarship and his contributions to the black community, most notably as the winner of the 1961 Spingarn Medal, the highest award given by the **National Association for the Advancement of Colored People (NAACP).** When he retired, Clark founded Kenneth B. Clark and Associates, a consulting firm specializing in **affirmative action** in race relations.

Clark, Septima Poinsette

EDUCATOR, CIVIL RIGHTS ACTIVIST
May 3, 1898–December 15, 1987

Septima Poinsette Clark was a teacher who believed that **education** was the strongest weapon in the fight for African-American civil rights. Septima Poinsette was born and reared in Charleston, South Carolina, to parents who taught her to share her gifts with the world and to believe there is good in everyone. Poinsette's early education brought her into contact with demanding black teachers who insisted that students have pride and work hard. As a result of these influences, she pursued a career in education and in 1916 received her teaching certificate from Avery Normal Institute, a private school for black teachers ("normal schools" were schools for training teachers).

Poinsette's first teaching position was on Johns Island, South Carolina, because African Americans were barred from teaching in the Charleston public schools. She tried to address the vast educational, political, and economic problems that faced Johns Island blacks by creating adult literacy and health education classes. In 1919 she returned to Charleston to work at Avery. She also led a campaign against Charleston's education system that resulted, one year later, in the overturning of the law barring black teachers from teaching in public schools. In addition, she led the fight for equal pay for black teachers in South Carolina. She taught in the Charleston public schools until 1956, when she was fired for her civil rights activities.

Unable to find another position in South Carolina, Clark moved to the Highlander Folk School in Monteagle, Tennessee, an interracial adult education center. There, Clark became director of education. At Highlander, Clark created the citizenship school program, an adult literacy program that focused on promoting voter registration and encouraging people to solve their own problems. The first citizenship school, founded on Johns Island in 1957, was a success, and Clark traveled throughout the South to open other schools. By 1970 more than eight hundred **citizenship schools** had been formed that graduated over one hundred thousand African Americans.

Clark worked for equality for women as well as for blacks In 1966 she spoke at the first national meeting of the National Organization of Women (NOW). In 1976 she was elected to the Charleston, South Carolina, school board. In 1987 she received an American Book Award for her second **autobiography,** *Ready from Within: Septima Clark and the* **Civil Rights Movement.** (*See also* **Civil Rights movement; Highlander Citizenship School.**)

Clarke, Kenneth Spearman "Kenny"

JAZZ DRUMMER, BANDLEADER
January 9, 1914–January 26, 1985

Remembered for his contribution to the development of **bebop** (a modern **jazz** style), drummer Kenny Clarke was revered for what fellow musicians called his "heartbeat," his effortless, pulse-driven rhythm work on the cymbals. Clarke is most known for contributing to two of the earliest compositions in modern jazz: "Salt Peanuts" (1942), cowritten with legendary trumpeter **Dizzy Gillespie** (1917–1993); and "Epistrophy" (also called "Fly Right," 1941), written with piano great **Thelonious Monk** (1920–1982).

Clarke was born in Pittsburgh, Pennsylvania, into a very musical family. Studying trombone, drums, vibraphone (a percussion instrument—one that is sounded by beating, like a drum; shaking; or scraping—that resembles the xylophone), and music theory in public school, by the age of fifteen Clarke was playing professionally as a drummer. In 1934 he left Pittsburgh to perform with a St. Louis (Missouri)–based jazz band, and one year later he moved to New York, joining the city's thriving music scene. By the end of the 1930s Clarke had toured Europe, made his recording debut, and issued his first record as bandleader.

Clarke redefined the role of drums in jazz music: Rather than simply keeping the beat, he used his drums to accent (or punctuate) the sounds of the other instruments in the band. His "punctuation marks" became known in music circles as "dropping bombs" or "klook-mops," earning him the nickname "Klook." This new style of drumming can be heard in Clarke's 1940 recording "One O'clock Jump," with saxophonist and clarinetist **Sidney Bechet** (1897–1959).

During **World War II** (1939–45), Clarke was drafted into the U.S. Army and served in Europe from 1943 to 1946. Returning to New York, the jazz musician continued his career, touring internationally and making numerous recordings. In 1956 he moved to Paris, France, then a hotbed of jazz music. He continued working and established a drum school. In 1960 Clarke joined with Belgian pianist Francy Boland (1929–) to form the Clarke-Boland Big Band, an all-star jazz group. They performed and recorded together for thirteen years. Clarke was semiretired and living near Paris when he died.

Clay, Cassius. *See* **Muhammad Ali**

Cleaver, Eldridge

WRITER, POLITICAL ACTIVIST
August 31, 1935–May 1, 1998

Eldridge Cleaver was a writer and political activist whose book *Soul on Ice* told the world how it felt to be a black man in a world dominated by whites. After a rough childhood and spending time in prison, Cleaver joined the **Black Panther Party for Self-Defense**. The Panthers were a group of black men who inspired racial pride and believed that blacks should be prepared to defend themselves against an unjust government.

In 1968 Cleaver was involved in a shootout with police and arrested. Afraid that he would be sent back to jail, Cleaver left the United States and moved to Cuba, France, and then Algiers. During the early 1970s he wrote about his experiences and beliefs for many magazines. In 1975 he returned to the United States and was sentenced to twelve hundred hours of community service.

In 1978 Cleaver published *Soul on Fire*, a book about his new—and less extreme—ideas. He continued to write poetry and political articles throughout the 1980s and 1990s and traveled the country speaking on religion and politics. (*See also* **Black Nationalism**.)

Clemente, Roberto

BASEBALL PLAYER
August 18, 1934–December 31, 1972

Roberto Clemente was a favorite of **baseball** fans, particularly those from his homeland, the West Indies island of Puerto Rico. He played eighteen years for the Pittsburgh Pirates, with a career batting average of .318 (he

got a hit more than three out of ten times at bat). Clemente's manner and actions made him as respected off the field as on it.

Clemente played baseball in Puerto Rico before beginning his career in Pittsburgh, Pennsylvania. During his long career he dazzled fans with 240 home runs, 3,000 hits, four National League batting titles (the Major League Baseball Association is broken into two leagues, American and National, the champions of which play each other in the World Series), twelve Gold Gloves (given for excellence in fielding), and two World Series titles (1960 and 1971). Clemente was voted into baseball's Hall of Fame in 1972.

Clemente was coaching in Puerto Rico in 1972 when there was an earthquake in the nearby Central American country of Nicaragua. Clemente was flying to the ravaged country to give assistance when his plane crashed. Clemente had had a dream of making a "sport city" for young people in Puerto Rico, but he died before he could finish it. His wife, Vera Clemente de Zabala, later made his dream come true.

Cleveland, James Edward

GOSPEL SINGER
1931–1991

Born in Chicago, Illinois, singer James Cleveland is often called "the king of gospel." He began piano lessons at the age of five, three years before he became a soloist in church. At age fifteen he joined the Thorne Crusaders singing group. At sixteen he wrote "Grace Is Sufficient," which became a well-known gospel song.

In the early 1960s Cleveland joined the choir at First Baptist Church in Nutley, New Jersey, to make a number of recordings beginning with "Peace, Be Still" (1962). During the 1950s and 1960s Cleveland wrote more than five hundred songs. He continued to compose into the 1980s and had a popular success with "I Get a Blessing Everyday" (1980), recorded with the singing group Mighty Clouds of Joy.

Cleveland preferred a style known as "call-and-response": on his live choir recordings he played the role of a preacher who "calls" to his congregation; choir members sing the "response." When Cleveland performed, he sang the highest and lowest notes in his vocal range and enjoyed improvising (making up the music) at the end of songs. His songs dealt with everyday concerns such as paying rent and buying food.

In 1968 Cleveland formed the Gospel Music Workshop of America, which had several hundred thousand members by the mid-1980s. Pop star **Aretha Franklin** recorded "Amazing Grace" with Cleveland in 1971 and studied his style when he was director of the radio choir at Detroit's New Bethel Baptist Church.

In 1970 Cleveland organized and became pastor of Cornerstone Institutional Baptist Church in Los Angeles, California. At his death in 1991, the church had more than seven thousand members.

Coasters, The

POPULAR MUSIC GROUP

Known as "the clown princes of rock and roll," The Coasters were famous for singing high-energy comic songs. They are widely regarded as the number one vocal group of the original rock and roll era of the 1950s. Named "The Coasters" because of their West Coast origins, the group was created by two members of a singing act known as the Robins, Carl Gardner (1928–) and Bobby Nunn (1925–1986). Gardner and Nunn were joined by Billy Guy (1936-) and Leon Hughes (1938–). In 1957 Nunn and Hughes left the group and were replaced by Will Jones (1928–2000) and Cornell Gunter (1938–1990).

Starting in the mid-1950s, The Coasters had numerous hit records, most of them humorous tunes written by songwriters Jerry Leiber and Mike Stoller (who also wrote for rock-and-roll great Elvis Presley). These songs featured a rough, energetic style and included "Yakety Yak" (1958), "Charlie

Brown" (1958), which reached number one on the charts, and "Poison Ivy" (1959). The Coasters lost popularity after the 1950s but have continued to tour (with several personnel changes over the years. Their albums include *On Broadway* (1973) and *Thumbin' a Ride* (1985).

The Coasters have sold more than one hundred million records. During their heyday they also appeared in six major movies. In 1987 the original members of The Coasters became the first vocal group to be inducted into the Rock and Roll Hall of Fame.

Cobb, Jewel Plummer

SCIENTIST, EDUCATOR
January 17, 1924–

Scientist Jewel Plummer Cobb had an early interest in biology as a high school student in Chicago, Illinois, where she was born. Cobb studied at the University of Michigan and later earned a degree in biology from Talladega College in **Alabama.** A budding researcher in a male-dominated profession, she acquired master's and Ph.D. degrees in cell physiology from New York University. Her thesis (a research paper required for a degree) outlined areas for her future investigations of melanomas (skin cancers) and cancer treatments. Cobb assumed her first major teaching position as an anatomy instructor at the University of Illinois Medical School in 1952. She married Roy R. Cobb in 1954.

In 1955 Cobb established a Tissue Culture Research Laboratory at the New York University-Bellevue Hospital Medical Center. Over the next thirty years she served as a professor, researcher, and administrator at New York University, Sarah Lawrence College, and Connecticut College. As the dean (head of the school) at Connecticut, she created a program to enhance science education for women and minorities.

In 1974, as a member of the National Science Foundation's National Science Board, Cobb established a task force on women and minorities in science. She wrote an article titled "Filters for Women in Science" which addressed the difficulty women have in entering scientific fields. The article was published in 1974 as part of a collection, *Expanding the Role of Women in Sciences.*

Cobb was appointed president of California State University in 1981 and successfully obtained funding for programs, including science facilities. She continued to work at securing funding and opportunities for minorities in the sciences.

Coker, Daniel

MINISTER, ABOLITIONIST
1780–1846

Daniel Coker was a Methodist leader active in the fight for **abolition,** or ending slavery. He began life as a slave in Maryland. He learned to read and write in New York City while he was his half-brother's servant. (Coker was half white and his brother was white; they had the same mother but different fathers).

In 1800 Coker ran away and became a minister. He wrote a pamphlet in 1810 explaining why **slavery** was wrong. Coker helped bring the Methodist church to blacks in the United States by helping form the **African Methodist Episcopal (AME) Church** in 1816. In 1820 he went to **Africa** to spread Methodism and created the West African Methodist Church. (*See also* **Allen, Richard.**)

Cole, Nat "King"

SINGER, PIANIST
March 17, 1919–February 15, 1965

Nat "King" Cole was one of the most beloved entertainers of the twentieth century and was known for singing romantic songs with a very smooth

Nat King Cole (Archive Photos. Reproduced by permission)

voice. Cole had his earliest musical experiences in his father's church, where he sang and played the organ. In 1936 he played piano in a touring production of *Shuffle Along*. Cole stayed in California after the tour ended and played piano in local clubs. In 1938 he adopted the name Nat "King" Cole and became popular for his swinging piano style.

The first recording on which Cole sang, "Straighten Up and Fly Right" (1943), was also his first hit. The song, based on a sermon of his father's, was taken from a traditional black folktale. Eventually, Cole became more well known for singing than for his piano playing. His 1946 recording of "The Christmas Song" was a turning point in his career. Cole went on to great success with such vocal recordings as "Mona Lisa" (1950) and "Unforgettable" (1951).

Cole's relaxed singing style was popular with both white and black audiences. He had the first black **jazz** combo (a small jazz or dance band) to have its own commercial-sponsored **radio** program (1948–49), and in 1957 he became the first black performer to have his own series on network **television**. Cole also made several **film**s, including *St. Louis Blues* (1958) and *Cat Ballou* (1965).

In the early 1960s Cole was sometimes criticized by black activists for his failure to actively participate in the struggle for civil rights. Cole resented the accusations, noting that he had made large financial contributions to civil rights organizations. Ultimately, Cole was the most successful black performer of his time. The appreciation of his contribution to popular music has increased since his death. Episodes of his television show are back in circulation, and many of his recordings have been reissued.

Coleman, Bessie

AVIATOR
January 26, 1892–April 30, 1926

Bessie Coleman was the world's first black female pilot and the first woman to receive an international pilot's license. She was born on January 26, 1893, in Texas to sharecropper (a farmer who rents land and gives part of the crop as rent) parents, the twelfth of thirteen children. Her lifelong love of airplanes and flying was to meet with disappointment in the United States: she could not gain admittance to an American flying school because of her race and her sex.

Influenced by a black American pilot, Eugene Bullard, who flew with the French in **World War I** (1914–18), Coleman learned French and went to Europe with an American Red Cross unit attached to a French flying squadron. She persuaded French pilots to give her instruction and in 1921 earned a pilot's license, making her a licensed pilot two years before the legendary Amelia Earhart (1897–1937) earned her license in the United States.

Coleman returned to the United States in 1922 and worked to establish an American flight school for blacks. To gain support for the school, she traveled across the country giving lectures and stunt-flying demonstrations. She died without accomplishing her goal when she was thrown from her plane during a flying exercise in Jacksonville, Florida, on April 30, 1926.

Coleman, Ornette

JAZZ SAXOPHONIST, COMPOSER
c. March 9, 1930–

One of the most influential figures of modern **jazz**, Ornette Coleman has taught and inspired a new generation of jazz musicians. Born in Fort Worth, Texas, Coleman grew up in a musical household, listening to **gospel**, **rhythm and blues**, and bebop (a form of modern jazz). He began playing saxophone in his early teens and was introduced early on to the works of American jazz saxophonist **Charlie "Bird" Parker** (1920–1955).

Coleman performed in church and in the high school band, from which he was expelled for improvising (making up passages of music) while playing a march. In 1949 he got his first professional work, with a traveling minstrel show, a popular music and comedy show of the day. He also traveled with

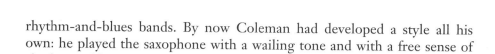
rhythm-and-blues bands. By now Coleman had developed a style all his own: he played the saxophone with a wailing tone and with a free sense of rhythm and harmony.

In 1950 Coleman moved to Los Angeles, California, where he married poet **Jayne Cortez** (1936–) in 1954 and found a circle of musicians to play with. Among them was trumpeter Don Cherry (1936–), who became his longtime friend. Unable to support himself as a musician, Coleman worked in a department store. In 1958 he was invited to make his first recording: *Something Else* marked a turning point for the innovative musician. The Ornette Coleman quartet soon began playing Five Spot, a popular New York City nightclub. Audience response was positive, and the performances earned rave reviews in the press. His "free jazz" had arrived.

Coleman's follow-up recordings, including *Tomorrow Is the Question* (1959) and *The Shape of Jazz to Come* (1960), were attacked by traditionalists, who heard nothing but noise in the loosely structured improvisations and daring harmonies. But his unique brand of jazz gained admirers as well; listeners with keen ears heard in Coleman's music the first significant development in jazz since bebop in the 1940s.

By the 1960s Coleman was hailed as one of the greatest figures in jazz. Scaling back his performance and recording work, the now-established musician studied trumpet and violin. In 1967 he became the first jazz musician to win a Guggenheim Fellowship. Throughout the 1960s and into the early 1970s, Coleman played with various trios and quartets.

Coleman has worked in a wide range of musical styles. He began composing classical music in the early 1950s. He has also dabbled in African **folk music.** In 1975 he began playing electric dance music heavily influenced by the rhythm-and-blues dance bands he played with in his youth. Coleman recorded this new style with a group of musicians called Prime Time. Today he continues to compose and record from his Manhattan, New York, home.

Coles, Charles "Honi"

TAP DANCER
April 2, 1911–November 12, 1992

Honi Coles's high-speed rhythm tapping was developed in contests on the streets of his native Philadelphia, Pennsylvania, where he was born in 1911. Coles first moved to New York in 1931 as one of the Three Millers, who tap-danced on top of pedestals, performing difficult dance steps. When the act no longer attracted an audience, Coles returned to Philadelphia to perfect his technique. He returned to New York in 1934, opening at the **Apollo Theater.** Coles earned a reputation for having the "fastest feet in show business" and was hailed as an extraordinarily graceful dancer. For three years he was a member of the Lucky Seven Trio, who, like the Three Millers, tapped on large cubes that looked like dice.

In 1940 when Coles was dancing with Cab Calloway's swing band, he met **Charles "Cholly" Atkins** (1913–). Several years later they formed the class act Coles & Atkins. Their best-known soft-shoe dance was danced to

Colescott, Robert H.

"Taking a Chance on Love," played at an extremely slow tempo. Coles and Atkins seemed suspended in midair as they tossed off gliding turns and smooth slides, all with crystal-clear taps.

Coles was known for the speed and swinging-rhythmic complexity of his dancing. From 1945 to 1949 Coles and Atkins appeared with the big bands of **Cab Calloway** (1907–1994) and **Louis Armstrong** (1901–1971), among others. On Broadway they appeared in a show-stopping routine that they created for the musical *Gentlemen Prefer Blondes* in 1949.

For the next sixteen years, Coles worked as the production manager at the Apollo Theater. He served as president of the Negro Actors' Guild and in 1949 was a founder of the tap dancers' fraternity **The Copasetics.** When Coles and Atkins last danced together in 1959, the big-band era was over and tap dancing was no longer so popular on Broadway.

In the early 1960s Coles helped spark a new interest in tap dancing. In 1978 he placed tap firmly in the world of concert art when he performed with the Joffrey Ballet. He returned to Broadway in several other shows. During the 1980s Coles taught dance and dance history at several colleges and universities. He received several awards for his contribution to dance.

Singer **Lena Horne** (1917–) said of Coles, "Honi makes butterflies look clumsy." Coles was also a singer, composer, and master of ceremonies renowned for his quick wit. He was a dancer whose personal style and technical precision epitomized what is known in the community of **tap dance** as the "class act" dancer.

> *"Honi makes butterflies look clumsy"*
>
> Lena Horne, describing Cole's dancing grace

Colescott, Robert H.

PAINTER
August 26, 1925–

Robert Colescott is famous for creating paintings that mimic well-known European art to make humorous social commentary. Born in Oakland, California, he earned bachelor's and master's degrees at the University of California at Berkeley. He lived in Paris, France, beginning in the late 1940s, before moving to Cairo, Egypt, where he was artist-in-residence at the American Research Center (1964–65) and a teacher at the American University (1966–67).

Borrowing from European paintings, Colescott created pictures that challenge racial and gender stereotypes. To do this, he puts cartoonlike, blackfaced figures (people with black facial makeup) into the settings of famous paintings, often changing a figure's race, sex, expression, or occupation. For example, *Eat Dem Taters* (1975) was modeled after *The Potato Eaters*, by French impressionist painter (one who tries to represent the effects of light on what they are painting) Vincent Van Gogh (1853–1890). In his version Colescott painted poor black farmers to compare the poverty of American blacks and nineteenth-century European peasants.

In the late 1970s and early 1980s, Colescott began focusing on women in his paintings. He also began to create satires (a type of humorous criticism) of American landscape painting, such as *Chocolate Cakescape* (1981). By the mid-1980s Colescott was exploring religious subjects, again using

European paintings as a source for visual puns (a humorous double meaning) and observations about people.

Colescott's work has been shown at many major U.S. museums and in a traveling exhibit organized in 1989. In 1997 he represented the United States at the internationally famous Venice (Italy) Biennial (held every two years) exhibition. In Colescott's painting of a police officer screaming racial slurs, *Bilingual Cop*, made news when a University of Nebraska gallery made it off-limits during elementary school field trips.

Colleges and Universities

Most historically black colleges and universities (HBCUs) were founded in the years immediately after the **Civil War** (1861–65). Many were set up to train teachers to work in black elementary and high schools, while others focused on well-rounded academic training, and still others concentrated on training students for particular kinds of jobs.

The founding of black colleges fell into one of four categories: (1) those established by missionary societies of the North; (2) independent schools not associated with any church or church group (nondenominational); (3) industrial colleges; and (4) state "land grant" institutions.

Work of the Missionary Societies

Before the Civil War, many Christians in the North were active abolitionists. Viewing **slavery** as morally wrong (the Bible condemns the practice), they were an important part of the movement to outlaw it. When the fighting ended and all slaves were declared free throughout the United States, many of these people were eager to move into the South to set up schools. It was part of their mission as Christians to teach black people, whom they viewed as spiritual equals, to read the word of God. First founding elementary schools, missionaries soon turned their attention to secondary schools and colleges, where future teachers could be trained to staff black schools in the South.

Associated with various churches, including the Congregational, Baptist, and Presbyterian, missionaries established such long-standing black institutions as **Fisk University** (Nashville, Tennessee) in 1866; **Morehouse College** (Atlanta, Georgia) in 1867; and **Huston-Tillotson College** (Austin, Texas) in 1877.

Black churches also supported higher education, and had been doing so even before the Civil War. For example, **Wilberforce University** (Tarawa Springs, Ohio) was founded in 1856 by the Methodist Episcopal Church, who jointly maintained it with the **African Methodist Episcopal (AME) Church.** Also, black **Baptists** were responsible for setting up colleges in the South.

Independent Colleges

With most missionary schools operated and controlled by whites, educated blacks moved quickly in the post–Civil War era to establish schools of their own. At **Howard University,** founded 1868 in Washington, D.C., and **Atlanta University,** founded 1872 in Georgia, black students could receive an education similar to that offered to white students at the nation's universities. They could also earn advanced degrees in subjects such as medicine and law.

Industrial Training

Virginia's Hampton University, founded as Hampton Normal and Industrial Institute (usually referred to as simply **Hampton Institute**) in 1868, was among the earliest schools to train black students in "useful skills." The institute prepared students to teach in black schools or take labor jobs that were traditionally held by blacks. Therefore, Hampton's program and policy did not threaten whites.

Among Hampton's first graduates was **Booker T. Washington** (c. 1856–1915). Using Hampton as his model of education, in 1881 he founded **Tuskegee University** (originally called Tuskegee Institute) in Alabama. These industrial schools, which focused on job skills (vocational) training and not necessarily on academics, were embraced by the white community. White lawmakers, who decided how schools were funded, favored the training institutes since they did not challenge the status quo (existing conditions in society).

Land Grant Colleges

In the 1860s the U.S. Congress passed laws that gave government land to states as long as the states used the land to build or support institutions of higher learning. At the time, most Americans believed the nation's future rested on agriculture and new machinery. Therefore, many states moved quickly to set up what were called A&M colleges, or agricultural and mechanical colleges (although sometimes the "M" stood for "mining" or "military"). Because of their funding, they were also called land grant colleges. The first of these schools set up to educate blacks was Mississippi's Alcorn A&M College (1871), today called Alcorn State University. By 1915 there were sixteen land grant colleges for African Americans.

The Great Debate

Just as black elementary and high schools struggled to secure enough money to operate a solid academic program, funding was also a problem for the nation's black colleges. After 1900 the support of the missionary societies declined. While other charitable organizations, especially the Julius Rosenwald Fund, stepped in to lend financial backing, black colleges found they were competing with one another for precious dollars.

This competition contributed to the ongoing debate in the black community about how its youths should be educated. Some agreed with Booker T. Washington's method, which trained black workers to become competent in a chosen skill. Others listened to scholar and educator **W. E. B. Du Bois** (1868–1963), who believed college education of blacks should be rooted in a strong academic tradition, with students learning a range of subjects, including Greek, Latin, history, geography, math, and science. Du Bois asserted

W.E.B. Du Bois believed college education for blacks should be rooted in a strong academic tradition, including Greek, Latin, history, geography, math, and science.

that black schools should produce leaders, who, in turn, would teach and encourage other African Americans to reach their full potential.

Historians have pointed out that the Washington-supported training institutions and the Du Bois-backed academic institutions both made needed contributions to society, since they prepared and educated workers and technicians, as well as educators and politicians. The HBCUs have trained generations of black professional and working people. They play a crucial role in the education of the nation's youths. (*See also* **Education.**)

Colorado

First African-American Settlers: One of the earliest recorded instances of blacks in what became Colorado occurred in 1776 when a Franciscan friar (Catholic monk) recorded the drowning of one of his black assistants. The first Anglo-American blacks arrived in Colorado in the early nineteenth century as participants in fur-trading expeditions and as laborers to staff new communities.

Slave Population: Colorado was admitted to the Union as the thirty-eighth state in 1876, fifteen years after becoming a U.S. territory. Some of the first blacks in the state were slaves, particularly those who were part of the fortune-seeking groups that originated in the Southern states. Some enslaved blacks were brought to work gold mines around Pikes Peak.

Free Black Population: By the 1860s several **free blacks** had arrived in Colorado seeking to improve their lives, and the black population increased to 456 by 1870.

Reconstruction: In the years following the American **Civil War** (1861–65), African-Americans in Colorado struggled successfully to gain suffrage (voting) rights and to integrate schools. Shortly thereafter came the first black police officers and jurors appeared. The opening of new gold and silver mines, as well as the arrival of the railroad in Denver, lured additional blacks to Colorado in the 1880s. Some areas of Colorado housed prosperous black communities, but the majority of black residents were isolated, underemployed, and discriminated against.

The Great Depression: The coming of **World War II** (1939–45) brought an enormous shift in the fortunes of Colorado's African Americans as many took advantage of the massive hiring of laborers in defense-related industries. From 1940 to 1950 the African-American population of Colorado almost doubled, and it nearly doubled again by 1960. By 1960 black income in the state was up to 75 percent of white income, and the gap narrowed somewhat thereafter.

Civil Rights Movement to the Present: In 1969 the Denver School Board adopted by a wide margin a school integration plan that included busing. White parents sued to cancel the plan, and the question went through the courts. In 1973 the U.S. Supreme Court, in *Keyes v. Denver School District No. 1*, ruled in favor of the school board. Desegregation was met with violence, and some school buses were bombed.

Current African-American Population: According to U.S. Census Bureau estimates, the total black population in Colorado was 171,904 (4.3 percent of the state population) as of July 1, 1998.

Key Figures: "Aunt" Clara Brown (1800–1885), the first female African American to settle in Central City; Emma Azalia Smith Hackley (1867–1922), singer and educator; Academy Award-winning actress **Hattie McDaniel** (1895–1952); **Jimmie Lunceford** (1902–1947), big-band leader; author **Clarence Major** (1936–); **Edwin Corley Moses** (1955–), track-and-field athlete.

(SEE ALSO EXODUSTERS; KU KLUX KLAN.)

Colter, Cyrus

NOVELIST, LAWYER, TEACHER
January 8, 1910–

Cyrus Colter was born and raised in Noblesville, Indiana. His mother died in 1916, and Colter's childhood and youth were greatly influenced by the learning and accomplishments of his father, a traveling organizer for the newly established **National Association for the Advancement of Colored People (NAACP).** Colter attended high school and college in Ohio. After earning a law degree, he began practicing law in Chicago, Illinois, in 1940.

Colter entered the U.S. Army in 1942, was eventually promoted to captain, and served in combat in Italy until the end of **World War II** (1939–45). In 1942 he married Imogene Mackay. He returned to Chicago in 1946 and embarked on a political career. He was appointed by Democratic governor Adlai Stevenson to the Illinois Commerce Commission, on which he served under six governors. In 1973 Colter retired from the commission and from the active practice of law. He became Chester D. Tripp Distinguished Professor at Northwestern University in Evanston, Illinois, where he built the Afro-American Studies Department and taught until his retirement in 1979.

Colter began to write for publication at age fifty and published his first book ten years later. *The Beach Umbrella*, a collection of short stories published in 1970, won the first Iowa Fiction Award, judged that year by novelist Kurt Vonnegut. His first novel, *The Rivers of Eros* (1972), is about the social, political, and psychological problems faced by working-class black men and women. It was followed by *The Hippodrome* (1973), *Night Studies* (1979), *A Chocolate Soldier* (1988), and *City of Light* (1993). *The Amoralist* (1988) is an expanded edition of *The Beach Umbrella*.

Coltrane, John William

JAZZ SAXOPHONIST
September 23, 1926–July 17, 1967

John Coltrane, often simply called "Trane," was by far the most popular **jazz** musician to emerge from the New York City jazz movement of the late 1950s and 1960s. Born in Hamlet, North Carolina, Coltrane received his

first instrument, a clarinet, when he was twelve, although he soon began to play the alto saxophone. After high school Coltrane moved to Philadelphia, Pennsylvania, where he studied at the Ornstein School of Music and the Granoff Studios.

In 1945 Coltrane joined the U.S. Navy, where he was exposed to the music of **Charlie Parker.** Awed by Parker's alto saxophone style, Coltrane switched to the tenor saxophone to avoid a comparison. When he returned to Philadelphia, he started playing in **blues** bands, and bandleader **Dizzy Gillespie** hired him in 1948. But Coltrane began drinking heavily and using drugs, and in 1951 he lost his job with the Gillespie band.

The recognition of Coltrane as a major jazz figure dates from his joining the **Miles Davis** quintet (a group of five) in 1955, an association that would last until 1959. In 1957 Coltrane overcame his drinking and drug problem, and in the process he underwent a spiritual rebirth. He began to play with **Thelonious Monk** and recorded his first album as a leader, *Blue Train*.

Coltrane left Davis in 1959, started his own group, and began playing the soprano saxophone (an instrument rarely used by jazz musicians). He developed a distinctive soprano style, different from the one he favored on the tenor saxophone, and soon recorded his most famous soprano sax solo, "My Favorite Things." Beginning in 1965, Coltrane explored free jazz improvisation (creating music spontaneously, not following a written score) until his death from cancer on July 17, 1967. Coltrane's personal style, his early death, and the power and grace of his solos contributed to a Coltrane "cult" (a group of followers) that has remained strong in the decades since his death. His influence on later musicians, which has been immense, includes not only his musical ideas but also his view of jazz as an ongoing quest for spiritual knowledge and self-wisdom.

Comedians

Early African-American Comedy

The role of the comedian in most cultures is to make humor out of the characteristics of a given society. African-American comedy is no exception, and much of the material that provided humor for many years focused on race relations between blacks and whites. In many ways, the condition of American society at the time black comedians began to emerge forced them to use racial themes. However, as society progressed and the **Civil Rights movement** began bridging the gap between blacks and whites, black comedians began entertaining crowds by spinning humor out of everyday human experiences (rather than "black" and "white" issues).

African-American comedy began before the **Civil War** (1861-65) with whites painting their faces black with burnt cork and imitating blacks with singing, dancing, and dialogue. These performances were called "minstrel" shows, and the performers were known as "minstrels." At the time, whites did not have much exposure to blacks, which made minstrel shows popular because they played on rumors about black culture. Unfortunately, the skits used by minstrels reinforced negative stereotypes (prejudiced impressions) suggesting that blacks were backward people with unattractive features. So it is curious that blacks found their way into show business by performing minstrel routines.

Popular black comedy routines that used the minstrel style of humor (dressing up in odd clothes, making strange faces, and imitating the way blacks spoke at the time) included "Mr. Tambo" and "Mr. Bones." Minstrel shows led to the development of the Theater Owners Booking Association (TOBA), which controlled black entertainment throughout the country. **Bert Williams,** the first famous black comedian, at one time performed in an enormously popular TOBA musical show called the Ziegfeld Follies.

In 1934 African-American comedy was given a boost by the start-up of Harlem's **Apollo Theater,** which provided a place where aspiring amateurs could compete for stardom. One of the most popular routines to get its start at the Apollo was Butterbeans and Susie (1930s), performed by Joe and Susie Edwards. Their act included sexual humor, which delighted many and enraged others. In general, the comedy routines of the 1930s and 1940s con-

EDDIE MURPHY

Eddie Murphy was born in Brooklyn, New York, and moved to Long Island, New York, when his father, a policeman, was killed in the line of duty. Murphy began comic routines with "ranking" (acting out the roles of two people exchanging witty insults). In 1979 he earned a spot on television's "Saturday Night Live," where he was an instant success.

Murphy entertained millions on "Saturday Night Live" with Bill Cosby and **Stevie Wonder** impressions and playing characters such as a grown-up "Buckwheat" from the "The Little Rascals" and "Mister Robinson," a mean-spirited version of television's "Mister Rogers." Murphy recorded an album of his stand-up routines, which went platinum (sold over one million copies). He then began a successful acting career, starring in box office hits such as *48 Hours* (1982), *Beverly Hills Cop* (1985), *The Nutty Professor* (1996), *Doctor Doolittle* (1998), and *Nutty Professor II: The Klumps* (2000).

sisted of song-and-dance routines and creative exchanges common to the minstrel tradition. One of the most popular early black comedy routines was Dusty Fletcher's "Open the Door, Richard." Fletcher prompted roaring laughter by playing a drunk trying to enter a house, falling down the stairs exclaiming, "Open the Door, Richard!"

The Emergence of Black Comedy

A new form of comedy began to emerge in the 1960s when **Jackie "Moms" Mabley** introduced her "dirty old lady" to audiences. The unique thing about Mabley's character was that she performed a stand-up monologue (one person speaking), a style that is still used today. Although Mabley used non-racist themes such as sex in her performances, she also included political themes such as segregation. The sex theme was also picked up by comedians such as George Kirby and Redd Foxx who made "party records" to circulate their material. Redd Foxx was one of the most successful among black comedians in the 1970s, starring in a television show called "Sanford and Son."

Dick Gregory, Bill Cosby, and **Richard Pryor** introduced three very different approaches to humor. Dick Gregory used comedy as a platform to comment on problems in American society. Cosby's humor focused on middle-class family problems that all Americans could relate to. Cosby is one of few modern comedians to gain international fame without resorting to the use of foul language. Cosby made a popular television show that was a take-off from one of his comic routines about a childhood friend called Fat Albert. Cosby then starred in the "Cosby Show," which portrayed middle-class family life. Unlike Gregory and Cosby, Pryor was unpredictable on the stage, a genius of impromptu (or making things up as you go along) comedy. Neither Cosby nor Pryor incorporated political activism into their routine, which is a reflection of the progress made in American society on racial issues. For perhaps the first time, African-American comedians were not seen as "black comedians," but simply as comedians.

In the 1970s comedians began to branch into different careers after getting their start on the stage. In the 1980s Arsenio Hall, Eddie Murphy, and **Whoopi Goldberg** continued this trend. Hall began a television talk show after making a name for himself doing stand-up comedy. Murphy and Goldberg took up acting after doing stand-up comedy and have become Hollywood stars. In the 1990s and the early twenty-first century, comedians such as Chris Rock and Martin Lawrence have also moved on to television and motion picture careers after getting their start on stage. Lawrence created a television show and starred in several movies while Chris Rock has also begun an acting career.

Early black comedians got their beginnings performing in small clubs and often got their material from the racial climate of American society. However, African Americans now enjoy greater opportunity to perform before large audiences and establish successful acting careers. In addition, the material used by black comedians has drifted away from politics and race. Social and political progress as well as the emergence of several talented performers opened the door for blacks to enrich our lives with the gift of laughter.

Comer, James Pierpont

PHYSICIAN, TEACHER
September 25, 1934–

James Comer: Selected Publications

Beyond Black and White
(1972)

School Power
(1980)

Black Child Care
(1975)

Maggie's American Dream
(1988)

Waiting For a Miracle: Why Schools Can't Solve Our Problems—And How We Can
(1997)

Psychiatrist James Comer is known for developing alternatives to negative methods of discipline for behavioral problems. Born in East Chicago, Indiana, he graduated from Indiana University and attended **Howard University** (Washington, D.C.) College of Medicine, where he earned an M.D. degree in 1960. In 1964 he earned a master's degree in public health at the University of Michigan.

While at the University of Michigan, Comer decided on a career in psychiatry, and later trained in psychiatry at Yale University. He believed that psychiatry offered a way to address the urban social problems that he had observed. In 1968 Comer directed a project at Yale that applied the principles of psychiatry to the problems of inner-city schools. He approached behavioral problems by using a sympathetic probing for the causes underlying disruptive or antisocial behavior. The "Comer Process" was an innovative alternative to negative methods of discipline and was adopted by many school districts nationwide.

Comer has served on the Yale faculty since 1968. He is a cofounder of Black Psychiatrists of America, and he served on the National Board to Abolish Corporal Punishment in the Schools.

Comic Books

In the early years of comic books, African Americans usually appeared only as minor characters, and for the most part they were depicted as stereotypes (as all having pretty much the same traits and features), which was

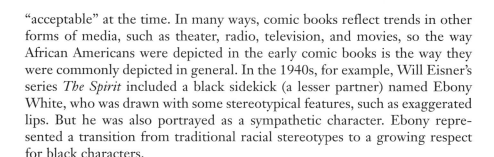
"acceptable" at the time. In many ways, comic books reflect trends in other forms of media, such as theater, radio, television, and movies, so the way African Americans were depicted in the early comic books is the way they were commonly depicted in general. In the 1940s, for example, Will Eisner's series *The Spirit* included a black sidekick (a lesser partner) named Ebony White, who was drawn with some stereotypical features, such as exaggerated lips. But he was also portrayed as a sympathetic character. Ebony represented a transition from traditional racial stereotypes to a growing respect for black characters.

Comic Books in the 1960s and 1970s

Not until the 1960s did blacks begin to appear as important characters in mass-circulation comic books, following the lead of a handful of television shows that were starting to portray black characters as educated, middle-class professionals. For example, the *Spiderman* comic book introduced Joe Robertson as city editor at the *Daily Bugle*, the newspaper where Spiderman's alter ego (the opposite side of a dual personality, like Superman's Clark Kent), Peter Parker, worked as a photographer. This trend continued in the 1970s, especially in comic books put out by Marvel Comics. Marvel's *Silver Surfer #5* (1969) featured a black scientist named Al B. Harper, who ultimately sacrificed his life to help the Silver Surfer save humanity from extermination.

Marvel also introduced the first major black superhero, the Black Panther, in 1966. The ruler of a fictional African nation called Wakanda, T'Challa, the Black Panther first appeared in *The Fantastic Four No. 52* and eventually became a regular member of *The Avengers*. He was featured in his own series, *Jungle Action*, in 1973. Marvel's first and most successful black title, however, was *Luke Cage, Superhero for Hire* (1972). The Luke Cage series was important because Luke was the first major African-American comic book character to be drawn by a black artist, Billy Graham.

Other noteworthy developments in black comics have included a 1970s special collectors' series published by DC Comics that featured a duel between Superman and boxer **Muhammad Ali** and *Sabre*, a series produced by Eclipse Publications. Created by Don MacGregor, *Sabre* features a main character modeled after the rock guitarist Jimi Hendrix.

New Trends

In the 1980s the rise of specialty comic-book stores and other economic factors led to changes in the comic-book industry. New companies were established to market and sell comic books to these speciality stores, which were starting to sell comics to audiences who were becoming more mature and more selective. This created opportunities for people who created speciality comics along certain themes (such as fantasy, science fiction, or horror), or who featured specific characters (such as women or African Americans), to reach a larger audience.

In the early 1990s some independently produced black comic books appeared, such as *Brotherman* by David, Jason and Guy Sims, and *Black Thunder*, by Ernest Gibbs Jr. African Americans working for major companies included the writers Dwayne McDuffie and Marcus McLaurin, an editor at Marvel. McDuffie went on to become cofounder of a DC Comics off-shoot company, Milestone Comics, in 1993. Milestone became the world's largest black comic-book company, one that was dedicated almost entirely to black superheroes and storylines. Unfortunately, because of dwindling readership and financial concerns, Milestone closed after four years. In 2000, however, the WB television network produced an animated series, *Static Shock*, based on a Milestone character.

Also in 2000, computer technology had made it possible for some adventurous African-American artists to bypass both the big companies and the newsstand altogether; serials such as *Tribal Science*, a futuristic saga of five interrelated characters created by Jimmie L. Westley Jr., were made available on the World Wide Web.

Comic Strips

From its beginnings in 1895, the American comic strip has generally featured characters from a wide variety of ethnic and cultural backgrounds. African Americans, however, typically served as background characters in early strips and were usually portrayed in stereotypical style (as all being the same). This was true even of the early work of the brilliant creator of *Krazy Kat* (1915–44), **George Herriman**, who was only recently discovered to have been of African ancestry.

Early African-American Strips

As it became evident after the turn of the twentieth century that the comic strip was a permanent part of the newspaper, many black newspapers encouraged staff artists to develop comic strips that would be more sensitive to black characters. The best known and longest-running of them was the *Chicago Defender*'s *Bungleton Green* (1920–63), created by Leslie L. Rogers. Other strips emerged in the wake of *Bungleton Green*, perhaps the best known of which is **Ollie Harrington**'s *Jive Gray* (drawn in the 1940s), a nationally distributed **World War II** (1939–45) adventure strip about a black aviator.

The most important strip to appear throughout the 1940s and 1950s—and one of the first to directly address the issue of race—was *Torchy Brown*, by Jackie Ormes, about an independent and attractive woman who fights racism and sexism, among other social problems, in exciting adventure narratives. Torchy was a powerful role model for young black women.

African American Strips Go National

The first African-American strip to achieve mainstream national distribution by a major syndicate (seller of materials for publication, such as comic strips, to multiple newspapers) was *Wee Pals*, by Morrie Turner, in 1964. The strip was integrated with children of different races and social backgrounds but was not really political. Turner's charming style and his gentle treatment of racial and political themes made the strip a great success during the years of the **Civil Rights movement.** Turner's success in breaking the racial bar-

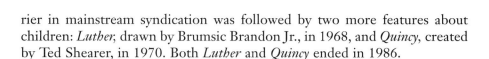

rier in mainstream syndication was followed by two more features about children: *Luther*, drawn by Brumsic Brandon Jr., in 1968, and *Quincy*, created by Ted Shearer, in 1970. Both *Luther* and *Quincy* ended in 1986.

Once Turner, Brandon, and Shearer had demonstrated a national interest in comic strips about blacks, the syndicates soon began to search out African-American talents. Ray Billingsley, a young cartoonist from North Carolina, achieved widespread success in 1988 with the appearance of *Curtis*. The strip features a black family, and Billingsley succeeds in balancing humor with family conflict. Occasionally the strip ventures into controversial areas such as drugs, drinking, smoking, and discrimination.

Another strip, *Jump Start*, created in 1988 by Philadelphia-born Robb Armstrong, examines the lives of an entire urban community and the stresses of careers and married life, while Stephen Bentley's *Herb & Jamaal*, begun in 1989, features two former high school friends who have opened an ice cream parlor.

Comic Strips of Today

In 1991 Barbara Brandon, Brumsic Brandon's daughter, launched a nationally syndicated strip called *Where I'm Coming From*, which features a small community of female characters who comment on social attitudes and politics. Another 1990s success was Jerry Craft's *Mama's Boyz*, which follows the lives of the urban Porter family. The strip was bought by King Features Syndicate in 1995 and appears in more than fifteen hundred newspapers around the world.

Concert Music

African Americans have provided concert music with some of its greatest talents. Black artists have also brought their own cultural heritage to the body of concert music, giving it unique characteristics. Audiences around the world have benefited from these important contributions.

Concert music is defined as music that is written so that when it is performed it sounds almost exactly as the composer (writer) intended it. Since African cultural heritage is rooted in the oral (spoken) tradition, black artists who first participated in concert music adapted to the European custom of passing music from one generation to the next in a written form.

Concert Music in the New Republic

Some of the earliest African-American concert musicians were slaves in the South. Written accounts and illustrations from the 1700s and 1800s describe blacks who were given the duty of learning to play an instrument (often the violin). Sometimes as talents developed, slave owners exploited them (used them to their advantage) by touring the musician around the country to make money. Other African-American concert musicians from the time of slavery were freeborn. Notable artists from the pre-**abolition** era included pianist and composer Thomas "Blind Tom" Bethune (1849–1908) and singer (soprano) Elizabeth Taylor Greenfield (1824–1876).

Concert Music after Abolition

After slavery was outlawed in the United States, black performers found that their talents were welcomed in few circles. For the most part, the concert stage was not open to them. In response, many African-American musicians devoted themselves to writing for or performing in other genres (styles), including minstrel shows, popular music and comedy shows of the day. Such was the case for the musician-composer **Will Marion Cook** (1869–1944). Since racial prejudices frustrated his efforts to pursue a career as a classical musician, he turned his attention to writing music for the Broadway stage, where he introduced **ragtime** music.

One of Cook's peers, the singer-composer Henry "Harry" T. Burleigh (1866–1949), became noted for performing and arranging spirituals, which had until then been limited to the oral tradition. Both Cook and Burleigh had studied with Czechoslovakian composer Antonín Dvorák at the National Conservatory of Music (New York City), where they were encouraged by their teacher to incorporate black traditions into their music.

African-American Musicians Make Headway

The first to be generally recognized as a black composer in the United States was **William Grant Still** (1895–1978). He blended elements of Native American music, African-American **folk music,** and **the blues** to create symphonies and **opera**s as well as chamber music and art songs—concert music in its truest form. He was followed by **Ulysses Simpson Kay** (1917–1995), a leading twentieth-century composer who also drew on African-American musical expression. Kay studied at Yale University with the great composer Paul Hindemith (1895–1963), who was forced to leave his German homeland for political reasons. In Kay, Hindemith found an eager student. Beginning his career during the post–World War II era (the years immediately following the war's end in 1945), Kay was faced with fewer restrictions than earlier African-American composers. At the same time, George T. Walker (1922—) gained recognition as a pianist, touring the United States and Europe before devoting himself to writing and teaching music. By the time of the Civil Rights movement, a new brand of concert music, called "ethnic nationalism," had taken hold.

While African-American composers made strides during the mid-1900s, black performers were also advancing in the world of concert music. Not only was opera singer **Marian Anderson** (1897–1993) a popular success with both black and white audiences, she is also credited with opening doors for black musicians. She was the first African American to sing at the famed Metropolitan Opera Company (New York City), known fondly by music lovers as "the Met." Aside from her many "firsts," Anderson inspired a new generation of concert musicians, among them the opera great **Leontyne Price** (1927—), whose career spanned three decades.

But racial prejudices have only slowly been pushed aside by the determined African Americans who have pursued careers in concert music. Even while Marian Anderson wowed audiences at the Met and other venues, African-American conductor **Dean Dixon** (1915–1976) could not secure a permanent position with a U.S. symphony orchestra, despite his impressive training and background. To advance his career he spent two decades in Europe (1949–70).

As the twenty-first century dawned, African Americans continued to enter the field of concert music as composers, singers, instrumentalists, and conductors. Audiences were being enriched by such great talents as the conductor **James DePreist** (1936–), the concert pianist **André Watts** (1946–), and the opera and concert singer **Kathleeen Battle** (1948–).

Congressional Black Caucus ▪▪▪

The Congressional Black Caucus (CBC) is made up of African-American members of Congress. The purpose of the CBC is to allow its members to jointly concentrate on government issues of concern to African Americans. The CBC originated in 1969 when Representative Charles Diggs from Michigan formed the Democratic Select Committee (DSC) as a way for the nine black members of the U.S. House of Representatives to address their common political concerns. They met with President Richard Nixon to discuss civil rights, anti-drug legislation, welfare reform, and U.S. involvement in the war in Vietnam. On June 18, 1971, at its first annual dinner in Washington, D.C., the group was formally organized as the Congressional Black Caucus, and Diggs became its first chairman. In 1973 Representative Louis Stokes from Ohio succeeded Diggs as caucus chairman. Stokes worked to get individual CBC members greater seniority and more powerful committee positions in Congress.

The CBC soon extended its influence both within and outside Congress. CBC members became chairs of seven out of twenty-seven congressional committees. The group developed nationwide networks of black voters and business leaders as well as networks addressing education, health, the justice system, and foreign affairs. In 1976 the CBC established the Congressional Black Caucus Foundation, which conducts and funds studies that help its members meet the concerns of the black community. The CBC was also involved in the successful efforts to pass the 1977 Full Employment Act, the 1982 Martin Luther King Holiday legislation, and the 1986 sanctions against South Africa, when the United States stopped trade with South Africa to protest apartheid, South Africa's policy of strict segregation of the races.

Over time, the CBC has become one of the most influential voting blocs in Congress. Although it has been divided on certain issues, such as the 1993 North American Free Trade Agreement (NAFTA), on many other issues (for example, health care, welfare reform, and crime) the CBC has emerged as a strong and effective advocate for African-American interests. (*See also* **Politics**)

Congress of Racial Equality (CORE) ▪▪▪

With a political legacy that spans six decades, the Congress of Racial Equality (CORE) is an important organization in the civil rights history of the United States. It was founded in Chicago in 1942 as the Committee of

The publicity generated by the Freedom Rides placed CORE in the forefront of the Civil Rights movement

Racial Equality (the name was changed in 1943) by a mixed group of white and black students. Among the most prominent of these founders was a black student named **James Farmer.** The founders of CORE believed in interracialism (different races living and working together harmoniously), and many were deeply influenced by the pacifist (nonviolent) strategies for social change introduced by the Indian activist Mahatma Gandhi (1869–1948).

Growing Pains

In their first year, CORE members organized **sit-ins** and other protests against segregation in public facilities, but they achieved few victories. It was clear to CORE's founders that to be effective they would need to attract more members and work at a national level. CORE grew throughout the 1940s, mostly through the efforts of its executive secretary, George Houser, who helped define CORE's mission and organize the group's first big project, the Journey of Reconciliation. The "Journey" was a two-week trip into southern states to test a 1946 U.S. Supreme Court ruling that banned segregation in interstate travel.

Despite CORE's efforts to become more coordinated and centralized, the group suffered during the early 1950s. Members fought about whether or not to use violence to further their message (cofounder James Farmer had always advocated a more militant stance) and about how to organize at the national level. By the mid-1950s, however, CORE found a renewed sense of purpose. The group was energized by the ***Brown v. Board of Education of Topeka, Kansas*** decision, which declared separate but equal educational facilities unconstitutional, and by the **Montgomery bus boycott** in Alabama, which mobilized thousands of African Americans to challenge segregated buses.CORE expanded its efforts, pulled together its national staff, and worked to become a major civil rights organization alongside the **National Association for the Advancement of Colored People (NAACP)** and the **Southern Christian Leadership Conference (SCLC).**

Finding a Voice

By 1960, with a stable national structure and increased visibility, CORE finally seemed ready to join the ranks of the major civil rights organizations. In Florida and South Carolina, CORE members pioneered a protest strategy called the "jail-in." During a jail-in, protesters who had been arrested for picketing or other public disturbances (which were considered "unlawful assembly") chose to serve out their jail sentences rather than pay bail. "Jail—no bail" became an important strategy in the **Civil Rights movement.**

In May 1961 CORE launched its most visible and forceful challenge to segregation: the **Freedom Rides,** protests against segregated interstate buses and terminals in the South. The publicity generated by the Freedom Rides placed CORE in the forefront of the Civil Rights movement.

Internal Conflict

By 1963, however, CORE was changing. CORE chapters began to create more community social programs that would help African Americans in need. CORE also began attracting more working-class black members, and individual chapters moved their headquarters into the black communities. The group's original mission was also being challenged by members who wanted to use more confrontational tactics, such as resisting arrest and obstructing traffic. These members identified with **Malcolm X** (1925–1965), who preached racial pride and black separatism, rather than with nonviolent means of protest.

By 1964 serious debates emerged within CORE about the roles of whites in the organization. In 1966 CORE endorsed the slogan "Black Power" and officially supported the ideas of black self-determination and local community control. In 1967 the word "multiracial" was removed from the constitution, and whites began to leave the organization. A year later, **Roy Innis,** the outspoken leader of CORE's Harlem, New York, chapter, took control of the national organization. Innis, arguing that blacks were a "nation within a nation," barred whites from active membership in CORE. He also pushed for a strong national center that would control all local chapters. By this point, however, CORE was a weakened organization with only a handful of chapters and dwindling resources.

Innis's beliefs and his approach to leadership caused more problems for CORE, and by the 1980s almost all CORE activities had ceased. In 1976 founder James Farmer cut off all ties with CORE in protest of Innis's methods. In 1981, after being accused by the New York State attorney general's office of misusing charitable contributions, Innis agreed to contribute $35,000 to the organization. In the early 1980s former CORE members, led by Farmer, attempted to transform CORE back into a multiracial organization but were unsuccessful. CORE chapters were involved in only a few activities in the 1990s, and Innis continued as national director of the organization.

Connecticut

First African-American Settlers: Africans originally arrived in Connecticut as a result of the triangular trade in rum, slaves, and molasses that linked New England, West Africa, and the Caribbean. As early as 1679 a governor of Connecticut recorded the importation of several Africans by the northern **slave trade.**

Slave Population: In 1750 the black population was recorded as 3,010, comprising 3 percent of the state population. In 1784 Connecticut passed a gradual emancipation law that allowed for a slave to become free at age twenty-five. Thus by 1820 the number of slaves had decreased to less than 100. Connecticut became the fifth state in 1788.

Free Black Population: The **emancipation** law led to an increase in the **free black** population and saw the movement of blacks from rural towns to urban centers, primarily to meet the demand for services by a growing urban population.

Civil War: Two all-black regiments from Connecticut fought during the **Civil War** (1861–65), returning home to be honored by the governor and residents of the state.

Reconstruction: Having secured the right to vote, Connecticut black residents began to seek inroads into the political system, most notably through the State Sumner Union League. At the same time, the black population continued to grow, from approximately 10,000 in 1873 to over 15,000 by the early twentieth century.

The Great Depression: By 1930 the black population had grown to approximately 30,000 as many southern blacks migrated north in search of industrial jobs. A similarly dramatic change occurred in the years following **World War II** (1939–45), when the black population in the state grew to 54,000 (1950).

Civil Rights Movement: Inspired by the southern **civil rights movement,** black communities in cities throughout Connecticut mobilized to struggle against chronic unemployment, inferior housing, political powerlessness, and persistent racism. The growing militancy of the black population culminated in a series of riots that swept Hartford, New Haven, and other cities throughout the state in the late 1960s.

Current African-American Population: According to U.S. Census Bureau estimates, the total black population in Connecticut was 303,721 (9.6 percent of the state population) as of July 1, 1998.

Key Figures: Venture Smith (c. 1729–1805), slave and writer; clergymen Amos Beman (1812–1874) and James Pennington (1807–1870).

(SEE ALSO **AMISTAD MUTINY.**)

Conservatism

Convervatism is the need to maintain, or "conserve," what currently exists. Someone who is conservative in politics believes in careful, gradual change (or no change), the opposite of someone who desires radical (and sometimes violent) change. In the United States, conservatives are usually linked to the Republican Party.

African Americans who are considered conservatives believe in the need to fight for civil rights and equality, but they generally support a slower, more peaceful approach to social change. They also believe that violent and combative methods will only hurt the cause. African-American conservatives argue that black equality can be achieved without fighting with whites and that the most effective way to change existing problems is for blacks to better themselves. Throughout American history, this has led to conflict between blacks who believe that change must come slowly and peacefully and those who think that African-American rights must be achieved at any cost.

Conservatism before the Civil War

Prior to the **Civil War** (1861–65), most blacks were slaves, and those that were not still had very few rights. Some **free blacks** were abolitionists, or people who fought to end **slavery.** Most of these African-American political leaders supported the early conservative political parties, including the

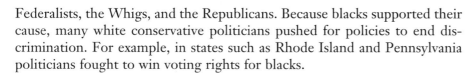
Federalists, the Whigs, and the Republicans. Because blacks supported their cause, many white conservative politicians pushed for policies to end discrimination. For example, in states such as Rhode Island and Pennsylvania politicians fought to win voting rights for blacks.

Considering, however, that most blacks were not involved in politics (in 1860 only five of the thirty-three states allowed blacks to vote), party politics were not really important. What was important was the development of **education,** which was seen as a means of real empowerment, and the need for blacks to become self-sufficient by owning their own businesses and farms. There was a push, especially among religious communities such as the **African Methodist Episcopal (AME) Church,** to create an educated black middle class.

Conservatism after the Civil War

When the Thirteenth Amendment ended slavery in the United States in 1865, 4.5 million slaves in the South were freed. Many of them were left without homes, and although they were "free," they still had no real rights. Some of them wanted radical changes to be made. One push was for the government to take over large Confederate (Southern) estates and divide the land among the slaves who had previously worked on them. Most black leaders, however, did not agree with such measures. Instead, they were convinced that the best way to eventually achieve political power was to live and work peacefully with the Southern whites and to avoid conflict.

Although few rights were given to blacks from the end of the Civil War to the 1920s, this was a period of some achievement in African-American history during which many important black organizations and colleges were formed. Some of these colleges were funded by white religious groups, organizations, and businessmen, and conservatives point to these partnerships as positive results of the two races working together. African-American conservatives of the time who worked within the system also befriended white politicians who helped change antiblack laws in their various home states.

The creation of black institutions was part of the central African-American conservative trend after the Civil War, which was an emphasis on self-help and the belief that blacks could only advance through their own efforts. The biggest advocate of this belief was educator and Tuskegee Institute founder **Booker T. Washington** (1856–1915), who was widely supported by blacks of all classes. Washington's beliefs were further reinforced by the black church, which at the time was very conservative. It was common for pastors to ignore social problems and to urge members of their congregation to treat whites with respect and to avoid conflict.

Conservatism in the Twentieth Century

Although most conservative black leaders supported Booker T. Washington, as the twentieth century progressed some began to disagree with him. Most of the disagreement was about segregation (the separation of blacks and whites). Although Washington was not consistent in his arguments, and he actually secretly helped fund lawsuits against segregation, in public he did endorse it. Some conservatives argued forcefully against segregation, but even so, they called for eliminating it gradually.

By the 1930s Washington's extremely conservative views were slowly disappearing, and after **World War II** (1939–45) the way in which conservative politicians and leaders approached change was slowly shifting. The postwar period produced a number of dynamic African-American leaders, such as **Martin Luther King Jr.** (1929–1968), who pushed for equal rights. As important cases such as *Brown v. Board of Education of Topeka, Kansas* (1954) were won and laws such as the Civil Rights Act of 1964 were passed, the number of conservative African Americans dropped. This can be seen in the 1964 presidential election, when 99 percent of African Americans voted for Democrat Lyndon Johnson (1908–1973; president 1963–1969). They did not vote for Republican Barry Goldwater, who opposed the Civil Rights Act.

Conservatism since the Civil Rights Era

Even within the **Civil Rights movement**, there were differences of opinion. A major disagreement was over **affirmative action**. Affirmative action is a policy to make up for past discriminations; for example, in business it means making an effort to hire a certain percentage of minorities, including African Americans. For conservatives, affirmative action is wrong. They argue that the main goal of the Civil Rights movement was to create a "color-blind" society that guarantees equal opportunity for all. Giving special opportunities to blacks reinforces the false belief that blacks are inferior and require special treatment in order to get ahead.

Conservatives also believe that government programs created during the 1960s to help African Americans in need have generally been unsuccessful. While some progressives (the oppositive of conservatives) such as **Jesse Jackson** (1941–) claim that the government does not give enough funding, conservatives insist that it is not the government's fault; it is up to African Americans to help themselves (the same belief held by Booker T. Washington and early conservatives).

The number of African Americans who support conservatism has never increased since the 1960s, and black conservative politicians are not very well supported by black voters. Black conservatives who are elected usually tend to come from areas that are mostly white. The question, however, still remains, How can African Americans prosper in a country that has a history of discrimination? And throughout that history the conservative answer has been, by working within the system for peaceful change.

Conyers, John Jr.

POLITICIAN, CONGRESSMAN
May 16, 1929–

John Conyers of Michigan is a longtime member of the U.S. House of Representatives. A founding member of the Congressional Black Caucus (CBC; a group of black legislators who meet to support common causes), he has worked to promote social welfare and civil rights causes. His most famous achievement was winning a fifteen-year fight to create a national holiday in honor of Dr. **Martin Luther King Jr.** The third Monday in January is now set aside to honor King's birthday.

Born in Detroit, Michigan, Conyers earned a bachelor's degree from Wayne State University (Detroit) in 1957 and a law degree from Wayne State Law School in 1958. After graduating he jumped right into **politics,** serving as legislative assistant to Michigan representative John D. Dingell. In 1964 Conyers ran for office and became the second black member of Congress from Michigan, winning by only 108 votes. He later became so popular that he won his 1992 reelection race with 84 percent of the vote.

Conyers supported President Lyndon Johnson's (1908–1973) Medicare program, a health insurance program set up for people sixty-five and over in 1964. He was also a strong advocate of the Voting Rights Act of 1965, which was passed to enforce the Fifteenth Amendment (1870), which had extended the right to vote to blacks. (Although the **Fifteenth Amendment** had given blacks the right to vote, violence, unfair taxes required to cast votes, and difficult "literacy" tests kept many blacks from voting.)

In 1992 Conyers spoke out against efforts to keep Haitian refugees from entering the United States. In 1998 Conyers, as ranking Democrat on the House Judiciary Committee, was a leading opponent of the impeachment of President Bill Clinton (1946-).

In 2000 Conyers became a strong promoter of Juneteenth celebrations, held in more than two hundred U.S. cities to celebrate June 19, 1865, considered the date when the last slaves in the country were freed.

John Conyers in his congressional office (AP/Wide World Photos. Reproduced by permission)

Cook, Will Marion

MUSICIAN, COMPOSER
January 27, 1869–July 19, 1944

Composer Will Cook introduced **ragtime** rhythms to Broadway, New York City's main theater district, around 1900. Attempts to revive Cook's music, remembered for its snappy melodies, have been controversial because his lyrics (words) reflect social stereotypes, or prejudices, of the day. Nevertheless, Cook was a groundbreaking musician whose influence was widely felt.

Part of the first generation born after **slavery,** Will Cook's father, John Cook, was treasurer of **Howard University** (Washington, D.C.). Will attended Oberlin College in Ohio, where he studied violin. In 1885 he gave his first recitals, in Washington, D.C. The Abolitionist and writer **Frederick Douglass** (1817–1895) was among Cook's sponsors.

For the next five years, the young musician studied in Berlin, Germany, with Hungarian violinist and composer Joseph Joachim (1831–1907). Returning to the United States, Cook began working as a concert violinist, performing at New York City's Carnegie Hall in 1895. At the National Conservatory of Music (New York), he studied with

Czechoslovakian composer Antonín Dvořák (1841–1904). But Cook's career as a classical musician was stifled by racial discrimination. To continue working in his field, he turned his attention to composing music for the stage.

Cook collaborated with African-American poet **Paul Laurence Dunbar** (1872–1906) on the ragtime musical (operetta) *Clorindy; or, The Origin of the Cakewalk*. It was the first black musical comedy performed at a major Broadway theater. He continued working with Dunbar over the next several years; their works included *In Dahomey* (1903), which featured the popular song "On Emancipation Day." The musical, the first full-length Broadway musical written and performed by African Americans, went on to tour Europe. In 1904 Cook wrote the music for *The Southerners*, the first Broadway show with an interracial (white and black) cast.

In the 1910s Cook toured the United States and Europe with a group he organized, the Southern Syncopated Orchestra. The group performed a wide variety of numbers that included classical music, early jazz, and compositions written by Cook. Settling in New York in the 1920s, Cook continued writing music for the stage and became a mentor to American jazz great Duke Ellington (1899–1974).

With titles such as "Jes' Lak White Fo'ks" (1899), "Who Dat Say Chicken" (1902), and "Darktown Is Out Tonight" (1902), Cook's music is disturbing and even confusing to modern audiences. But historians have noted that the words should be viewed as a product of their time and the music valued for its originality, for introducing an early African-American influence on Broadway, and for its popularity.

Cooke, Samuel "Sam"

SINGER, SONGWRITER
January 11, 1935–December 11, 1964

The son of a Baptist minister, Samuel "Sam" Cooke began his musical career singing **gospel music** with his seven brothers. Eventually, Cooke became one of the most important figures in gospel, touring and recording with a group called the Soul Stirrers for more than five years.

In 1956 Cooke turned to popular music. "You Send Me" (1957), his first hit, sold more than two million copies worldwide. In 1960 Cooke signed with RCA Records, where he wrote songs that, although still popular, were slightly closer to the **rhythm-and-blues** tradition. Among his most well known songs are "Wonderful World," "Chain Gang," "Sad Mood," "Having a Party," "Bring It on Home to Me," "Another Saturday Night," and "Twistin' the Night Away." In addition to writing and performing, Cooke also produced records for his Star label and ran Kags Music, a publishing company.

Cooke was killed by a white woman who claimed he was attacking her in 1964. Since then, his songs have been re-recorded by countless artists, and he continues to influence new generations of singers and songwriters.

Cooper, Charles "Chuck"

BASKETBALL PLAYER
September 29, 1929–February 5, 1984

Charles "Chuck" Cooper was the first African American drafted to play in the National Basketball Association (NBA). In 1950 the Boston Celtics selected Cooper in the second round. Although this was a historic event for American society, Cooper was very modest about it, giving baseball player **Jackie Robinson** (1919–1972) credit for opening professional sports to blacks.

Born in Pittsburgh, Pennsylvania, Cooper played **basketball** in high school and college, at West Virginia State. He then decided to put off college to serve in **World War II** (1939–45). Upon his return, Cooper attended and graduated from Duquesne University (Pittsburgh, Pennsylvania). He played for six years in the NBA, four of those with the Boston Celtics. After retiring from basketball, Cooper earned a master's degree in social work from the University of Minnesota. He worked hard to improve African-American life in Pittsburgh and was loved and respected by everyone who knew him.

The Copasetics

TAP DANCE GROUP

The Copasetics, a dance fraternity (social group) of mostly African-American tap dancers, was established in 1949 in memory of Bill "Bojangles" Robinson (1878–1949). The group was founded by Charles "Cookie" Cook (1917–1991), the musician **William "Billy" Strayhorn** (1915–1967), and others. They took the name of their club from Robinson's famous phrase "Everything's copasetic" (meaning fine or all right). Early members of The Copasetics included well-known performers during the golden years of tap in the 1920s and 1930s, including **Charles "Honi" Coles** (1911–1992) and **Charles "Cholly" Atkins** (1913–).

In the mid–1950s, **tap dance** became less popular as more and more people became interested in rock and roll and pop music. However, tap regained some popularity in the 1970s and 1980s. Veterans (former or long-time members) of The Copasetics were in demand as teachers and performers throughout the United States and Europe, and the members started performing as a group. The Copasetics' excellence in performing and their technical dance skills laid the foundation for a new generation of tap dancers.

Cortez, Jayne

POET
May 10, 1936–

Born in Fort Huachuca, Arizona, poet Jayne Cortez moved with her family to the Watts area of Los Angeles, California, when she was seven. **Jazz** was an early and significant artistic influence on her life; in 1954, while still a teenager, she married saxophonist **Ornette Coleman**. They divorced in 1960, and Cortez began to write poetry and pursue an acting career. After spending the summers of 1963 and 1964 in Mississippi helping to register voters, Cortez returned to California transformed by the experience: "I saw history being made." She continues to be a highly political poet.

Shortly after her return to California, Cortez founded the Watts Repertory Theater Company. In 1967 she moved to New York City, where she founded Bola Press and later published her first collection of poetry, *Pissstained Stairs and the Monkey Man's Wares* (1969). From 1977 to 1983 she served as writer-in-residence at Livingston College of Rutgers University (New Brunswick, New Jersey).

Music continues to influence Cortez's poetry, especially in its rhythms. She often performs and has on occasion recorded with jazz musicians, including, in 1997, the record *Taking the Blues Back Home*. The record is a story of personal history and African heritage, and Cortez is accompanied by a group of jazz and **blues** performers—including her son, drummer Denardo Coleman. African imagery, poetic forms, and language are also important forces in Cortez's work, which is collected in *Coagulations: New and Selected Poems* (1984) and in a more recent book, *Somewhere in Advance of Nowhere* (1996).

Cosby, William Henry Jr. "Bill"

COMEDIAN, PHILANTHROPIST, AUTHOR
July 12, 1937–

Bill Cosby is arguably the most successful male African-American entertainer of the twentieth century. His career as a **comedian**, actor, and author has spanned forty years and is going strong in the twenty-first century. Born in Germantown, Pennsylvania, Cosby studied at Temple University in Philadelphia but dropped out to pursue a career as a stand-up comic.

After four years on the television series *I Spy*, Cosby appeared as Chet Kincaid, a bachelor high school coach, on the comedy series *The Bill Cosby Show*. A few years later, Cosby created *Fat Albert and the Cosby Kids* (1972–1977), a cartoon series for children. The series set the course for **television** in the vital new area of values, judgment, and personal responsibility.

In the fall of 1984, *The Cosby Show* began on NBC, featuring Cosby as Cliff Huxtable, a doctor living with his wife and children in New York City. The characters on *The Cosby Show* represented a real African-American upper-middle-class family, rarely seen on American television. Cosby sought black artists who had not been seen on network television in years for roles. He also included black writers among his creative staff, and by the third year, he insisted on using a black director for some of the episodes. In its first year, *The Cosby Show* finished third in the ratings; from the second season through the fourth season, the show was rated number one in the United States. Cosby also became a spokesman in advertisements for Jell-O, Coca-Cola, and Kodak. He appeared in **drama**, action-adventure stories, comedies, and children's programs. In 1992 he also entered into prime-time syndication (making available to a number of television stations, to be shown at the time of day when the most people are watching) with a remake of the old Groucho Marx game show *You Bet Your Life*. In 1996 he began a new hit

series, *Cosby*, in which he played a working-class man from Queens, New York. The series lasted until 2000.

Throughout his career, Cosby has appeared at highly popular concert performances across the United States. His comedy focuses on his own life as a reflection of universal human needs. Cosby has also produced more than twenty comedy-musical record albums, many of which have won Grammy Awards.

Cosby has also written many best-selling books, including *The Wit and Wisdom of Fat Albert* (1973), *You Are Somebody Special* (1978), *Fatherhood* (1986), *Time Flies* (1987), and *Love and Marriage* (1989).

Cosby is one of the most important contributors to African-American institutions. In 1986 he and his wife gave $1.3 million to **Fisk University** (Nashville, Tennessee); the following year they gave another $1.3 million to be divided equally among four black universities. In 1988 they divided $1.5

million between Meharry Medical College and Bethune–Cookman College (Daytona Beach, Florida). In 1989 Bill and Camille Cosby announced that they were giving $20 million to Spelman College (Atlanta, Georgia), the largest personal gift ever made to any of the historically black colleges and universities. In 1994 the couple donated a historic landmark building in downtown Washington, D.C., to the National Council of Negro Women to help them establish a National Center for African-American Women.

Cotton Club

The Cotton Club was a popular night club open from about 1920 to 1940. It was first located at the corner of Lenox Avenue and West 142nd Street in **Harlem**, a mainly African-American section of New York City. Even though it was open only to whites until 1928, the greatest African-American **jazz** musicians and dancers of the time performed there, including **Duke Ellington** (1899–1974) and his orchestra, **Cab Calloway**'s Missourians, Jimmie Lunceford and his swing band, trumpet player **Louis Armstrong** (1900–1971), and dancers **Bill "Bojangles" Robinson** (1878–1949) and the **Nicholas Brothers**.

First opened in 1920 as the Club Deluxe, the Cotton Club was given its name in 1922 by new owner Owney Madden, who wanted to attract an upper-class white audience. Before long, high-society whites were coming from all over the city to see top black performers in the lower-class Harlem neighborhood. Soon after Ellington took over as bandleader in 1927, the orchestra was broadcast nightly over a national radio network. Another attraction at the club was the women dancers.

By 1928 blacks were demanding to be admitted to the club. Management agreed but continued to charge high prices that kept most blacks away. Calloway's Missourians took over as the club band after Ellington's orchestra left in 1931. In 1934 the Missourians were replaced by Lunceford's band.

The Cotton Club closed in 1935, after riots in Harlem, but it reopened at a different location, 200 West 48th Street, in 1936. The club closed for good in 1940.

Court Cases. *See* **Antelope Case; Brown v. Board of Education of Topeka, Kansas; Dred Scott v. Sandford; Hill-Thomas Hearings; Odell Waller Case; Plessy v. Ferguson; Scotsboro Boys**

Creed, Courtlandt Van Rensselaer

PHYSICIAN
April, 1835–August 8, 1900

Courtlandt Van Rensselaer Creed was born in New Haven, Connecticut. After attending the Lancasterian School in New Haven, Creed was employed briefly as a book agent before entering Yale Medical School

in 1854. He earned an M.D. degree in 1857 and opened an office in his family home. There, in a predominantly white part of town, he built a successful general practice that included several prominent citizens.

During the **Civil War** (the war between the American South and the American North from 1861 to 1865), Creed volunteered as secretary for a local Colored Freedmen's Aid Society. In 1864, following several failed attempts to offer his services to the Union army, he was appointed acting surgeon of the 30th Connecticut Volunteers, a black regiment. He was one of a few black physicians to receive an officer's commission. He was discharged from the army on November 7, 1865.

Creed settled in New York but found life difficult there and returned to New Haven in 1873. He spent the remainder of his life in relative poverty and obscurity. His family house was sold to pay off debts and legal expenses. While continuing to practice medicine, Creed lodged in dingy rooming houses in New Haven and in Brooklyn, New York. On August 8, 1900, he died of kidney disease while attending to a patient.

An African-American FIRST

Physician Courtlandt Van Rensselaer Creed was the first African American to earn a degree at Yale.

Creole

The word "creole" comes from the Portuguese term *crialla*, which means "to raise" or "to be born." In the seventeenth century, it was used to describe people who had been born in the Spanish, French, and Portuguese colonies of the New World, as opposed to individuals who had been born in Europe or slaves who had been born in Africa.

In the United States, and especially in Louisiana, which formerly was a French colony, Creoles were the children of French settlers or blacks born in America. By the eighteenth century, however, the term was associated strictly with the aristocratic families of French-speaking whites. But descendants of free blacks continued to use the term and people in Louisiana (both white and black) eventually began to describe African-American creoles as "Negro Creole" or "Creole Negro."

Over time, "Creole" has come to describe a unique culture that blended influences from many different traditions: Spanish, French, African, Caribbean, and West Indian. This blending created a particular way of life, including a style of cooking, a way of speaking, types of music and dancing, and forms of literature. The Caribbean Creole way of life, for example, is explored in the plays of **Derek Walcott** (1930–).

Crichlow, Ernest

ARTIST
June 19, 1914–

Artist and illustrator Ernest Crichlow was born in Brooklyn to parents who were originally from the West Indies island of Barbados. He studied art in the early 1930s at the Art Students' League and also at New York University. Later in the 1930s, he traveled to Greensboro, North Carolina, as a federal Works Projects Administration (WPA) artist (the WPA was a jobs program started by President Franklin Delano Roosevelt in the 1930s to help unemployed people during the **Great Depression**). He did not return to New York until the 1950s.

Crichlow is best known for cofounding the Cinque Gallery in New York City in 1969, along with fellow artists **Romare Bearden** (1912–1988) and Norman Lewis (1909–1979). Named after the African leader of the 1839 **Amistad mutiny** aboard a Spanish slave ship, the gallery provided exhibition space for black artists under thirty years of age.

Crichlow is also a painter and an illustrator of children's books. His work addresses social issues, particularly those relating to the lives of urban children. He has illustrated children's books on African-American culture and history, including *Freedom Train: The Story of **Harriet Tubman*** and *African Folk Tales* (1969).

Beginning in the 1930s, Crichlow taught art at such institutions as the Harlem Art Center, the **George Washington Carver** School, and the City College of New York. He exhibited at the Federal Art Gallery and the ACA Gallery in New York City, the Newark (New Jersey) Museum, and Smith College Museum of Art in Northampton, Massachusetts.

The Crisis

The Crisis is a monthly magazine published by the **National Association for the Advancement of Colored People (NAACP).** Since its founding, *The Crisis* has documented the struggles and achievements of African Americans. The magazine's first editor, **W. E. B. Du Bois** (1868–1963), explained that the name *The Crisis* was chosen for the publication because the founders believed that the period in which it was started was a critical point in American history for the advancement of blacks.

While Du Bois was editor, the magazine published literary works, editorials, current events, and reports on NAACP activities. *The Crisis* has chronicled each step of America's ongoing fight against racism, recording the positive and the negative alike. During its early years the magazine concentrated on black achievements in college and the impact of the NAACP on American society and politics. Among the famous thinkers who have contributed to *The Crisis* are the British playwright George Bernard Shaw (1856–1950), the Indian social reformer Mahatma Gandhi (1869–1948), the author Sinclair Lewis, and the writer **Langston Hughes** (1902–1967), author of *The Ways of White Folks*.

Under editors **Roy Wilkins** and James W. Ivy, the magazine focused on issues such as racism against blacks in the military, reporting on **Jim Crow** policies (racist laws instituted in the South), and **lynchings.** As the fight against racism shifted from the streets to the courts, the magazine began recording legal battles, such as school desegregation, voter registration, and housing discrimination. *The Crisis* continues to record America's progress in the fight against racism. When Du Bois retired in 1934, the magazine suffered a drastic reduction in subscription (one hundred thousand to ten thousand). However, an increase in corporate advertising and policy changes, such as requiring NAACP members to pay for their subscription, turned the financial condition of the magazine around. In 1988 the magazine had 350,000 subscribers. Sondra Kathryn Wilson put together some of most notable publications that have appeared in the magazine in a book called *The Crisis Reader: Stories, Poetry and Essays From the NAACP's Crisis Magazine* (1999).

Crite, Allan Rohan

PAINTER, ILLUSTRATOR, ART HISTORIAN
March 20, 1910–

The artwork of Allan Rohan Crite represented the black working- and middle-class, although his compositions later took on a spiritual tone. Crite was born in Plainfield, New Jersey, but spent most of his life in Boston, Massachusetts. After showing early talent, he studied at Boston's School of the Museum of Fine Arts. His works of the 1930s and 1940s show the people of his neighborhoods and reveal the sensitivity of an artist working within his community. These pieces contrast sharply with the negative depictions of blacks that were prominent at the time.

A deeply committed **Episcopalian,** Crite in the late 1930s began to produce religious works in a variety of media. His best-known works are book illustrations that were radical for the times, showing biblical characters as black. He also created murals and devotional objects for churches throughout the United States. In 1948 Crite published a book of religious illustrations, *Three Spirituals from Earth to Heaven.*

Crite also created lithographs (prints made from a metal plate) of nude men and women. One piece featured a clothed character on one side of the canvas, and the same character in the same poses but nude on the other side. Crite called this "using fantasy to cover reality." Crite's work, including several exhibitions of sacred art, has appeared in the United States and abroad. He has greatly influenced the representation of African-American life in art.

Crummell, Alexander

NATIONALIST, ABOLITIONIST, MISSIONARY
March 3, 1819–September 19, 1898

Alexander Crummell was born in New York City, the son of a former slave and a **free black** woman. At an early age, he was influenced by Rev. Peter Williams Jr., a supporter of back-to-**Africa** movements. Crummell attended school in Williams's church and at the African Free School until his early teens.

Encouraged by Williams to become a minister, Crummell applied to the General Theological Seminary in New York but was rejected. He informally attended lectures at Yale University and studied privately with clergymen in New England. While in New England he preached to congregations in New Haven, Connecticut, and Providence, Rhode Island, and worked as a correspondent for the *Colored American* newspaper. Crummell became an Episcopal priest in 1842 and worked with small congregations in

Philadelphia, Pennsylvania and New York. He went to England in 1848 to raise funds for his parish and began preparing, with the aid of a tutor, to apply to Cambridge University. He was among eleven out of thirty-three candidates who passed the entrance examination, and he was awarded a bachelor's degree in 1853.

Because he wanted his children to attend school in Africa and to be part of African society, Crummell became a missionary to West Africa for the Protestant Episcopal Church. Many of his writings during these years address the topics found in "God and the Nation" and "The Relations and Duties of Free Colored Men in America to Africa." These, along with other essays on black nationalist themes, were collected for his first book, *The Future of Africa* (1862).

Crummell spent sixteen years between 1853 and 1872 in Liberia. He established St. Luke's Episcopal Church in Washington, D.C., in 1879 and remained the pastor there until 1894, when he retired. He continued to write and lecture actively until his death in 1898. Among his important writings during the Washington years were "The Destined Superiority of the Negro" and "The Black Woman of the South, Her Neglects and Her Needs" (1883). These and other sermons were collected in his books *The Greatness of Christ and Other Sermons* (1882) and *Africa and America* (1891).

In the year before his death, Crummell organized the American Negro Academy, which was dedicated to the pursuit of higher culture and civilization for black Americans. (*See also* **Black Nationalism**.)

Crumpler, Rebecca Lee Davis

PHYSICIAN
February 8, c. 1831–March 9, 1895

Rebecca Davis Lee Crumpler was the first African-American woman to receive the M.D. degree in the United States. Sources differ on her birthdate and birthplace. She was born in either Richmond, Virginia, or in Delaware to Absolum Davis and Matilda Webber. She was raised in Pennsylvania by an aunt.

Crumpler had moved to Charlestown, Massachusetts, by 1852 and for eight years worked as a nurse. On recommendation of the physicians whom she had served as nurse, in 1860 she was admitted to the four-year medical program at New England Female Medical College. The Boston Female Medical College, the name under which the school opened in 1848, was the world's first women's medical college.

Crumpler sat before the faculty for her final, oral examinations on February 24, 1864; however, the faculty hesitated in Crumpler's case, suggesting some deficiencies in her education. The faculty overcame their reservations, however, and on March 1 the trustees conferred on her the doctress of medicine degree. The college closed in 1873 without producing more African-American graduates.

Around graduation time, Rebecca Lee married Arthur Crumpler. She practiced in Boston for a while. When the **Civil War** ended in 1865, she moved to Richmond, Virginia, where the Freedmen's Bureau arranged for

her to treat black patients, many of who had left the plantation and had no medical provisions. Crumpler met resistance, however, as male doctors snubbed her and druggists grudgingly filled her prescriptions.

Crumpler's enthusiasm for practicing medicine had been reinvigorated by the time she returned to Boston in 1869. Apparently, her services were in no great demand there, however, and by 1883 she was no longer in active practice. That year, Crumpler published a book of medical advice for women and their children called *A Book of Medical Discourses* and dedicated the work to mothers and nurses. She died in Fairview, Massachusetts, in 1895. Crumpler remained an inspiration to women in medicine; her pioneering work led to the formation of the Rebecca Lee Society, the first medical society for African-American women.

Cruse, Harold Wright

WRITER, PROFESSOR
March 18, 1916–

Harold Cruse wrote the influential book *The Crisis of the Negro Intellectual* (1967) and went on to become a college professor. Born in Petersburg, Virginia, Cruse moved with his father to New York, where he was educated in the public school system. As a young man, he became involved in the cultural and political life of the Harlem neighborhood of New York City. After serving in the army during World War II (1939–45), Cruse attended the City College of New York following his discharge but dropped out within a year.

Holding a series of part-time jobs and occasionally writing, Cruse became involved in left-wing (radical) Harlem politics. It was thought that he was involved in the Communist Party, but later he fiercely objected to its politics. In 1963 he began work on *The Crisis of the Negro Intellectual*, publishing it four years later. In it Cruse criticizes black leaders for not expressing a nationalist consciousness: while African-American thinkers had attacked black assimilation (absorption) into white America, they had not developed black culture or politics.

Cruse criticizes black leaders for not expressing a nationalist consciousness

In the fall of 1968 the University of Michigan (Ann Arbor) hired Cruse as a visiting professor. He cofounded the Center for Afroamerican and African Studies and continued teaching at the university, becoming a full professor in 1977. He retired ten years later. In 1982 Cruse published *Plural but Equal*.

Cuffe, Paul

MERCHANT, EMIGRATIONIST
January 17, 1759–September 9, 1817

Considered by some to be the father of **black nationalism**, Paul Cuffe was born to a former slave and an American Indian woman. Early in life, he was upset by racial discrimination and took action. In 1780, to protest the

Massachusetts state constitution, which did not allow blacks to vote, he refused to pay his taxes.

As a teenager, Cuffe went out on whaling expeditions. As an adult, he owned several farming, fishing, and whaling businesses. He built at least seven boats at his Westport, Massachusetts, docks and amassed a fortune in trade. His property in 1806 was valued at approximately $20,000, making him Westport's wealthiest resident.

In 1808 Cuffe became a devout Quaker. Because of his religious beliefs, he became involved in the movement to end the **slave trade.** He was particularly interested in the idea of resettling former slaves in **Africa.** In 1811 he made the first of two trips to Sierra Leone, England's West African colony for former slaves.

It was on this first trip that Cuffe started to imagine the possibility of a three-way trade route between the United States, England, and Sierra Leone. His hope was that the trade route would bond African descendants on three continents. During the trip, Cuffe also sailed to England, where he protested the effects of Britain's trading policies on black merchants.

Cuffe's efforts were blocked by the War of 1812 between the United States and England. Each country forbade trade with the other, and when Cuffe asked to continue trading, both the U.S. Congress and the British Parliament refused him. Cuffe, however, remained convinced that it was necessary for blacks to return to Africa to lessen the plight of black Americans and to bring a measure of prosperity to Africa. His death in 1817 came before he could fulfill his plan.

Cullen, Countee

POET, NOVELIST, PLAYWRIGHT
March 30, 1903–January 9, 1946

Countee Cullen, a major figure of the 1920s artistic and cultural movement known as the **Harlem Renaissance,** was born on March 30, 1903. Few details of his birthplace and early life exist, but it is known that in 1918 he was adopted by a Rev. Frederick Cullen and his wife, Carolyn. Cullen was very close to his Methodist father, but his poetry, often full of conflict between the physical body and the spiritual soul, shows a clear discomfort with his strong and conservative Christian training.

Cullen was an outstanding student at DeWitt Clinton High School, where he helped edit both the school newspaper and the literary magazine. He also wrote his first award-winning poetry, capturing a citywide competition. Later, while a student at New York University, Cullen wrote most of the work that was to make up his first two volumes, *Color* (1925) and *Copper Sun* (1927).

By the time Cullen earned a master's degree in English and French from Harvard University (Cambridge, Massachusetts) in 1927, he had become the most popular black poet in the United States. He won more major literary prizes than any other black writer of the 1920s, and he was only the second

"HERITAGE"

What is Africa to me:Copper sun or scarlet sea,
Jungle star or jungle track,
Strong bronzed men, or regal black
Women from whose loins I sprang
when the birds of Eden sang?
One three centuries removed
From the scenes his fathers loved,
Spicy grove, cinnamon tree,
What is Africa to me?....

(Source: Excerpt from "Heritage," by Countee Cullen. *My Soul's High Song: The Collected Writings of Countee Cullen.* New York: Doubleday, 1991.)

African American to win a Guggenheim Fellowship (a grant of money that allows recipients to take a break from their regular job to pursue their creative interests). Lines from Cullen's popular poems, such as "Heritage," "Incident," "From the Dark Tower," and "Yet Do I Marvel," are still commonly quoted.

Cullen was also at the center of one of the major social events of the Harlem Renaissance. On April 9, 1928, he married Yolande DuBois, the only child of the intellectual **W. E. B. Du Bois,** in one of the most lavish weddings in black New York history. The wedding was a symbolic event, linking the grand black intellectual patriarch (founding father) and the new breed of younger African Americans, but the marriage was a disaster and ended in 1930.

Cullen's most ambitious work, *The Black Christ and Other Poems,* was published in 1929 but received lukewarm reviews. Cullen was bitterly disappointed, and from the 1930s until his death he wrote less, limited partly by his job as a French teacher at **Frederick Douglass** Junior High—where he taught the young **James Baldwin.** But he turned out significant work during this period, including the children's books *The Lost Zoo* and *My Lives and How I Lost Them.*

Cullen's poetry during this period includes perhaps some of his best and gloomiest works. He was working on a musical with the writer **Arna Bontemps** at the time of his death from high blood pressure and kidney disease. For many years after his death, Cullen's reputation was eclipsed by those of other Harlem Renaissance writers, but more recently there has been a renewed interest in his life and work.